FLOOD OF LIES

FLOOD OF
LIES

The St. Rita's Nursing Home Tragedy

JAMES A. COBB, JR.

PELICAN PUBLISHING COMPANY
GRETNA 2013

*The word "Pelican" and the depiction of a pelican are
trademarks of Pelican Publishing Company, Inc., and are
registered in the U.S. Patent and Trademark Office.*

Library of Congress Cataloging-in-Publication Data

Cobb, James A.
  Flood of lies : the St. Rita's nursing home tragedy / by James A. Cobb, Jr.
     p. cm.
  Includes index.
  ISBN 978-1-4556-1789-0 (hardcover : alk. paper) — ISBN 978-1-
4556-1790-6 (e-book) 1. Mangano, Salvador—Trials, litigation, etc. 2.
Mangano, Mabel—Trials, litigation, etc. 3. Trials (Homicide)—Louisiana—
Saint Bernard Parish. 4. Nursing home administrators—Legal status, laws,
etc.—Louisiana—Saint Bernard Parish. 5. Nursing home patients—Legal
status, laws, etc.—Louisiana—Saint Bernard Parish. 6. Hurricane Katrina,
2005—Social aspects. I. Title.
  KF225.M36C63 2013
  345.763'02520976336—dc23
                                                                2013005942

Printed in the United States of America
Published by Pelican Publishing Company, Inc.
1000 Burmaster Street, Gretna, Louisiana 70053

For Christopher, Collette, and Debbie

"And the rains fell, and the floods came, and the winds slammed against that house; and yet it did not fall, for it had been founded on the rock."

—Matthew 7:25

Contents

Chapter 1: Has the Jury Reached a Verdict?

The courthouse stood on a bluff overlooking the Mississippi River in quaintly gorgeous St. Francisville, Louisiana. A Civil War battle was fought here. Union artillery shells rained down near here. The streets leading to the courthouse were lined with antebellum mansions, stately homes with sculpted front yards and second-story wrap-around balconies behind huge white columns. It was a place suspended in time and it was beautiful. For the past four weeks, the courthouse had been host to another kind of battle, one which was anything but beautiful. The townspeople of St. Francisville were about to decide the most horrific criminal case in America. Thirty-five helpless nursing home residents had drowned in their beds and wheelchairs, unable to escape the tsunami spawned by a killer named Katrina. The government had charged the owners of the home with murder—"negligent homicide," to be legally precise.

Now six residents of the bucolic St. Francisville area were about to render a decision that would affect hundreds of people forever—both the survivors of the dead and the defendants, a tough, self-made couple named Mangano.

The courtroom was packed on this last day, just as it had been packed every day for four weeks. Some two hundred people, thrown together for a month of gut-wrenching evidence and raw emotion, sat in silence enforced by a judge's warning. All were drawn to this same place for the same reason, and many had much in common. All were physically, mentally, and emotionally exhausted. Dressed symbolically in black for this final day of their ordeal, family members of the thirty-five victims sat behind the prosecution team on one side of the aisle that divided the courtroom into warring camps. Their grief and outrage sent a compelling message to members of the jury. Across the aisle sat the family, friends, and supporters of the elderly but still vigorous Sal and Mabel Mangano. Everyone in the room was hopeful and prayerful, but for diametrically opposed outcomes. Who would God favor on this day?

Sal and Mabel had been demonized around the world. Media reports of their conduct two years earlier had preceded authorities even talking to them. It was reported that the couple had abandoned their residents before Katrina struck, leaving them to fend for themselves. Others reported that the residents of St. Rita's were tied to their beds or shackled to their wheelchairs as the flood waters rose, their fate sealed by their involuntary restraints. It was further reported that the Manganos were spotted shopping in Mississippi in Katrina's immediate aftermath and merrily gambling at a casino, just as they had gambled with their residents' lives in failing to evacuate them ahead of the epic storm. Follow-up reports had them attempting to flee the United States on a cruise ship, bound for Mexico and points south. Some sensationalist print journalist had bestowed on them a title; he called them the "Monsters of Katrina." They had become the most hated couple in America. In the court of public opinion, fired by a 24/7 media frenzy, they had been convicted before the state of Louisiana even arrested or indicted them.

Earlier on this final day of the trial, the walls of the courtroom had reverberated with the closing arguments by the lawyers for both sides. Their harangues had lasted well into the afternoon. The lawyers were punch drunk from four weeks of trial—physically, mentally, and emotionally exhausted. I know this because I was one of those lawyers. Our clients? Sal and Mabel. And when the closing arguments were over and the jury began their deliberations, my two associates and I repaired to our war room, a tiny, wood-frame building directly across the street from the courthouse. A marker on the front lawn certified that the building had been in continuous use as a lawyer's office since 1842. We were only its latest temporary inhabitants. I retreated to a small office in the back and closed the door. I pulled out a few sheets of white paper and began to write. Minutes later, my co-counsel knocked and stepped into my sanctuary.

"Are you okay?"

"Not really," I said.

"What are you writing?" he asked.

"I'm writing a statement for the press after the jury returns its verdict."

He paused, looking down at the floor and asked quietly, "You writing one or two?"

"Just one," I said.

He nodded and quietly backed out of the room, closing the door without a sound.

I finished my handwritten composition, blue ink on unlined white paper. I read it to myself a couple of times, folded the paper lengthwise, and slid it into a pocket inside my suit jacket. After four weeks of trial, the most maddening part was about to begin—waiting on the jury's verdict. The laws of physics are suspended at such a time. Minutes feel like hours; hours feel like days. It's impossible to avoid replaying pivotal moments in one's mind—second guessing strategies employed, questions asked, and arguments made or not made. But the matter was over and done with and we could no longer affect the outcome. The overwhelming feeling was of helplessness and doubt as minutes stretched into hours. I emerged from my sanctuary with an announcement: "I can't take it anymore. I'm heading to the Magnolia Café for a margarita. Anybody coming with me?" Yes, the town's watering hole and best restaurant was indeed named the Magnolia Café. I told the sheriff, if the judge needed us, that's where we'd be. By car it was all of two minutes from the courthouse. We could be back on very short notice.

A few team members joined me. It was a Friday night and there was a gathering thunderstorm in the distance. The Magnolia Café was packed as we entered. We bypassed the maitre d' and went straight to the back bar. Everyone knew who we were, in our pinstriped blue suits and ties, and why we were there. As soon as she glimpsed me, the bartender reached for a large margarita glass and, unbidden, started mixing me a double. I had been her customer many times in the previous four weeks and she knew what I required. She slid the icy concoction across the bar. "Good luck," she said quietly. "This one's on me."

I sat up against the wall, withdrawn from my colleagues, lost in thought. I munched on some chips and tried to become part of the woodwork. There was chatter all around me but I couldn't speak.

I had spent a professional lifetime defending those who were, at law, entitled to a defense but were often unworthy of one. I had represented large corporations and insurance companies regularly accused of negligence and greed in causing some calamity that took a worker's life or left him crippled and unable to provide for his family. Occasionally, it was my calling in life to deprive widows and orphans of compensation for the deaths of their husbands and fathers, or, at the very least, to minimize a client's exposure to some nominal sum. I was very good at what I did.

On those occasions when I was besieged by guilt for having skillfully deprived people of compensation to which they were justly entitled, the cure was sure: Bombay Sapphire, rocks. Thirty years of competence and achievement had left me more than comfortable and had left my soul utterly unfulfilled. And then came Katrina.

The circumstances that brought me to the defense of Sal and Mabel Mangano were unusual, but from the perspective of those who had lost loved ones in their nursing home, the Manganos were not all that different from my typical clients. They were not Exxon Mobil. A drunken sea captain on their payroll had not washed the coast of Alaska with oil. But on a smaller scale, they were the owners, the capitalists, the Lincoln-town-car-driving administrators of a corporation in which families had placed their trust and people had died—thirty-five people, more than three times the number that went down on BP's Deepwater Horizon oil rig.

The intimate scale of the case only made it more profoundly personal. Mabel, a deeply religious woman, had come to believe it was neither circumstance nor coincidence that had brought her together with me for two stressful and horrendous years. It was Divine Providence. *He* sent *me* to *her,* she believed—a sense of destiny that I found more than a little burdensome, given the odds against our keeping her and her husband from prison. But while it was my view that the Almighty had been a bit too busy in the days and weeks following Katrina to be concerned with, must less to direct, Mabel's selection of counsel, I was not inclined to contest a belief from which she drew strength.

And anyway, we knew from the start that we would need all the help we could get—divine or otherwise—because there was no doubt we were up against a devil.

It had become clear to me from the start that the government's attempt to blame only two people for all the sins associated with Katrina was a gross miscarriage of justice. Hadn't the collapse of the federal levee system been responsible for the flooding that killed some 1,600 human beings? The Army Corps of Engineers had as much as conceded the point in its own post-mortem within a year of the disaster. And yet the State of Louisiana had persisted in its effort to imprison Sal and Mabel Mangano for the rest of their lives. The question was not why. The question was, who? And the answer was a man named Charles Foti, the state's attorney general and someone the Mangano defense had come to detest with a special passion. At the time of Katrina, Foti could claim a law degree, but he had never really practiced law. For thirty-two years he had been the Orleans Parish criminal sheriff, whose job it was to incarcerate the hundreds of thousands of souls who passed through his prison complex over the course of those three decades. He was a jailer, not a lawyer. So when it came time to exercise judgment and discretion commensurate with his office as the state's freshly elected "minister of justice," he saw the world through the eyes of a prison warden—everybody was guilty. It's all he knew.

In 2003, shortly before Katrina, the people of Louisiana in their wisdom had made him their attorney general. So when disaster struck, he was new to the office and still learning to flex the considerable muscle that came with it. During his decades as sheriff he had amassed power the old-fashioned way, through the exercise of political patronage and the personal benefactions that came with it. A cousin had given him his first job and then the political support that secured his first election as sheriff. The cousin was named Moon Landrieu, in due course mayor of New Orleans, U.S. secretary of housing and urban development, and a Louisiana appeals court judge. Landrieu, as in U.S. Sen. Mary Landrieu, his daughter. Landrieu, as in Lt. Gov. Mitch Landrieu, who would soon follow in his father's footsteps and become mayor of the state's largest city. Foti and the Landrieus supported each other politically, used massive organizations in the black community to turn out monolithic votes, and won bunches of elections.

For thirty-two years before Katrina, Foti's most notable achievement was his annual Thanksgiving Feast, which he put on for thousands of people each year, at taxpayer expense. Costs were further eased by "contributions" from people and companies who wanted his favor. The crowds were mostly poor, black, and, you guessed it—the elderly. (Nursing homes bussed their residents by the hundreds to Foti's groaning board.) I had never attended the event, for I did not qualify for membership in any of the three constituent groups: I was not poor, black, or elderly, at least not yet. But by all accounts Foti's annual feast was a bright spot in these people's lives. If an ancillary dividend was to secure their eternal loyalty on Election Day—well, that was nice, too.

Understandably then, Foti had seen the unfortunates at St. Rita's as "his people." Some might even have dined on his turkey. I did not doubt the genuineness of his affection for the elderly, nor his personal outrage and sadness over what happened at St. Rita's. First-year law students are taught to keep passion and prejudice from overcoming logic and reason. From his reaction to the tragedy, one can assume Attorney General Foti had long since forgotten this elementary lesson learned in law school almost forty years earlier.

There was also a personal side. His own father had lived well into his nineties and Foti, a lifelong bachelor, and his brother, a medical doctor, were the old man's primary caretakers. They knew firsthand the ravages of age and the difficulty of evacuating an elderly parent in the face of a hurricane. They had done so themselves on several occasions—and they could pride themselves on an outcome a hell of a lot better than what went down at St.

Rita's. There, but for the grace of Charlie Foti, went his own father. Whoever allowed this to happen had to be a criminal. And Foti knew what to do with criminals. Lock 'em up. There is, however, a step between personal outrage and a lifer's jail cell. It's known as trial by jury, and in St. Francisville, on this September afternoon in 2007, this one was coming to its climax.

Jury trials are much like an election, a battle for hearts and minds. Foti had never lost an election, and he did not intend to lose this trial. He was politically astute enough and sufficiently aware of his own limitations to have put someone else in charge of the prosecution. Lead counsel for the state was the head of the attorney general's criminal division, assisted by the department's head of trials. For the all-important task of managing media, they retained a political fix-it guy. The trial lawyers for the state were smart and tough and, like their boss, inexperienced at losing. They had prosecuted criminal cases for thirty years or more. I hadn't tried a criminal case in twenty-five years, something I was acutely aware of as I sat there in the Magnolia Café, sipping my margarita and trying to press myself into the wall of the back-room bar.

I desperately wanted a verdict—but not just yet. Quick verdicts after long trials are usually guilty verdicts. I was less than halfway done with the first of what I hoped would be many margaritas when a house phone rang and the bartender took the call. She looked at me while she listened to the voice on the other end. She hung up. "Jim, that was the sheriff. He says the judge wants all of you back right away." I looked at my watch. The jury had been deliberating for barely three hours. After four grueling weeks, it was too soon. I looked at my colleagues, raised my eyebrows, and said, "Looks like a quick verdict." The air went out of the room. I picked up my glass and slammed its contents down my throat. "Thanks, honey," I said as I left. She looked at me with an unmistakable trace of sadness on her face. Somehow, even the bartender sensed that a quick verdict spelled doom for us.

Within minutes we had rejoined our teammates and clients in the courtroom. On both sides of the center aisle, people scurried to claim a seat. There followed a knock on the door and the sheriff said loudly, "All rise." The judge entered, took the bench, and ordered us to be seated.

On cue, a half-dozen deputies—very large and fully armed—entered the courtroom and took up strategic positions in the gallery and at the one exit. We had experienced intense security during the trial, but this show of force was unexpected and dramatic.

The judge began to speak. "The jury has reached a verdict," he said, "and I am about to receive that verdict here in open court. I know this case has been very emotional for many of you. I will not tolerate any outbursts from

The "old" courthouse in St. Francisville, with a Confederate memorial guarding its entrance.

A lawyer's office since 1842, this was our command center during the trial.

Louisiana Atty. Gen. Charles C. Foti, Jr., rails against the Manganos at a press conference. Courtesy of CBS News, from *48 Hours: No Way Out* (02/02/08).

Mabel and Sal Mangano. Courtesy of CBS News, from *48 Hours: No Way Out* (02/02/08).

anyone, either side, when the jury delivers its verdict. If you believe you will be unable to control your emotions, then you need to leave now. Does everyone understand me? If anyone in the audience utters a sound, I will hold you in contempt of court and put you in jail immediately, where I promise you, you will spend the night. Does everyone understand me?" An already quiet courtroom got even quieter. I turned around to see if anyone was leaving. No one did. I caught a glimpse of my wife in the gallery, her eyes closed, her hands clasped, deep in prayer, worry written all over her face. I wished in that instant that I could pray, too. I couldn't and didn't and felt empty because of it.

"Sheriff, bring in the jury," the judge boomed. There was a loud knock on the jury room door as it opened. "All rise for the jury," the sheriff said. I had developed an eye-contact relationship with one of the jurors over the previous four weeks. When things had gone well for us, he was visibly supportive. When we had been the victim of an unfair ruling from the court, he appeared as disappointed and outraged as we did. He was, I believed, solidly in our camp. I fixed my gaze on him as he entered the jury box. For the first time in weeks, he wouldn't look back. He was staring down at his feet, his hands crossed, folded in his lap. He looked unhappy. I turned to my colleagues and whispered, "We're cooked." My heart was racing at a hundred miles an hour.

"Has the jury reached a verdict?" the judge asked. The foreman stood and said, "Yes, we have, Your Honor." The judge then ordered the sheriff to bring the paperwork to him. Because there were 118 criminal counts alleged against both defendants, each required a separate individual verdict. The form was almost twenty pages long. The judge perused it slowly and carefully. As he did so, there was a flash of lightening followed in less than an instant by a crack of thunder that rattled the windows and shivered the timbers of the old building. The storm was on top of us. Other than the pelting rain, the courtroom was completely silent as the judge looked down his nose and through his reading glasses. He came to the last page and cleared his throat.

He had to raise his voice to be heard over the storm: "Will the defendants please rise and face the jury?" As was our custom, my colleagues and I rose with our clients. In that moment I touched Mabel's arm in an attempt to give her support. She was trembling. The judge continued, "In the case of State of Louisiana versus Salvador and Mabel Mangano, on the charge of thirty-five counts of negligent homicide, we the jury find the defendants . . ."

Chapter 2: Whataburger Meltdown

My family and I had fled New Orleans in advance of Hurricane Katrina, a completely different decision from the one made by Sal and Mabel. We found shelter with friends in Lafayette, Louisiana's Cajun capital located west of New Orleans, and stayed about a week. Upon learning that floodwaters had destroyed our home and that the children's school was closed indefinitely, we decided to try Houston, to find a school for the kids and, God willing, work for me. In addition to Louisiana, I was licensed to practice law in Texas and had some clients and contacts there. Debbie, my wife, found a hotel in Houston that had one room left and was also pet friendly. She jumped on it. We packed up everything we had brought to

A sad Collette, after learning that our house had flooded, her school had closed, and we were moving to Houston to start over. Lucky appears sad too.

Lafayette, which took all of about thirty seconds, and hopped in our cars. The decision to take both of them out of New Orleans had proved to be a good one; the car left behind would have flooded and been a total loss. My son Christopher and I got in my ten-year-old BMW and led the way. Debbie and our daughter, Collette, followed in the Escalade. They also took with them my wife's "baby," our two-year-old Bichon Frise named—I should say misnamed—Lucky.

On the way out of Lafayette we passed a Home Depot. An Allstate Insurance disaster response team had set up shop in its side parking lot. Our flood and homeowner's insurance was with Allstate, a company I quickly would come to despise. We pulled over and got in a line that was a half-block long. It was 90 degrees in the shade and it felt like twice that on the asphalt where we stood with hundreds of other displaced people. At the head of one line, we were directed to get in another, and then another, and lastly a fourth line where we were promised a check for living expenses: the princely sum of $1,500. A couple of nights earlier, unaware that we were homeless and poor, we had spent almost half that amount at a steakhouse in Lafayette. At least we'd gotten something. A painfully long time would pass before we would receive another red cent from this despicable insurer, and then only after I threatened to sue them. Most, not all, of the insurance companies treated the victims of Katrina abominably. They made it so hard to recover that thousands and thousands of people just gave up and withered away, no doubt as intended all along.

Interstate 10 to Houston was crawling with cars and trucks and National Guard vehicles in both directions. The eastbound traffic was headed to New Orleans to assist in ongoing relief and rescue efforts. Westbound vehicles contained people like us, going someplace—anywhere—to start their lives over. As one car passed another, the looks on people's faces were the same, no matter which direction they were going: bewilderment, fear, and sorrow. A trip that would normally take four hours lasted more than eight. Tired and exhausted, we pulled into the parking lot of our new home—the Sheraton Suites Houston Near the Galleria on a service road, close to the intersection of I-610 and Westheimer Drive, by Houston's famous Galleria shopping center. We would soon spend time there buying clothes as our three-day supply had already run out. And that was about it for Allstate's measly $1,500.

Check-in at the hotel was a mob scene with dozens of New Orleans evacuees jockeying for a room. We finally sealed the deal, got keys, and went upstairs. Our new "home" was one room, with smallish double beds in which the four of us would have to sleep. There was a single bath, and while the kids were excited to be in a hotel, the reality of four people living in this small space, in such close quarters—with a rambunctious dog—was a prescription for frayed nerves and sudden outbursts.

Mission number one was to get the kids into a school, put some structure into their lives, occupy their minds, and keep them from watching the 24/7 cable news coverage of the destruction of their hometown. I arranged for an interview at St. Mark's, an Episcopal school in Bellaire, Texas, some fifteen minutes away from our new hovel in the sky. As we toured the school the next morning, I lagged behind so the kids could be up front with the tour guide, the school's director of admissions.

It was an uneasy experience in spite of the administration's efforts to make it otherwise. I couldn't help but notice how the students looked at our kids and whispered to one another as we passed by. "There are some of those Katrina people," I imagined them saying. But the headmistress couldn't have been more welcoming. She told me the tuition was $14,000 per year, per student, and when I told her I had already paid that to St. Martin's Episcopal School, Chris and Collette's school back in New Orleans, and didn't, under the circumstances, have $28,000 at my immediate disposal, she said not to worry. St. Mark's would take our kids anyway, and we would deal with the money issue later on. This was a huge relief and some good news at last.

All of the St. Mark's kids were dressed in smart uniforms. St. Martin's had not required uniforms. This was a big deal, especially for Collette. She was an athlete and a tomboy and didn't even *own* a skirt or a dress at her then age of not-quite-eleven. Wear a skirt and pressed white blouse to school every day? Uh, Dad, puhhleeze? "Couldn't the kid wear regular clothes?" I asked. But the headmistress was way ahead of me. "It's bad enough that your kids have to be here under these circumstances," she said. "It would be even worse if they looked different than everybody else." She was, of course, correct. Picking up the phone, she got her mothers' club president on the line and within minutes, a platoon of St. Mark's moms had swept down upon us, fitting the kids with used uniforms, socks, shoes, and other apparel so they could enter school the next day at least looking like they belonged. It was a wonderfully generous thing to do that still brings a tear to my eye. Unlike Blanche DuBois in Tennessee Williams' New Orleans-based *A Streetcar Named Desire*, we had never before had to rely upon the kindness of strangers.

The joy of finding a new school faded quickly for Chris and Collette. The next morning was bedlam. Get some kind of breakfast in an under-staffed hotel jammed with evacuees and coordinate two kids taking consecutive showers in one bathroom, then getting dressed in a stranger's worn clothes.

I was the designated driver for an early morning trip through heavy traffic to a school we had visited once before. Debbie stayed behind to walk Lucky.

The ride to school was quiet. I tried to lighten up the mood with some talk about how it was going to be fun to meet new people in a new place. My small talk was met with big questions to which there were no legitimate answers. How long are we going to be in this school? What about *our* friends? Is our old school ever going to reopen? When will we be able to go home? I didn't have answers, and they were way too smart to let me put a happy face on our unimaginable situation. "Look," I said, "all we can do is to try to do the best we can, one day at a time, confronting the challenges each day presents. Everything's going to be okay." Even I didn't believe the words coming out of my mouth, but I could think of no others.

We arrived at the school. I parked the car and walked them in. We were greeted efficiently. Someone took Christopher, the eighth grader, off in one direction. I waited with Collette for a few minutes. She was quiet and stared down at her shoes. Her new teacher came into the office to take her to her new class. I watched them walk down the hall and before they turned the corner, another student stopped the teacher asking her for something. Waiting, Collette turned and caught me looking at her. Her face was sad; her lower lip trembled as she bravely fought back tears. She was losing the battle. Her look screamed, "Why is this happening to me? Dad, how could *you* let this happen to me?" She turned the corner and disappeared from view. I was crushed.

En route to the parking lot, I bucked an incoming tide of suburban moms hustling their kids to school. I started to tear up, Collette's look haunting me. How could I have allowed the pain I saw on my daughter's face? I turned away from the happy children—kids whose fathers had clearly done a much better job than I when it came to protecting their innocents from pain. The more happy faces I saw, the worse it got. I couldn't look them in the eye. I had to get to the car before all these kids and moms noticed this old guy in rumpled clothes crying like a baby in broad daylight.

Anonymous in rush-hour traffic, but unable to stop crying, I pulled into the parking lot of a fast food joint, Whataburger, angled into a parking space, placed the vehicle in park, and broke down completely. It was a pathetic moment, wholly uncontrollable and thankfully private—until someone pulled into the space next to me. So much for self-pity. Snap out of it! You're in Texas now; real men don't cry in Texas. In the coming two years, I would shed more than a few tears of anger, frustration, hurt, and disappointment, but this episode was by far the worst, taking place as it did in a fast food parking lot, of all places. I guess there are worse venues for such a meltdown, but none come presently to mind.

For twenty-seven years, I had solved other people's problems: big problems, intractable problems, life-and-death dilemmas. But now I couldn't solve my own. Lawyers identify issues and problems to be solved. We marshal evidence and weigh the pros and cons. We consider options, carefully analyze those options, and then make a decision. I was very good at that end of the business and very good at predicting outcomes. I needed to come up with a solution, a scenario, a game plan to publish to my family, and then at least act optimistic about it. Our morale depended on it, maybe our sanity, and surely our survival. Our predicament was not a matter of perspective, of optimism versus pessimism. It was not a question of the glass being half empty or half full. Our life's glass was, at that moment, unable to hold any liquid whatsoever. It had shattered. How do you put *that* back together?

This was the riddle I had to solve and solve quickly. I stumbled back to the hotel and did not mention my Whataburger meltdown to Debbie. I turned on the news and there, for the first time, I saw a story about the discovery of thirty-five bodies in a flooded nursing home in St. Bernard Parish, just outside New Orleans. St. Bernard Parish had been completely destroyed in the storm. More than 95 percent of the buildings in the parish, homes and businesses, had sustained flooding reaching up to their rooftops. Larry Ingargiola, St. Bernard's director of homeland security and emergency preparedness at the time, had said in an interview that St. Bernard Parish was "literally dead." The CNN anchors were terming the discovery at St. Rita's nursing home the worst, most horrific news in a week full of horrific news. How could this happen, I thought? Why didn't they evacuate? I was glued to the screen. This terrible news made my problems seem insignificant by comparison. At least we're alive, I thought to myself.

Chapter 3: Divine Intervention?

We went and looked at some apartments while the kids were in school, but two weeks would pass before we escaped the hotel at $149.95 a night, plus tax. Two weeks, four people, one dog, two females, one bathroom. Challenging is one word to describe those two weeks; miserable is another.

After watching more cable news about the death of our hometown, I returned to pick up the kids at school. I was, of course, very early and I spotted a Starbucks in a strip mall close to the school. I pulled in and had a coffee. This store had "house" newspapers, where customers could peruse several national publications for free. Free was good. I glanced at a *New York Times* piece wherein St. Bernard Parish officials were confirming at least thirty-two deaths in the St. Rita's nursing home debacle. The story reported that the bodies, one week after Katrina made landfall, still lay where the patients died, draped over wheelchairs, wrapped in a shower curtain, or lying on the floor in several inches of muck. Thankfully, there were no photos accompanying the *Times* piece. There were stories in the Houston and Dallas papers, too. The *Morning News* article was especially graphic. Their reporter must have gained access to the facility. One elderly woman clothed in a thin house-dress was on the concrete floor of a patio, according to the reporter. More than a week after the storm, ". . . the smell of rotting human flesh clung to clothing of searchers going through the building." There were enough bad stories happening in my life without reading this one to the end. Anyway, it was time to pick up Christopher and Collette.

Idling in the carpool line, I saw Chris and Collette before they saw me. They were standing alone, off to the side, separate from the other kids. "Well, how was it, guys?" I asked, trying to sound upbeat as they clambered into the car. In unison and without the benefit of a rehearsal, they let loose: "I hate it. I want to go home!" So much for the positives of finding a school and getting them into a structured environment. I had worked my tail off to make this day happen and they hated it at first glance. Oh well, just another kick in the groin for dear old dad.

Returning to the hotel we set about trying to establish a normal routine. But what's normal about living in a hotel full of people from New Orleans who had lost everything in their lives in the blink of an eye? It was not exactly a happy place, but we were determined to make the best of it. We allowed the kids to order room service instead of going downstairs to eat in the packed restaurant. They had always enjoyed ordering room service on our previous vacations, so this was a feel-good concession on our part. Chris took full advantage, ordering hamburgers, French fries, steaks, mashed potatoes, ice cream, cheesecake, and chocolate malts. He was determined to work his way through the entire room service menu. Just how much he enjoyed his stay would be driven home by the gargantuan size of the room service bill presented to me as we finally checked out. While still worried about the money we were spending, and with no sign of income ahead, I had resorted to that time-tested and truly American way of dealing with financial crisis. I was charging everything. American Express, MasterCard, and Visa could not find me here. I had not exactly left a forwarding address from our flooded digs in Lakeview. It would take months for the bills to catch up with us. And, of course, given the interest rates they charged, the credit card companies were more than happy to overextend my credit. A day of reckoning would come, of course, but at this point we were fighting for sanity and survival, so I tried not to worry about it.

The St. Rita story was now on cable news constantly. It was the lead story for several days and in the competition for ratings and exclusives, the networks began aiming for the fences with reports that the owners had evacuated before the storm, leaving patients lashed to their beds and wheelchairs. I was as appalled as anyone. Somebody needs to find these people, take them out, and shoot them, I thought.

Apparently Attorney General Foti was thinking the same way. On September 8, 2005, only ten days after Katrina struck, he took to the airwaves, essentially putting out an international A.P.B. (all points bulletin). "Anyone knowing the whereabouts of the owners of the St. Rita Nursing Home should contact our office," he said. He announced that his Medicare/Medicaid, Fraud and Abuse investigators were looking to find out why St. Rita's residents were unable to get help. At a well-attended press conference, his voice cracked with anger and emotion:

> "This is a horrific tragedy and the story is one of the worst I have heard. I am deeply saddened to learn of the fate of so many elderly

citizens. I will investigate this case fully. . . . I want answers! I want to know why these people were trapped and were not evacuated."

More stories followed, including a report that the owners were attempting to flee the country to Mexico. Why Mexico, I thought? Another story had them trying to get on a cruise ship to flee the country. The verifying detail was some "source" who claimed that St. Rita's owners were known to be fans of cruise-ship vacations. An escape by cruise ship? Wait a minute, I thought. That's a pretty sluggish and rather traceable getaway escape vehicle. But illogic and non sequiturs never get in the way of a good story, and I was as riveted to this one as the rest of America.

At a second press conference, Foti waxed even more strident and outraged. The presumption of innocence had by now been completely suspended. Foti had caught, tried, and condemned these people before even determining their location. As I watched the non-stop coverage, the defense lawyer in me began to wince at how these people were being brutalized by the media. Where were the owners, I wondered. More to the point, where were their lawyers? Why weren't they feeding the press alibis and punching back. With media hungry for a conviction, if you fall too far behind a prosecutor's rantings you can never get public opinion back on an even keel and there goes your jury pool. Thankfully, it wasn't my problem. My plate was already quite full, what with trying to hold our family together; figuring out a way to restart my law practice in a new city; finding a place to live; reconnecting with our law firm staff and dealing with their issues and personal tragedies; and contacting clients and letting them know we were okay and that the firm was going to open a Houston office and continue to handle their cases, old and new. Surely there would be a lot of legal insurance business on the heels of Katrina, and we had to be in position to capitalize on that. Somehow, I had to make some money to cover all these extraordinary expenses and credit-card bills. I had to accomplish all these tasks simultaneously, while trying to avoid another Whataburger meltdown.

I fell into a routine. After driving the kids to school, I would stop for coffee and read the papers. The St. Rita's tragedy was everywhere; it was the Katrina tragedy du jour. Comments by disgruntled former employees of the nursing home were reported as fact. From the hundreds of cases I had handled for employers, I knew that no former employee ever told the whole truth, instead focusing on details that would put the former employer in a bad light. Every rumor, every whisper about St. Rita's had begun whirling through the news industry's twenty-four-hour cycle. With the news outlets fighting for attention, the most outrageous and unsubstantiated fantasies were being reported as "breaking news"—whereupon bobble-head commentators would dissect them day and night, as though the veracity of these tidbits had long since been established.

Back at the hotel room, I would flip on CNN or one of its rivals, drink more coffee, and work the phones trying to put our law practice back together. The big problem was that ninety percent of our cases were in litigation in a flooded city to which residents were forbidden to return. There would be no work, no court appearances, no depositions, and no legal research for the foreseeable future. Accordingly, there would be no income. First things first: the city was still being drained of floodwaters; no one was in any rush to restart the tort bar, one of New Orleans' bigger industries. My firm was, quite simply, stuck in neutral. Each day that passed was another eight hours of missed opportunity to bill by the hour, multiplied by ten billing attorneys and paralegals. We were bleeding from it and losing the opportunity to even make a living. It was depressing and there was no end in sight.

I was sitting there before the TV sinking deeper and deeper into the quicksand of despair when, one morning, the telephone rang. This was odd in and of itself, as hardly anyone knew where we were. I hadn't even communicated yet with my extended family to let them know our whereabouts. Probably the front desk, I thought, calling to kick us out of the hotel in order to accommodate a longstanding reservation. I had already turned the corner onto Pessimism Drive and begun to expect the worst of every encounter, phone call, or news item. It was my way of steeling myself for the truly horrific news that I feared lay just ahead.

I picked up the phone. The voice on the line, male, asked: "Is this Jim Cobb?" I said yes. "Are you the lawyer from New Orleans?" Strange question, I thought. The caller introduced himself as Jeremy Goux and said he was a lawyer in Covington, a New Orleans suburb on the north shore of Lake Pontchartrain. He said he was the son of Ron Goux, president of the Louisiana Nursing Home Association. I knew his father from some previous cases I had handled. Goux *père* was a nursing home owner and, as president of the state's Nursing Home Association, a political force in Baton Rouge, the state capital, and a wily and cagy operator.

"Sure, I know your dad," I said. "What can I do for you?" Goux *fils* said: "I'm on the line with my client, Mabel Mangano; she's the owner/administrator of the St. Rita's Nursing Home." Before I could respond, a woman was saying: "Mr. Cobb, this is Mabel Mangano. We need a lawyer. Could you please help us?"

I had neither met nor spoken to either of these people before. How had they even found me? Pondering how to respond to Mabel Mangano's entreaty, I glanced at the television. By sheer coincidence, the video was of dozens of body bags being hauled out of St. Rita's and placed in ambulances. The TV voiceover reported, "We are now seeing images of some thirty bodies or so being removed from a nursing home; all of these elderly citizens drowned in Katrina floodwaters in what has become the most shocking tragedy associated with this storm. Why weren't they evacuated is the question on the minds of law enforcement officials." I was speechless. I was on the phone at that very moment with the only person in the world who could answer that question.

The mystery of how they tracked me down came packaged with a deeper question: Why? Why me?

As I would later learn, like most everyone else, Sal and Mabel Mangano had indeed fled Louisiana in Katrina's aftermath—not by cruise ship, however. They had escaped to the west bank of the Mississippi River by ferry and had been part of a throng driven to the New Orleans airport in school buses. From there, without any say in the matter, they found themselves being hauled to a high school gym in suburban Dallas where they spent a wretched interlude of several nights on cots. This was not a place you would want to stay under any circumstances, but the last straw for Sal was waking up at 3 A.M. one morning to see the gentleman on the next cot over bury his face in a handful of white powder and start to snort it into his nostrils. Enough! The Manganos contacted friends in Lafayette and arranged to stay with them. They were greeted with hugs and kisses and then this: "You're all over the television. They're looking for you."

"They" included their lawyer, Jeremy Goux. Goux handled civil issues for St. Rita's, including the nursing home's dealings with the State Department of Health and Hospitals. And as cable news went berserk over the St. Rita's story, he became increasingly concerned that he hadn't heard from his clients, not knowing they were in a TV-less limbo between Dallas and Lafayette. As St. Rita's registered agent and lawyer, Goux had been contacted by representatives of the attorney general's office asking to speak to his clients. He told them the truth: "I haven't heard from them and have no idea where they are." He then called his father, Ron Goux, president of the Louisiana Nursing Home Association. The senior Goux was very influential in the nursing home industry. He owned or operated three or four homes, lobbied the state legislature on behalf of the association, and was point man for political contributions by nursing home owners in key legislative races. A player in gubernatorial politics, he had also raised money among nursing home owners for Attorney General Foti's campaign three years earlier. Sal and Mabel had contributed to that campaign at Goux's request.

Jeremy informed his father that he had received a call from the A.G.'s office inquiring as to the whereabouts of the Manganos. "What should I do?" he asked. "You don't handle it," was the elder Goux's immediate response. He correctly perceived that this was a witch hunt and that the entire nursing home industry would likely be put on trial for the tragedy. As president of the association, Goux senior could not have his son out front in such a case. Jeremy was an up-and-coming lawyer, but he was young and had never handled a case of this magnitude. "You need to find Jim Cobb, put Sal and Mabel in his hands, and then step back and let him take the lead and the heat." The elder Goux sensed the political implications of such a case instantly. "You get behind him, out of the line of fire, and learn how to handle such a high profile case. But you can't be out front." His son had a question. "Who's Jim Cobb?" he asked.

For three years starting in 1982, I had been lead counsel for three not-for-profit hospitals in a showdown with then-governor Edwin Edwards. That's how Ron Goux had first come to know me. For reasons having a bit more to do with politics than public health, Edwards had ordered approval of applications to create new hospitals in communities that didn't need them—in flagrant disregard of DHH standards, criteria, and plans. These new for-profit ventures would have attracted doctors and put my clients out of business. Jeremy Goux was maybe ten years old at the time and had no memory of the case. We filed suit and discovered that the proponents had paid Edwards $2 million in "consulting fees" the year before he was once again elected governor. His payback was to give them Certificates of Need, which they could sell or develop for millions more. The case created a firestorm in the healthcare industry and garnered much media attention. One morning, I had gotten a call from the federal prosecutor in New Orleans asking if he could send some FBI agents to my office to look at the information we had developed. They did, and months later Edwards was indicted by a federal grand jury on racketeering and bribery charges, with mail and wire fraud thrown in for good measure. His first trial, as a sitting governor, ended in a hung jury. I testified as a witness for the prosecution in the re-trial. This was not a very smart career move, taking on Louisiana's most powerful governor since Huey P. Long, but it established my reputation as a lawyer who backed down to no one. Edwards was acquitted in the second trial, but the scandal cost him re-election. We were successful on the civil side in preventing these unnecessary and expensive hospitals from being built. All of my clients prevailed and remained in business, maintaining their market share in their respective communities.

"Cobb knows healthcare, he knows how to handle the media in a big case, he didn't back down to Governor Edwards, and he certainly won't be intimidated by Foti. Get him," the senior Goux concluded. "Everybody's scattered to the four winds. How do I find him?" the son asked. "Look, I've told you what to do. Now you figure out how to do it." With that, Ron Goux hung up. He had better things to do than look for one aging, gin-swilling needle in the haystack that was the Katrina diaspora. All of Goux's nursing homes had evacuated ahead of the storm. His residents were scattered and dropping like flies, as commonly happens when very frail geriatrics are moved abruptly.

Jeremy got back on the phone and began calling every phone number that could possibly lead him to me—office, home, office building managers. None of it worked. The State Bar Association had set up a clearing house for lawyers to check in and leave numbers where they could be contacted by clients. Jeremy tried the clearing house; no luck. I was in a hotel room in Texas, totally unaware of what the Bar Association was doing back in Louisiana. Jeremy contacted other lawyers far and wide. Typical response: "Sure, I know who Cobb is. You're trying to find him? No idea where he is."

It was at this point that Jeremy got the long-awaited call from a very panicky Mabel Mangano. "Jeremy, what's going on? What are we supposed to do?" The bull's-eye shifted to Jeremy's back. He now knew that Sal and Mabel were in Louisiana, in the Lafayette area, and were the subject of a televised manhunt. He had been counseled not to handle their case, but could not find the lawyer his father—the industry leader—had told him to hire on their behalf. The A.G.'s office called back, and now he was in a trick bag. He knew where these "fugitives" were, and were he to misspeak or mislead investigators, he could be charged with obstruction of justice. The young lawyer was growing older by the minute. He dodged their pressing inquiry without misleading them. He told them, "I'm swamped right now, working on something. I'll get back to you tomorrow." This sufficed. What the authorities did not know was that he was "swamped" trying to find representation for the very people they were looking for, now that he was aware of their precise location. That bought time but brought him no closer to a solution. He worked the phones all day into the early evening, striking out again and again. Katrina was pitching him a no-hitter. True to his profession, he wound up in a bar with a pal, crying in his beer, trying to figure out what he would do when, at first light, the cops called him back.

He muttered to himself and, as the liquor loosened his tongue, moaned aloud: "I'm looking for this guy, Jim Cobb. I don't know where he is, what he looks like, or have any clue of how to find him. For all I know, he could be sitting on the roof of his house waiting for a helicopter. I have to find him by tomorrow. I am totally screwed."

A young woman at the end of the bar was listening in on the conversation. "Excuse me," she said, "are you speaking about Jim Cobb, the lawyer from New Orleans?"

"That's the one. Do you know him?"

"No, but I have a friend whose mother is friends with Cobb's wife. Do you want me to try to reach her?" Telephoning feverishly and with great difficulty, as cell service was still largely out of commission, the young woman located her friend Rachal Bezou. Amazingly, for the first time since the storm, Rachal had spoken to her mother that very day, as the older woman reached a friend's house in Houston. "Do you know where Debbie and Jim are?" she asked. "As a matter of fact, I do," the mother said. "I just spoke with Debbie this afternoon, and they're at a Sheraton here in Houston." Rachal got the hotel phone number and gave it to Jeremy. First thing the next morning I received the call that would change my life. Small world? Uncanny coincidence? Or, as Mabel came to see it, divine intervention? Those are the facts. Make of them what you will.

Chapter 4: Facts Are Stubborn Things

"We need a lawyer. Could you please help us?" Those were Mabel's words but not hers alone. I had heard these words more than a thousand times in my almost thirty years of practice. As a younger lawyer, I would have answered "yes" immediately, excited by the prospect of a new case and flattered by the notion that someone, somewhere, needed my help. As I grew older and, hopefully, wiser, "yes" was uttered less frequently and never immediately. Every lawyer bears the scars of representations they should never have undertaken. Unreasonable clients who were impossible to please. Unpaid bills and unrealized expectations leading to terminated relationships—these were occupational hazards unknown to the young and the free. By this time in my career, I more often said "no" immediately, and always avoided saying "yes" without first pondering the consequences, because getting out of a representation, once you've signed on, is a whole lot harder than getting in. Aware of the pitfalls of each and every case, burdened and weakened by the weight of carrying other people's problems on my back for three decades, and in the homestretch of a thirty-year race that invariably leads to a clubhouse labeled *burnout*, why would I want to help these people whom I didn't even know and to whom I owed nothing? If only one-tenth of what had been said about them were true, then they were terrible and despicable people, and why would I want my good name associated with theirs? Why would I want to represent them in small claims court, let alone on a worldwide stage?

And so when this notorious stranger named Mabel Mangano asked for my counsel so pleadingly, what did I say? "Yes," I said, and I said it immediately. "Yes, I will help you." So much for caution, reflection, and the careful weighing of consequences.

I had been led to this rash response on the strength of an inspiring example. I had recently finished reading David McCullough's brilliant biography, *John Adams*. I was so moved by the power of his writing and the elegance of his prose that I choked back tears reading his description of Abigail's death and John's reaction to it. I could not remember ever being so moved by a book. McCullough's depiction of Adams' ability and principles as a young trial lawyer had been enough to restore faith in my dubious profession. The most outrageous case in eighteenth century America was the Boston Massacre. We all learned as school children that British troops fired upon unarmed colonists, killing many. Right? The term "massacre" has survived through the centuries and resonates to this day. The great patriot Samuel Adams (he now makes a great beer) termed the killings a "bloody butchery." Paul Revere published a print portraying the scene as the slaughter of the innocent and unarmed by a brutal British garrison.

The day after the massacre the thirty-four-year-old Adams was approached and asked to defend the soldiers, all other lawyers having refused. Adams had political ambition and did not suffer public criticism easily. Why should he defend these butchers and imperil his political career and standing in the Commonwealth? Adams did not hesitate for a second, immediately accepting the defense of these "bloody butchers." Adams' "Yes, I will help you" was strongly rooted in the belief that no man in a free country should be denied the right to counsel and a fair trial. And if scorn and ridicule were heaped upon the lawyer who chose to defend pariahs, so be it; his duty was to a higher calling and he must answer that call.

I learned in McCullough's book that not only did Adams defend the hated British at trial, he did it twice in two trials. First, he represented the British captain in charge of the detail, one Thomas Preston. McCullough wrote in *John Adams*:

> Whether Captain Preston had given an order to fire, as was charged, could never be proven. Adams' argument for the defense, though unrecorded, was considered a virtuoso performance. Captain Preston was found not guilty.

In the second trial, Adams defended those who pulled the triggers, sending their musket balls into the unruly crowd, killing five and injuring many more. These clients were the rank and file, the enlisted/conscripted men of the British army: the grunts. Adams' closing argument on their behalf lasted an astonishing two days—a tour de force.

"Facts are stubborn things," Adams told the jury, "and whatever may be our wishes, our inclinations, or the dictums of our passions, they cannot alter the state of facts and evidence." His language was so gripping, the argument so compelling, that I wrote it down for future use. It was seared into my memory as was the strength of Adams' example in representing the "bloody butchers," for whom he obtained seven out of nine acquitals.

They weren't butchers at all, it turned out. Years later, after having served as America's first ambassador to the Court of St. James, then as the first vice president and second president of the United States, Adams conceded that the Boston Massacre case was the most exhausting work of his career. Ever the trial lawyer, he concluded that his part in the defense was "one of the most gallant, generous, manly and disinterested actions of my whole life, and one of the best pieces of service I ever rendered my country." His story and example were fresh in my mind as I took Mabel's unlikely call and acceded to her request.

Adams wasn't my only inspiration. Closer to home and two centuries later, I had become close friends with another lawyer who had received "the call" to defend a bloody butcher, a man the media had nicknamed "the most hated man in America." Stephen Jones of Enid, Oklahoma, was lead defense counsel for Timothy James McVeigh, the man accused of blowing up the Alfred P. Murrah Federal Building in Oklahoma City. It was, at that point, the most heinous act of terrorism ever committed in the United States. McVeigh killed 168 people, including dozens of women, children, and even infants in a nursery and daycare center for federal employees. The television images of rescue teams carrying out burned and bloodied babies was the worst thing I had ever seen—until I viewed photographs of the thirty-five innocent elderly who drowned at St. Rita's.

I followed Jones' representation of McVeigh from afar, on television. I wondered how he could possibly defend this murderous, rotten son-of-a-bitch. Media coverage had co-opted any presumption of innocence on my part. Jones acted with dignity, competently and aggressively defending his client. He had been so successful in pre-trial maneuverings that some legal publications speculated on the possibility of a not guilty verdict for McVeigh. It all unraveled when a trusted member of Jones' team betrayed the defense by leaking to the *Dallas Morning News* that McVeigh had confessed to his lawyers.

I watched the trial play out and was pleased with the guilty verdict and death sentence. If anyone deserved the death penalty, I thought, surely this baby killer did. But I was actually more interested in the lawyer who defended McVeigh than I was in McVeigh. Jones had acquitted himself with dignity, self-respect, and decorum, while fighting against overwhelming odds. I could scarcely imagine the toll the representation must have exacted on him and his family for defending "the most hated man in America." In 1999, two years after the McVeigh trial, I was in my eighteenth year as an adjunct professor of law at Tulane University and co-director of the law school's trial advocacy program, where we teach senior law students how to try cases before they are set loose on an unsuspecting public. Part of our program was a distinguished speakers' series, where once a semester I would select someone to give a talk about the practice of trial lawyers, a talk designed to be informative but also inspirational. Impressed as I was by Jones, one day I picked up the phone and cold called him—no introduction whatsoever. I invited him to visit Tulane and speak to my students about the case, and more importantly, about how and why he had decided to undertake the representation and the effect it had on his life. He agreed.

He came to New Orleans and spoke to my class and to many invited lawyers and faculty members on February 17, 2000. He spoke for an hour and fifteen minutes, which passed in the blink of an eye. His audience of one hundred was so quiet you could have heard a pin drop on the carpeted floor. As to the question of why he agreed to undertake the defense, his answer was blunt: "McVeigh was in desperate need of counsel. I did not have a conflict of interest with any of my other clients in accepting his case. I felt reasonably qualified and competent to defend him and would commit to him my all. I said, 'Yes,' to the question of the chief judge for the United States District Court in Oklahoma City."

He returned year after year delivering the same message to each new class of senior law students. We became close. He and his wife visited our home; we went out to magnificent lunches and dinners in New Orleans, with more than our fair share of adult beverages, although Stephen rarely drank. We over-nighted as a family in the Jones' home in Enid, Oklahoma, on a twenty-two hour drive back from Aspen, Colorado. It was the best pot roast and the most challenging political discussion in which I had ever been engaged. I forgave Stephen for being a Republican and for having worked as an aide to Richard Nixon. He forgave me for being a southern Democrat, who, on occasion, spoke too loudly and drank too much. We made each other laugh a lot and kept up an active correspondence: real letters, typed on paper. No emails for us.

So when "the call" came to me, my course of conduct and my response had already been set. I had in my mind both Adams' lofty philosophizing and Stephen's simple and direct analysis of why *every* lawyer must say "yes." As we say in my business: case closed. I was going to help these people, despite the obvious and dangerous pitfalls that their case would present. I had no idea, however, in saying "yes" that helping them would turn out to be the hardest choice of my life.

Chapter 5: St. Rita, Pray for Us

"Speak to no one, Mrs. Mangano," I said, "not even friends or relatives. I don't want to talk about this on the phone so I will come to you immediately. How about tomorrow?" She was, of course, available and desperate to start disentangling herself from what was already a legal nightmare. The Manganos were in Lafayette, Goux was in Covington, and I was in Houston. The attorney general's office was in Baton Rouge, so we decided to meet there, at the Nursing Home Association office. Jeremy told me the A.G.'s office was hot on his heels for an answer regarding his clients' whereabouts. I told him I would take care of that. I called the assistant A.G. with whom Jeremy had been dealing and informed him that I had just been retained by the people the state sought. I was evacuated to Houston, my house in New Orleans had flooded, but I would come to Baton Rouge and meet with my new clients and call him after that. He seemed relieved that the "fugitives" had been "found" and grateful that they had counsel with whom he could speak. My call bought us another couple of days.

I told Debbie about the call and that I would be leaving almost immediately. This would necessarily increase her duties and burdens with the kids, but as a trial lawyer's wife, she was used to me picking up and suddenly disappearing to chase some far away catastrophe. Still in shock from the greater calamity, the annihilation of our home and the world we had known, she voiced no objection, although had she thought about it, she might have said: "Wait a minute; you're not leaving me in a hotel room with two kids in a new school on the edge of nervous breakdowns! Your place is here with us." Neither of us could imagine at that early moment in time how things would play out in the coming twenty-four months. Otherwise, we both might have said: "No way. We don't need this in our lives right now! They've got plenty of lawyers in Louisiana, in fact, too many. Let somebody else handle it." That discussion never took place and the thought of it never entered either of our minds. Always the practical one, Debbie had one question: "What are you going to wear?" She was on to something. Lead defense counsel for Katrina's biggest criminal case? I didn't have a pair of long pants or a clean shirt.

I sped off to the Galleria, bought some khaki pants and a couple of golf shirts, underwear, socks, a pair of shoes, legal pads, pens and pencils, and, oh yes, a briefcase. I started to make calls to find a place to stay in Baton Rouge. With a million people having fled the New Orleans area, there wasn't a hotel room to be had from Houston and Dallas in the west to Birmingham and Memphis in the east. There were certainly none in Baton Rouge as it was high, dry, and only seventy miles away from the Big Uneasy. Even private homes were bursting at the seams. Good Samaritans took in people that they knew, and occasionally even strangers. Some people slept in cars, others in shelters and on buses—any place they could lay their weary heads. I contacted a lawyer friend to see if he had some room in his "inn." All the beds were taken, he said, but I was welcome to come and "grab some floor." I jumped at the opportunity. My host, Andre LaPlace, was a character. His ménage included waiters from Galatoire's, musicians, jugglers, fire-eaters, and upon my arrival, a high-wire act; I would be working without a net. Andre's place was a circus and so was Baton Rouge.

I drove over from Houston early the next day, leaving my homeless family in a hotel room on an interstate service road. In a brief discussion with the kids, I told them I was leaving to go meet some clients in Baton Rouge in a case that was all over television. I didn't know what was going to happen or when I'd be back. Collette asked why I was leaving. I answered that there were two people back in Louisiana who needed my help. "We need your help, too," she said. Dagger, straight through the heart. I had no answer for her and left anyway. Interstate 10 was still packed in both directions. Hundreds of relief trucks and military vehicles were headed east with me. Similar numbers were headed west; hundreds of cars were stuffed with people and belongings looking for a place to land. Confusion and anxiety still reigned supreme.

I had no idea what to expect when I met the Manganos. I reminded myself of something I had said in opening statements on behalf of defendants for thirty years: "there are two sides to every story, ladies and gentlemen. Please withhold judgment until you hear *our* side of the story." I was skeptical that there even would be an "our side of the story." I could not imagine why the Manganos had not evacuated their helpless residents. I gave myself a pep talk in the six hours it took me to get to Baton Rouge, a drive of less than three hours usually. I had time to play back the mental tape of myself excoriating the Manganos' lawyers for not rushing to their defense as I sat in front of the TV set listening to the attorney general and an army of hack reporters vilify them on cable broadcasts. They had been railroaded and lynched without so much as a whimper. Okay, smartass, I thought, what are you gonna do about it? I hadn't a clue.

Something very odd happened before my first scheduled meeting with Sal and Mabel. I didn't have an office in Baton Rouge so, with the permission of the Nursing Home Association, we had arranged to meet at their offices. The day before the meeting someone from the association called and suggested we meet someplace else. Sal and Mabel were long-standing members of the group and were well liked and respected, or so I was told. The meeting had to be moved to the conference room of a downtown law firm, I was informed. I said nothing; I really didn't care where we met, so long as we could meet privately and comfortably, but I wondered if this was a first whiff of the public disgrace that would come with representing "monsters" like the proprietors of St. Rita's. Sal and Mabel were evidently taboo, even to their own association. At this stage of the hysteria which reigned in Baton Rouge, no one wanted to be associated with them. It also meant, by definition, that no one wanted to be associated with me. It was not the worst instance of the shunning we would be exposed to over the coming two years, only the first. It was a stinging rebuke to Sal and Mabel. They felt it and so did I.

I got to the unfamiliar law office first. One of the senior partners met me, showed me the conference room we could use, pointed out the facilities and the coffee pot, and said we would not be disturbed. Then he disappeared. I could hear the sound of shuffling feet beyond the conference room door. It opened and there stood Sal and Mabel, along with a fair-sized clan: their son, "Little Sal;" his wife, T.J.; their son, Tanner; and the Manganos' other grandson, Johnny White, the son of their daughter, Tammy. As I would soon learn, all of them had been at St. Rita's when the flood suddenly struck the nursing home. All of them had had to swim for their lives. They appeared disheveled, distracted, and unsure of themselves. Sal and Mabel looked like two deer frozen in the headlights of an onrushing eighteen-wheeler.

I figured them to be in their mid-sixties, both of them short and compactly built. Mabel's skin was a bright white, topped off by big white hair, teased and curled in a coiffure stuck in the late 1950s. She had pencil-thin dark eyebrows, in striking contrast to her hair. The web of smile lines around her eyes became more pronounced when she actually smiled—not that it was happening very often these days. Sal was Mabel's dermatological opposite, with an olive-toned complexion that bespoke his Italian roots. He was solid with strong, well-worn palms and short, thick fingers. His handshake was like vise-grip pliers. He looked me squarely in the eye as we met as if he were taking my measure. Given what I had seen and heard about this duo on television, I returned just as hard a look. I needed to take their measure, too. First impressions count: they were clearly shaken and ill at ease.

I decided to start the conversation by telling them something about what had happened to our family. Our home had flooded in Lakeview, I said, and I had left my family in a hotel room in Houston to come and meet them. We had lost everything, but we had gotten out in advance of the storm and were struggling to make it, just as they were, I assumed. I asked them to tell me something about themselves, their family, and their life. I wanted them to relax as much as I wanted to know their story because, in the months to come, I knew that everything they told me would have to be filtered through the prism of their life's experiences.

Mabel, it seemed, had been born and raised in St. Bernard Parish. She was from Delacroix Island down in the Parish. The "island," as locals called it, was home to fishermen, oystermen, hunters, and trappers. Mabel's family had raised or caught the food they ate. Her father fished and shrimped and eventually landed a job as a St. Bernard Parish sheriff's deputy. He was in law enforcement for some twenty-five years. His boss, the sheriff of St. Bernard Parish, was one Jack Rowley, who held the office for decades. Rowley had tired of the sheriff's office, gone to law school, and gotten a law degree. He then ran for district attorney of the parish and had been elected easily. He still held the D.A.'s job in 2005, the year of Katrina; that would give him the ultimate say on whether to prosecute the Manganos—or so I thought. Mabel had known Rowley her whole life, and her father had been a trusted deputy. I made a mental note of this connection, for surely it should redound to our benefit later on. Mabel's uncle had risen to captain in the parish fire department and was buried with full honors. In the 1970s, when Mabel's grandmother was institutionalized in a nursing home in St. Bernard, Mabel had gone to care for her on an almost daily basis. These were the dark ages of the nursing home industry when homes acquired a reputation as dirty, dark, and smelly places where people went to die with little or no care or affection. That's why Mabel came almost every day—to see that her maw-maw was cared for. Her grandmother had died in that nursing home in St. Bernard. Her name was Rita.

Sal was not from St. Bernard. He was born up the Mississippi River from New Orleans in Ascension Parish, just outside Baton Rouge. He and his family had moved to New Orleans and settled in the French Quarter, then something of an Italian ghetto. He quit school early on in life and went to work with his hands. He was a mechanic, a heavy-equipment operator, a repair man, a blue-collar jack of all trades. He could build or fix anything from plumbing to electrical systems and he was a master of ceramic tile. He and Mabel had met at a dance in New Orleans some forty-five years earlier, quickly fell in love, and married just as quickly. They had two children, Sal Jr. and Tammy, each of whom was married and each of whom had two children. There was a pattern emerging here.

Sal Jr. had two sons: Sal III and Tanner. Earlier in the summer of 2005, before Katrina, Tanner had completed basic training in the United States Marine Corps. Out of a basic training class of some three or four hundred recruits, Tanner had finished first in his class. Mabel spoke with pride as she recalled her grandson's graduation ceremony just months earlier. She and her family sat in a place of honor on the stage alongside the commanding general, an honor bestowed only on the family of the soldier who finished at the top of the class. Her other grandson, Sal III, was a police officer in the City of Kenner, a suburb of New Orleans, and had been decorated for bravery.

Slowly but surely, a family portrait of these people was emerging: one quite different from what I had heard about them on television. For generations they had been first responders—policemen, firemen, and soldiers. They didn't brag; these were their roles in life. They spoke of them as matters of fact. Something didn't compute with the story the media told: the Manganos appeared to be stoic and self-reliant, hardly the type to abandon ship and flee to Mississippi casinos, much less to leave nursing home patients to die lashed to wheelchairs and beds. Desultory chitchat had had the desired effect. They began to seem relaxed, and so I summoned all my courage and quietly asked the question I had been scrupulously avoiding: "So what happened at the nursing home?" Mabel looked down at her pale hands on the conference room table; her fingers were interlocked as if she were praying. She took a very deep breath. I could tell she was fighting back tears.

It was a bad question asked too soon in the conversation. I was feeling the heat of finding out as quickly as possible what had happened so I could respond to the attorney general's office that was pressuring us for an interview. I immediately retracted the question as Mabel struggled to answer it, and asked instead, "How did you get in the nursing home business in the first place?" Much better question, I thought. Mabel settled back in her chair, off the hook at least for a few more minutes.

Prior to running a nursing home, Sal and Mabel ran a feed-and-seed store, catering to the agricultural and farming community in rural St. Bernard, a place with plenty of crop farming and animal husbandry. Theirs was a mom-and-pop business and they were successful at it. Mabel's interest and attention had shifted as a result of the time spent with her grandmother in the nursing home before she died. The conditions were deplorable, the food awful, the activities for residents non-existent. She got the idea, which then became an obsession, that they could do a better job. She vowed never to treat her residents as her grandmother was treated, and they never were. I was intrigued that she named the nursing home in honor of the named patron saint of her grandmother, Rita. I was a devotee of lives of the saints and could rattle off which saint was the patron saint of which cause with annoying accuracy. But I did not know St. Rita—internet to the rescue. St. Rita was born near Spoleto, Italy in 1381. She lived a hard-scrabble, miserable life under the yoke of an abusive husband who was eventually murdered by his enemies. His much deserved, early departure from this earth freed Rita to join an order of nuns, where she did charitable work and was completely devoted to prayer. She became the patron saint of impossible cases. Truth, always stranger than fiction, could not have supplied us a more astonishingly appropriate patron saint.

Mabel had no training or expertise but nonetheless began a quixotic quest to build, open, and run a nursing home in her home parish. The bureaucratic red tape to license such an enterprise is mind boggling. Without the aid of lawyers or accountants or healthcare consultants, she began the process of applying to the state for a nursing home certificate. It took seven or eight years, but she persisted. She went back to school and trained to be a nursing home administrator. She filled out application after application and went back and forth to Baton Rouge maybe a hundred times or more. She had been told dozens of times that she couldn't do it, that she was wasting her time. She refused to give up. Finally, she prevailed, securing the all-important Certificate of Need to build, open, and operate a nursing home. St. Rita, pray for us.

They had been successful in their seed-and-feed business, but not nearly enough to finance a one hundred bed skilled-nursing facility on their own account. They went to the banks, personally guaranteed loans, put up their life's savings, and borrowed the money. They were, as poker players put it, "all in." I was transfixed by the story. It was an amazing and uniquely American tale of two people realizing a dream through hard work, persistence, and incredible risk-taking. Except that the dream had now turned into a nightmare. Law enforcement was searching for them; they were accused of negligently murdering their own patients. In deciding not to evacuate, the risk-taking had tragically caught up with them.

They bought a tract of land deep in the parish, perhaps a forty minute drive from downtown New Orleans. The land was four to six feet above sea level, which may not sound like much, but in southeast Louisiana qualifies as a Himalayan elevation. When St. Bernard Parish flooded horribly in 1965 during Hurricane Betsy, their tract of land remained dry. Sal supervised construction, and the building exceeded all minimum requirements. He built it specifically to withstand hurricanes and it was, in his own words, "as solid as a brick shit-house. It wasn't going nowhere on account of wind." The 30,000-square-foot building was, in fact, made of concrete and brick and had a metal riveted roof. It was, he thought, an impregnable fortress. It was not water-tight, however; no building in south Louisiana was.

They opened for business in 1985, twenty years before Katrina. The whole family worked in the business. The tract of land on which the home was located eventually became the location of every family member's personal residence. Sal Jr. lived closest, no more than fifty yards from the rear entrance to the facility. Sal and Mabel had a home maybe two hundred yards away, as did Tammy and her husband. Everyone clustered around the business, which had become the centerpiece of their lives. Because of their proximity and the fact that it was *their* business, Sal and Mabel were in the facility night and day. Sal Jr. and T.J. also worked in the home and were on call 24/7. As the grandchildren were born and grew, they too spent time with the old folks in the home, first as toddlers then as teenagers. T.J. was particularly affected, emotionally, by the tragedy and was unable to speak of it without breaking down. Later, she would tell me that they didn't just lose thirty-five residents whom they cared for and loved; her kids lost thirty-five grandmothers and grandfathers.

The home prospered and was an operational and financial success. It gained a reputation as the best home in the parish. There were only three others. During their twenty years of operation, and through twenty hurricane seasons, they had never evacuated the facility because of an approaching storm. Other homes in the parish had evacuated, on occasion, with uneven results. The complicated and gut-wrenching decision of whether or not to evacuate the elderly in the face of a storm, how to evacuate them, and to where, had suddenly become more than simply a healthcare policy decision. It had become the subject of a major criminal investigation broadcast in real time around the world. "So," I asked, trying again to steer the conversation in a direction I knew it had to go, "what happened at St. Rita's during Katrina? And why were you guys still there?" The conference room got real quiet. Again.

Chapter 6: Sophie's Choice

St. Rita's had an emergency operations plan—state law required such a document. The plan was on file in the clerk's office in the St. Bernard courthouse, as required. The plan also had been submitted to the State Department of Health and Hospitals in Baton Rouge, the agency that inspected and regulated nursing homes. The plan was a cookie-cutter, one-size-fits-all model circulated by the Nursing Home Association to its members in order to help get them in compliance with state law. Thus, like most government-required documents, the plan was long on platitudes and generalities, but woefully lacking in mandates for critical decision making. I asked the Manganos if they had a copy with them or could access one quickly. They had left their copy in the nursing home, still awash in ten feet of water. Accordingly, we would be flying blind with respect to whether or not they had complied with their own plan. What we could say, positively, to the attorney general's office was that we had a plan. Check. We submitted it to the Louisiana DHH as required. Check. The local authorities in St. Bernard had a copy of it. Check. We were in compliance with all state requirements regarding the existence and the submission of emergency and hurricane preparedness planning. Check. I desperately wanted to see the document, but that wasn't going to happen any time soon. The decision I was facing was whether to let the Manganos talk to authorities and respond to their questions. Not having their emergency operations plan in hand argued for not allowing the Manganos to speak with the attorney general. There were other considerations, however.

They told me how their preparations for hurricane season began on June 1, every year. They had an established protocol for stocking up on supplies and medicines and placing them in a specific space—not to be used unless there was an emergency. They reviewed their procedures, conducted an in-service training session with staff and personnel, and pronounced themselves ready for the season, which runs from June through November, with the majority of storm activity occurring in August and the first half of September. Check. As Katrina formed in the Atlantic and struck Miami as a tropical storm, crossing the Florida peninsula and entering the warm waters of the Gulf of Mexico, they were aware of her presence. They followed her progress as we all did. She was expected to enter the Gulf, head north, turn east, and strike Florida's west coast around Tampa, said forecasters with the National Hurricane Center in Coral Gables. Slowly but surely the forecast shifted further up Florida's west coast until the weather folks began to predict a strike in the Panhandle. This change in direction was moving the storm closer and closer to Louisiana. One other fact was extremely disturbing—the warm Gulf waters were exponentially increasing the storm's strength and intensity. Katrina was growing into a monster. Predicting the precise location of a hurricane's landfall is an extremely inexact science. Information is fed into computers with variables plugged in to provide forecasters with a range of possible landfalls. That "cone of danger" is then plotted on a map and broadcast on television. The cone kept moving closer and closer to Louisiana. The Manganos and their staff were following matters closely on television. They couldn't help it. Televisions are often on 24/7 in nursing homes and blaring loudly for the hard of hearing; they could not have missed the increasingly alarming news about Katrina if they had tried.

By early Saturday morning, the situation began to look truly ominous. Returning from a golf game, I had looked at the news and made a very quick decision: we were evacuating, something we rarely did. Things looked that bad to me. I did not tell the Manganos about the Cobb family's very different response to Katrina, but I had to wonder how they could possibly have decided to stay put. To leave or not to leave: it was the question an entire region faced on that Saturday morning—and most of us took to our heels or did so the following morning. Of course, the Manganos' decision was more complicated than mine—but their responsibilities were also much greater. I had to worry about a family and two elderly parents. My parents lived in Metairie, a suburb of New Orleans, and were in their late seventies; they were nursing home material. They had toyed with the idea of staying put for Katrina. In a reversal of roles, I told them they were coming with us, and our caravan of three vehicles left the city early in the morning the day before Katrina struck. The Manganos had to consider the lives of sixty-five elderly and infirm residents—people who were in a nursing home in the first place because they couldn't make it in the outside world without round-the-clock care. My decision matrix was dramatically different. What was theirs, I asked.

The attorney general had stated repeatedly on television that the

Manganos had ignored a mandatory evacuation order from the parish government. I didn't know whether St. Bernard Parish had, in fact, declared a mandatory evacuation. I knew that New Orleans, on Sunday morning, had declared a mandatory evacuation for the first time in the city's history. I had seen Mayor Nagin declare the mandate on live television with Gov. Kathleen Blanco by his side. Surely, I thought, if New Orleans had gone mandatory, St. Bernard must have done the same. Since St. Bernard is closer to the coast, lower in elevation, and surrounded by water on nearly all sides, it is clearly a more vulnerable geographic location than New Orleans. The Manganos maintained that no one had told them to evacuate nor had anyone communicated to them a mandatory evacuation order issued by the civil authorities. Thus, the best we had on this issue was that *if* the parish had declared a mandatory evacuation order, nobody had communicated such an order to St. Rita's—a frail reed on which to build a defense against thirty-five counts of negligent homicide.

Mabel said her major concern was that she had six or seven "special needs" patients in St. Rita's at that time. "Special needs" meant that they were extremely fragile, on oxygen and/or feeder tubes, and couldn't stand or walk or even sit up for any extended period of time. Moving patients like that, she felt, was the equivalent of signing their death warrants. They would not make it through a multi-hour trip to another facility and would likely die in the bus in front of the other patients, engendering dismay or perhaps even panic. She hesitated at decision time, emotionally torn by the question of whose plug to pull first, in moving someone onto an evacuation bus. She remembered being frozen in indecision, a caring woman in exactly the wrong place at exactly the wrong time.

She was also guided, or misguided, by her own past experience with storms. But past as prologue doesn't work when it comes to hurricanes. The home had been in business for twenty years. For twenty years of hurricanes and tropical storms and bad weather, they had never evacuated and they had never experienced so much as standing water in their parking lot, much less catastrophic flooding. They had watched on television in previous years as other nursing homes evacuated and patients died on buses in gridlocked traffic. Though we couldn't know it yet, just weeks later something like that would happen on a Texas interstate as nursing home residents fled Hurricane Rita, their oxygen tanks ignited, and twenty-three of them died in a bus fire. In 2004, just a year earlier, a home in Louisiana had evacuated for Hurricane Ivan, which ended up making landfall in Alabama. Many patients had died on that evacuation bus, and the state had charged the operators with improperly implementing their emergency operations plan and had yanked the home's license to operate. Of this, Mabel had been certain: she was trapped between a rock and a hard place. She faced Sophie's choice: whom do I pick to live, and whom do I condemn to likely death? Faced with such an impossible decision, she chose what she knew—she stayed put. In twenty years of staying, she had never lost a patient during a hurricane. She wasn't about to start losing them to Katrina. Her choice was known in the industry as "sheltering in place," an option allowed under state regulations and one contained in her own plan, she told me. Sheltering in place was both legal and preferable, as it did not expose fragile patients to the multiple hazards of evacuation. Check.

As I tried to put myself in her shoes and ponder her decision, I had to concede that, while Mabel's choice was understandable, in the light of hindsight it could hardly be called wise. It was tragically wrong. But did that make it criminal? I concluded instantly that it was not. But I had done no research on the applicable law, whatever that might turn out to be, and didn't really know the potential charges or defenses. However, my gut spoke to me with the eloquence of Shakespeare's Portia: these people weren't criminals. They certainly weren't murderers. The chilling story I would hear next only supported that conclusion.

Chapter 7: Wall of Water

Katrina struck around dawn on a Monday. On the prior Saturday, St. Rita's had been a beehive of activity. Staff ordered and picked up additional meds for the residents just in case. Their standby diesel generator was tested and found to be fully operational. They had thousands of gallons of fuel, enough to power the place for weeks if necessary. Thousands of gallons of fresh drinking water were on hand. Soon members of the extended Mangano family began arriving to shelter in place, as they had for twenty years. Sal and Mabel were there, along with their children and grandchildren, nieces and nephews, Mabel's brother, family members of staff who always came to stay, and even family members of residents who came to ride it out with their loved ones. The men set about boarding up windows and securing the outside of the home, tying down furniture, flowerpots, and other objects that might become missiles in hurricane-force winds. Sheltering in place had its drawbacks, of course. The generator was reliable, but its capacity limited. It ran the lights and other essential electrical components, but it could not power the air conditioning for a 30,000-square-foot building. Instead they had huge shop-fans to circulate air and keep residents as comfortable as possible in the high heat of late August. New Orleans is oppressively hot in July and August with average temperatures in the mid-90s. Combined with an ever-present, suffocating humidity, the city often feels like the hottest place on earth. The summer of 2005 was particularly hot.

Nor could they run the big commercial washers and dryers St. Rita's used for towels and linens and residents' clothes. This had proved problematic in previous storms. So Sal went out and bought two gas generators on Saturday, brought them back to the home and, somehow, hooked them up to the circuits that controlled only the washers and dryers. He brought a supply of gasoline to run these new generators, not an easy purchase as every motorist in the parish was filling up their car and truck tanks in order to flee. Sal was filling his in order to stay. I was struck by the irony, and the window it provided into the Manganos' mindset. Sal had been out buying gasoline generators so St. Rita's could wash clothes after the storm hit. In this way, he thought, they would be better prepared than ever to survive the inevitable delay in re-establishing electrical power after the storm. They were worried about clean sheets and towels when, with the benefit of hindsight, they should have been packing people into buses and fleeing for their lives. Having chosen to shelter in place, there was only one item they could have purchased on Saturday that would have done them any good. Unfortunately, that item would have been a submarine with sufficient space for sixty-five elderly patients. Not exactly the kind of item you could pick up at Wal-Mart.

Saturday turned into Sunday and the news about the storm got even worse. Photos from space showed Katrina covering the Gulf of Mexico almost in its entirety. Her winds had increased to 150 mph, and the storm surge of water mounding ahead of her was predicted to reach a height of 25 feet as it crashed ashore. She was a hurricane and a tsunami, all wrapped into one deadly display of nature's power and fury. "Category 5"—the Saffir-Simpson Scale's highest storm rating—was headed for New Orleans for the first time I could remember since Camille in 1969. Early Sunday morning an elderly resident had passed away in the home from natural causes. Everyone knew the body had to be removed before the electrical power and air conditioning failed. It would decompose rapidly in the summer heat, and the smell would be unbearable. Several calls were made to an ambulance company to come and pick up the remains. Finally, someone called Dr. Bryan Bertucci, the parish coroner. St. Rita's former medical director, Dr. Bertucci was also a private physician who treated many St. Rita's residents as their physician of record. As coroner, he ordered the ambulance company to come by and it did so, at about 3 P.M. Thus there could be no denying that an elected official, in the person of the parish coroner, had unambiguous knowledge that St. Rita's was sheltering in place, as they had done for twenty years. But Dr. Bertucci's recollection of conversations and events would clash irreconcilably with Mabel's, and he would become a key witness in the prosecution's case two years later.

The weather had been picking up all day, with low, fast-flying clouds rocketing over the nursing home in a south-to-north direction. These clouds were what is known as feeder bands, heralds of the tsunami to come. The residents were fed dinner and gradually put to bed. Some understood that a hurricane was coming, but most didn't. None of the thirty-five who were to die the next morning could have imagined that they had just eaten their last supper. But among the staff and the Manganos, there was a whole lot of praying going on.

As darkness fell, the winds picked up dramatically and the feeder bands gave way to the storm itself. The rain was torrential and deafening on the home's nearly acre-sized metal roof. It went on all night. As the winds increased, so did their howl. The building was standing up to Katrina, but it was moaning and groaning audibly. Windows began to blow out, so the men raced to put up plywood. Water then started to stream through the roof. Little Sal and his son, Tanner, crawled up in the attic space to survey the damage. The winds were so strong that the roof was literally heaving up and down. Fearing for their lives, Little Sal and Tanner clambered down out of the attic and went to Plan B: placing buckets here and there to catch the cascades. The danger was that if the wind managed to pry one metal sheet free, it would then tear off the whole roof, like the skin of an onion. Little Sal and Tanner didn't want to be in the attic if that happened.

The battle between wind and building raged on all night. At over 100 mph, the wind sounded like a jet engine at full throttle for takeoff. Around 2 A.M., the building lost electrical power. The diesel generator kicked on dutifully and partial power was restored. But it was still dark inside the nursing home and fear and prayer was everyone's companion for the long, long night ahead. I remembered Betsy and Camille and the sounds associated with those storms and the fear I had, huddled in the dark, praying to be spared and praying for the dawn's early light, as if daylight would somehow save everyone. It rarely did.

Around 6 A.M., with water streaming through the roof and the walls still heaving in the howling wind, they began preparing breakfast. Sal and Mabel were intent on feeding their residents a hot breakfast, just as they did every day. They also had to feed family, staff, staff family, and a handful of residents' relatives who came to ride out the storm on what years of experience had proved to be safe ground. In total at St. Rita's that day there were fifty-nine residents asleep in their beds and another three dozen or so non-residents.

Everyone pitched in and breakfast was served without a hitch, with the Manganos hand-feeding many of the residents. Once breakfast was consumed and cleaned up, Sal turned his attention to preparing lunch. It's cultural. In New Orleans, a $60 "breakfast at Brennan's" may not be quite over when the topic at hand becomes lunch. And you may have just topped off a cup of garlic soup and a cashew butter and pepper jelly with duck sandwich with a coffee pot du crème at Bayona, when it's time to start thinking about the day's really important repast. *C'est la vie*—even in the middle of a hurricane.

Always a step ahead, Sal had prepared the main lunch course the day before—red beans for eighty, a Monday tradition in New Orleans—and put it in the refrigerator. To lighten the mood, I asked him about his secrets as a red bean chef. Did he use ham seasoning or sausage or both? Did he use a ham bone or ham hocks or both? "How the hell do you measure when you're cooking for that many people?" I asked.

It was around 10:30 A.M., Monday August 29, 2005. Sal Mangano put the rice on and looked out the kitchen window. It was daylight now, but still dark outside because of the storm. He could see downed trees everywhere, but the storm seemed to be weakening. The rain had stopped. There was even a patch or two of blue sky. Sal Jr. and Tanner, Mabel's brother Tony, and some other men ventured outside to do a quick inspection of the roof. The wind was still blowing but at nowhere near gale force. A huge sense of relief came over all of them. They were still here. It was daylight and they were outside walking around. They had dodged the bullet, they thought. Everyone had survived.

As the men made their way around to the side of the building that fronted the highway, Little Sal heard a distant, dull sound. They were all looking up at the building and its damaged roof with their backs to the road. The noise persisted and Sal remembered thinking it sounded like a far-off train. What idiot is running a train in a hurricane, he wondered. He turned around to face the strange sound. Across the road, perhaps two hundred yards away, he saw something he could neither process nor believe. A six-foot wall of water was rushing straight toward the nursing home. Ahead of the advancing water, he observed all manner of four-legged animals fleeing their pursuer. Dogs, horses, wild pigs from the marsh, anything that could run was hauling ass, fleeing for its life. He and the others spun around and sprinted back to St. Rita's main entrance, screaming: "Water is coming! Water is coming! Get everybody up. Put 'em on mattresses. There's water coming!"

There was no panic, just the sober realization that the sense of salvation they had savored minutes before was a snare and delusion. They had not made it; they had not dodged the bullet. They were about to be under withering attack by something far worse than bullets—they were being attacked by a tidal wave. One could get lucky and dodge a bullet. There was no dodging water. It was instantly everywhere. And it was rising.

Within seconds of the men re-entering the building, the wall of water slammed into the structure with the force of a bomb. Mabel was standing by the nurse's station and the rush of water blew out the half-wall she was leaning against, knocking her to the ground and sending her sprawling some thirty to forty feet. It was as if she were at a water park on a waterslide, unable to control where she went or how far. Little Sal ran through the building in the direction of his house, some 150 feet from the back door. As he exited the building, he found himself in two to three feet of water. By the time he reached the five-foot fence around his house, he was swimming over it, that's how fast the water was rising. He ran with his wife and son. Instinctively, they tried to get to their boat, which had been parked on the lawn but was now snagged in a tree. Somehow he managed to locate the boat's ignition key and a box of spark plugs in the house. He swam back out with these items in his mouth, desperate to reach his boat and release it before it became swamped in the furious floodwaters.

Right behind Sal Jr. and family were Tanner and Emmett Unbehagen, the husband of one of the nurses, Angela. Emmett had always come to the home to shelter with his wife and the residents. He had always brought his boat with him on a trailer, because he thought this was the best place to be. Emmett's boat was chained to the trailer to prevent it from blowing away in the storm. By the time he and Tanner got to it, the chain was holding the boat under water and it was threatening to sink it before they could release it. Fumbling for his keys to unlock the chain, Emmett was pre-empted: Tanner pulled out his gun and shot the lock and the chain off, freeing the boat to do what it was supposed to do—float. It wouldn't be the last time Tanner would use his pistol on this day.

Incredibly, both boat engines started on the first attempt and they headed back to the nursing home, less than a hundred yards away. Some residents were already dead, some were dying, and others were being rescued. When the boats rounded the corner and the front entrance came into view, people could be seen hanging from the gutters up under the eaves. Big Sal had gotten onto the roof by swimming out of the building as the rising waters reached a height of ten feet. He was on the roof straining to keep the front doors open against the pressure of the rising tide. Mabel, almost five feet tall and unable to swim, was half hanging from the gutter, half standing on a raised flower box. She was holding onto a woman named Janie, a borderline retarded resident who was Mabel's favorite. Janie had panicked as the water rose and frantically grabbed Mabel, dragging her under. They had managed to get outside and now were literally hanging on for their lives. Inside the nursing home, the scene was dark and eerily quiet. After running all night, the generator had fritzed out when rising water hit the wall outlets, about eighteen inches off the floor. From that point forward, and all at once, everything shorted out and the place became immediately dark. The building was coming apart at the seams, from the inside out. Windows and doors were popping out. Walls and partitions were exploding from the sheer force of the tidal surge. Little Sal re-entered the building in a frantic attempt to get people out. The only safe place was the roof. The men formed a rescue chain, passing residents out on anything that floated, putting them in boats and lifting them up onto the roof. Tony was wading down the hallway, checking rooms, yelling to see if anyone was inside. If he found someone, he'd put them on a mattress and pass them on to Sal or Tanner, who would pass them outside to the boats.

The brief lull in the weather as the eye of the storm passed overhead ended abruptly. The wind was again at hurricane strength but blew now from a different direction. The rising water became a lake replete with whitecaps—Lake St. Rita. The wind-driven rain returned again, stinging those holding on to each other on the roof. As the water rushed into the building, the back entrance became blocked with debris and floating furniture, an impediment to rescuers trying to get through the glass patio doors. Tanner pulled out his gun and blasted the doors to smithereens. By this time, water had risen above the tops of the door frames and Uncle Tony and Tanner had to dive into rooms in their search for survivors, then take them back under water to get them out of their rooms. They swam their way down the hallway until they found no one and heard no one. The nursing home where love and care and affection had been dispensed in large quantities for twenty years to thousands of people had turned into a water-filled tomb in a matter of minutes. Over the course of the next several months, I would debrief numerous witnesses. Everyone had the same recollection. From the time the water first struck the home until it filled to a depth of eight to ten feet was no more than fifteen to twenty minutes—at most. Mabel recalled hoping and praying that the rising water would just stop rising, level off, and give them a chance to save everyone.

There was only one place for the living, and it was on the roof. Some fifty to sixty people clung to life up there, amid pelting rain and winds that threatened to turn them into sodden tumbleweeds. That two dozen of the people on the roof were elderly residents of the home bespoke a rescue effort that was no less than heroic, I thought. But I said nothing, as the Manganos' stories spilled forth. Instead I scribbled furiously, uncertain what small details in the welter of information might prove crucial or even relevant.

Stuck on the roof, the men quickly came to the conclusion that no one would survive riding out the hurricane up there. God only knew how much longer this weather would last. So Little Sal and his son, Tanner, and others began loading the residents into the two boats and taking them away. They went first to Tammy's house, a couple of hundred yards away. Tammy's house had something the nursing home didn't—a second floor—and that ultimately became the difference between life and death. They unloaded the residents in the violent, choppy waters that now formed Lake St. Rita, carried them up to the second floor, laid them down as carefully as possible, and then returned to the nursing home to pick up another load of passengers. They repeated this process over and over and over until all were removed from the roof. The men were physically, completely exhausted.

The water, still rising, was lapping at the second story in Tammy's house. Without much discussion, it was decided to move the residents again to the abandoned Beauregard Middle School, about a half-mile away. It was an old courthouse and it had something Tammy's house didn't have—a third story. It was also closer to the Mississippi River and on slightly higher ground. Because of uncertainty as to how high the water would rise, "slightly higher ground" meant a lot. Little Sal and Tanner carried residents upstairs again, until the father and son were utterly drained of strength. They constructed makeshift beds out of desks and filing cabinets and placed the residents on top of these crude structures to keep them out of the water. Sal Sr. and Emmett grabbed a fireplace poker and some metal pipe and returned to the nursing home by boat. They tore a hole in the metal roof with their bare hands and an improvised tool kit. They yelled into the opening, and, amazingly, heard a response. Several people were clinging to a floating ice machine and had been for five or six hours, defying death. Five of them— three staffers and two residents—were pulled through the hole in the roof, the last people rescued from the building on that terrible Monday.

Darkness fell, a starless and moonless night darker than anyone had ever seen, and the water below was as dark as the sky. The Manganos stayed on Tammy's second floor and soon passed out from sheer exhaustion. The residents and staff members stayed at Beauregard Middle School, on a second floor more spacious than Tammy's. The dead at St. Rita's, some three-dozen of them, stayed where they fell, in the watery mausoleum that, hours earlier, had been their home. I bit my lip and shook my head slowly at the unbelievable story I was hearing. Interviews with hundreds, if not thousands, of clients and witnesses over the years had given me a deeply reliable sense of whether someone was telling the truth or lying. The glistening in Sal and Mabel's eyes told me I was hearing the truth, the whole truth, and nothing but the truth.

"Oh yeah," Little Sal piped in, "there's more." I wasn't sure I could take any more. As daylight broke on Tuesday morning, Sal and Tanner and Tanner's cousin Johnny got in Sal's boat and went back to see if there was anybody left other than the dead. "And Johnny heard someone hollering, 'Little Sal, Little Sal, don't leave me!' It was Miss Janis. She was in her room when the water came. A dresser fell over, she climbed aboard and floated out into the hall. The only person she was looking for was me. I was her favorite, and she didn't care

Outside St. Rita's, after the storm. Courtesy of CBS News, from *48 Hours: No Way Out* (02/02/08).

about the moon and the sun, but that's the way it was all the time. She said, 'I knew you wouldn't leave me, Little Sal, I knew it.'" The men got Miss Janis to Beauregard, cleaned her up, got her some water, and laid her down. Little Sal kissed her on the forehead and told her to close her eyes and try to get some rest. The two generations of Manganos then got back in their boat and raced back to the nursing home, hoping for another miracle. There would be no more miracles. Miss Janis was the last soul pulled out of St. Rita's alive. As for those residents who remained in the home, "we couldn't do nothing for them now," Sal concluded.

I broke the uncomfortable silence, "Why don't you all take a break," I said. "You've been at this for hours. Stretch your legs and walk around." What I was really saying, to myself, was, "*I* need a break! I can't take it anymore." The sadness was crushing.

As I got up to get my tenth cup of coffee, it hit me suddenly and hard: I'm defending these people, and we are at that point in the conversation where they're going to ask me, what do I think? I needed to ponder what to say. I got the coffee, left the building, and sat on a park bench out front beneath an oak. From the bench I could see the Old State Capitol in the distance, a

Bodies recovered from St. Rita's placed on the highway leading to the facility.
Courtesy of CBS News, from *48 Hours: No Way Out* (02/02/08).

beautiful, historic building. I was alone on the bench for just a few minutes.

Tanner came outside to burn a cigarette and walked right over to me. "Want one?" The implication in his voice was that after hearing what I just heard, I *needed* one. I hadn't smoked in decades, but I immediately said, "Sure." My personal and business world had crashed and burned, my fragile family was homeless and stuck in a hotel room in Houston, and I had just heard the most disturbing client's story in my three decades of practice. I was about to render counsel and advice that would forever impact the lives of people I had just met and instantly liked. I couldn't imagine a better time to take up smoking again. I put a cigarette in my mouth and Tanner held a match to it. "You got a shot of gin to go with this?" "No, Mr. Jim," Tanner said, "but I can go find you one." I told him I was just kidding; never touched the stuff while I was working, a complete fabrication.

"Are my grandma and grandpa going to be okay, Mr. Jim?" I took a deep, long drag on the cigarette and looked Tanner up and down. He had just gotten out of Special Forces basic training, was slightly shorter than my 5'9", but powerfully built. A bulldog, just like his grandpa, he had obviously been lifting weights frequently and for a long time. I looked at him and thought about the amazing acts of bravery others had attributed to him during our now six-hour meeting. Stalling for time, I repeated his question:

St. Rita's from the air, with floodwaters receding but still present, 2005. Courtesy of CBS News, from *48 Hours: No Way Out* (02/02/08).

The inside of a resident's room, mold on the wall to the left. Courtesy of CBS News, from *48 Hours: No Way Out* (02/02/08).

"Are they going to be okay? I don't know, Tanner," I said, "I don't know. What I've heard makes you and your family heroes as far as I'm concerned. All that bullshit that's been on television is just that—bullshit! If I were ever in a fight or a life-and-death situation, I'd want you on my side, kid. Anyone who wants to mess with your grandma and grandpa is going to have to come through me to do it, and they'll have to kill me first," I said. "Thanks for the smoke, and I'll take a rain check on that shot of gin. Now let's get back inside; it's hot as hell out here."

We created a bond that day that grew stronger over the next two years. Tanner was very protective of his grandma. He was even more protective of his mother who was fighting, without the benefit of counseling, a nervous breakdown from all that she had seen and endured. If ever I needed some Special Forces muscle in the coming months, I had found my guy. We went back inside and everyone was seated at the conference room table, anxiously awaiting our return. Maybe they had sent Tanner outside on a reconnaissance mission, with me as the object of his recon.

Chapter 8: Everything's Going to Be Okay

Sal Sr. spoke first. "So, what do you think, Mr. Jim?" This is *the* critical moment in every attorney-client relationship. Some lawyers always focus on the negative, the problems, the downside, and the risks. They predict a loss before the game even starts. They do this, in part, to disguise their own inability to accurately and correctly see how a particular drama will play out over time, based on the facts they have just been given. They also want to make everything seem so dicey, abstruse, and complicated that no client can understand what they really think. In this way, if things go wrong, they cannot be accused of having provided incorrect advice or unwarranted optimism. If you paint the picture darkly, and then achieve some degree of success, you are a hero. If it goes badly, the lawyer can always say, "I told you so," from the very beginning. It is a cowardly approach that disconnects the lawyer from the client and his or her problem. It is a disincentive to risk taking and almost puts the lawyer in a conflict situation, as a good result would be something different from what he had originally predicted. It is a setup to settle everything on the best possible terms. To this kind of lawyer, everything is always complicated and terrible, the jurisdiction is bad, the venue is hostile and unfavorable, and the facts are bad and will likely get worse when the process of discovery has led to disclosure of all the evidence. In this way, the client is prepared for the worst possible outcome, and anything short of that is a victory engineered, of course, by the lawyer who has painted the picture so darkly to begin with.

I am not that kind of lawyer. More importantly, these people had just experienced unimaginable horror. They had lost their homes and all their possessions. In a flash they had lost their business and their livelihood. They had, as well, lost the lives of some three dozen people for whom they were responsible. Surely, they did not need a lawyer painting a picture even darker than it already was. They needed some light in their lives, and I was determined to give it to them. I was well aware of the media and the government's drumbeat for a scapegoat on whom to visit vengeance for the unspeakable deaths at St. Rita's. I genuinely believed that if someone in authority heard the story I had just heard, a criminal prosecution would be out of the question.

"Mr. Sal," I said, "I believe what you all went through—your actions once the flood hit, your directing the rescue of some twenty-four of your residents, as well as all the other folks staying with you at the nursing home—is nothing short of heroic. Once all the false rumors that have been circulating on television are put to rest, I believe you guys will be okay. Once the A.G.'s office hears this story, I can't imagine that they will bring charges against anyone." I had spoken one sentence too many. What I could not imagine was the standard by which these folks were going to be judged. But my words brought a visible sense of relief to these devastated people. Mabel took a deep breath, as if the weight of the world had been lifted off her shoulders. "Good," she said. "What do we do now?"

Desperate for some advice that was positive and encouraging, she took my words as gospel. Neither of us knew that within twenty-four hours, we would both be reading John's Apocalypse, the book of Revelation.

I explained that I would call the A.G.'s office and engage in discussions and negotiations over how and when we would come to talk to them. "In fact, why don't I do that right now while you guys wait. I'm sure they'll want to meet as soon as possible," I said. I asked a secretary if I could use an empty office to make a local call and she directed me down the hall. I entered a room containing a desk, a chair, and a phone with nothing else. I closed the door behind me and called the attorney general's office. I asked to speak to Fred Duhy, an assistant A.G., who was the head of the Medicare/Fraud & Abuse section. I had spoken with him briefly once before to get him off Jeremy's back and to announce that I would be representing the Manganos and would call him after I met with them. This was that call.

I told him that I had been with the Manganos for hours and that we had all decided that it would be in everyone's best interest to meet with him. I informed him that everything he and I had heard about the St. Rita's tragedy on television was 100-percent incorrect. Their story was moving and amazing, I said, and you really need to hear it. He expressed relief and sighed audibly. I got the impression that he wanted to obtain information so that he could clear the matter up. There was no hard edge or rush to judgment in his tone of voice. "How about tomorrow?" he asked. I said, "Tomorrow is perfect. Let me continue to meet with them in the morning and we'll come to you mid-afternoon." He agreed. Since this was an interview to find out what happened, I insisted on being present throughout the interview. "No problem," he said. Further, I did not want the interview recorded or transcribed. "Agreed." Finally, I reserved the right depending on the direction in which the interview headed, to instruct my clients not to answer a question, should, in my judgment, their constitutional rights be imperiled. "No problem," he said again. We set the meeting for 2 P.M. at his office. "I'll see you tomorrow," I concluded.

I came away from the conversation convinced that he had no agenda or preconceived notions. He appeared to be genuinely interested in quickly obtaining the information necessary to report to his boss on what really happened at the nursing home. He agreed to all the conditions I set. I reported back to Sal and Mabel, outlined my conditions for the interview which were accepted, told them I would be there with them throughout the process and once again expressed the belief that upon hearing their story, no fair-minded prosecutor would charge them with anything. Mabel was now doubly relieved. I told them to come back the next morning to this office, and we'd spend the day preparing for the interview and then go meet with the authorities. I shook hands with Sal and put my arm around Mabel's shoulder to give her a hug of reassurance. "It's going to be okay," I said, "I'll see you tomorrow morning at 9:00 sharp."

Everyone's focus had changed. Looks of fear and trepidation had given way to at least a glimmer of relief and hope. Although the meeting had been wrenching and emotional, I had done some good this day, I thought. I watched the family cross the lawn outside the office and enter their vehicles, their heads held higher than when they had arrived. Less than twenty-four hours later, my perception of the situation, my instinct as to what the prosecutor would and wouldn't do, my comforting hugs and words of encouragement, and my prediction that everything would be "okay" would be revealed as the most colossal mistake I had made in thirty years of practice. That list of mistakes was not a short one, mind you, but this blunder rocketed instantly to the pinnacle of the top ten list. Within less than twenty-four hours, the prosecutor would trump mine with an even bigger mistake of his own. Had camera crews been following the two sides in this case as we stumbled into contact, the title of the documentary would have been "Dumb and Dumber."

I had been piloting this plane in peril now for some forty-eight hours and I was desperate for a co-pilot. I hadn't been actively involved in a criminal case for some twenty-five years and felt more than a little uncomfortable making decisions and judgments and recommendations on my own, with no co-counsel as a sounding board. Many times over the past thirty years, I had defended companies in civil cases which, all of a sudden, had taken a turn toward becoming potential criminal cases. On those prior occasions, I had always sought out criminal counsel to separately advise the employees of the company I was defending. Legal ethics required such an approach, but it also made good sense and gave me another mind, steeped in the criminal law, to participate in decision making and advice giving. These kinds of cases usually involved multiple deaths and high-profile disasters.

The most spectacularly sad case of that sort had occurred about a decade earlier. I was representing a marine dredging company that had obtained the contract to dredge the Jacksonville, Florida, ship channel. In setting up the job off the coast of Florida, at night, and in bad weather, one of my client's A-frame crane barges capsized and sank. Seven Hispanic workers were aboard. Two were rescued. The other five died in the incident and three bodies had not yet been recovered. The bodies were presumed to be trapped in the sunken equipment. To compound matters, the barge sank in the middle of the ship channel, shutting down all marine traffic until the wreck could be raised and removed, and the bodies recovered. It was front page news in Florida and elsewhere. My client flew me to the site in a private plane to observe and supervise recovery and wreck removal operations and to deal with the Coast Guard and the National Transportation Safety Board (NTSB), which was also investigating.

The Coast Guard acts as the police for accidents that happen on the navigable waterways of the United States. And they were pissed off, mighty pissed off. Turns out our sunken barge didn't just close the channel to commercial marine traffic; it also shut down access to the Jacksonville Navy base. American warships started to stack up off the coast awaiting cleanup of our unfortunate mess so they could get into port. I was taken out by boat to the scene and climbed aboard the recovery barge. Off in the distance I could see two large, gray Navy vessels, a destroyer and a cruiser, I thought, stuck, waiting on us. I borrowed some binoculars to look at the fleet and they appeared to have their guns pointed in our direction. Shit rolls downhill and I'm sure the Navy was ordering the Coast Guard to unclog this mess as their warships were sitting ducks in the Atlantic Ocean. To put it mildly, defending the company which caused this situation was intimidating. I asked the captain of the recovery barge if he had a white flag to run up, because I didn't believe the Navy could fire on us if we were flying the white flag. He didn't think it was funny. I wasn't kidding.

After several days of inconvenience, the barge came up, and sure enough, there were three young bodies trapped in it. The Coast Guard jumped all over it. The barge was in deplorable condition and had, obviously, been poorly, if not negligently, maintained. At the first interview of some of my client's crew, the investigating lieutenant read them their Miranda rights. I said, "Whoa, Whoa, Whoa, what's going on here?" The lieutenant, bucking for captain, pointed out that there was a statute that made it a federal crime for someone (a company or individual) to cause the death of someone at sea through "gross negligence." I had heard enough. "Well, lieutenant," I said, "you said my witnesses have the right to remain silent. I think that's what we'll do. See you later." I shut the interview down before it got started.

I needed separate counsel for these witnesses as we were now under attack by the Coast Guard, the United States Navy, and the U.S. Attorney's Office in Jacksonville. I thought of only one guy: Big Bad Bob Habans.

I had known Bob for a long time. He was a giant of a lawyer, literally and figuratively. He was big, real big. He was tall and barrel-chested, with a deeply intimidating baritone voice and a beard that made him look like a pillaging Viking. He was on my side and he scared the shit out of me. He entered the case and he and his clients walked out on two interviews with the Coast Guard until he got what he wanted: full immunity for everyone he represented in exchange for their testimony. As it turned out, their testimony did not expose the company or its managers to criminal charges and no charge of negligent maritime homicide was ever brought. Habans made mincemeat of the Coast Guard, and I successfully defended the civil wrongful death cases brought by the families of those who perished. We settled all of the cases inexpensively. I had done my dirty work once again— minimizing the recovery of orphans and widows caused by my client's negligent maintenance of its barge. For me it was, after all, still a living.

So it was a natural for me to seek out Bob to help me with the St. Rita's case. There was one problem. I couldn't find him. A fellow Louisiana resident, he had disappeared before or after Katrina, and I had no idea where he was or how to find him. I was flying the plane solo, in black-out conditions, and I wasn't rated to fly on instruments only; I didn't have enough criminal law experience. My search for Bob continued into the night. I decided to employ the methodology Jeremy had used to find me—bar hopping. Certain to run into hordes of displaced lawyers, I combed Baton Rouge restaurants and lounges. Plenty of people knew who Bob Habans was, but no one knew *where* he was. My zeal to find Bob knew no boundaries. I left no bar untouched, no drink unfinished. As a result of my unflagging devotion to my clients in this search, I would likely have a severe hangover in the morning, if not the flu. The events of the next day would prove it a terrible time to be suffering a hangover. Within twelve hours, issue would be joined and the war would begin.

Chapter 9: Nancy Grace Strikes

I got back late to my Baton Rouge flophouse. I was delighted to learn that one of our residents had moved on, allowing me to trade floor space for the bottom bunk bed in an outdated kids' room. I was moving up in the world. Before crashing, I clicked through the cable news shows to see what was being said about my new clients. It was more of the same inaccurate information, most of which had been recycled for days. There were more old clips of the attorney general pontificating and trampling on constitutional rights and the presumption of innocence. Just as I was about to click off the TV and crash, the screen teased the next show, one devoted entirely to the St. Rita's story, including allegedly new information. I quickly woke up.

It was the evening of September 12, 2005, and the show, appearing on

Nancy Grace calling for criminal charges on her evening television show. Courtesy of CBS News, from *48 Hours: No Way Out* (02/02/08).

CNN, was titled, *Nancy Grace*. A more accurate title would have been, *Nancy Dis-Grace*. It was appalling. She proceeded to conduct a public lynching of the Manganos, by using a posse looped in by satellite from remote locations. CNN correspondents, a psychotherapist who specialized in elder care, a defense attorney, and Ms. Dis-Grace herself committed multiple assaults on the presumption of innocence and caused one to question whether there should really be freedom of the press in this country, if that freedom applied to people like her.

She began with this intro:

Nancy Grace, Host: Tonight breaking news. Homicide charges could be handed down against the owners of a New Orleans nursing home who left wheelchair and bed-bound seniors to slowly drown to death. More than thirty seniors found dead in their beds and wheelchairs at St. Rita's Nursing Home. Contemptuous! Lady Justice brings down the hammer!

I couldn't believe my ears. It was totally false and I knew it. The banter and highly prejudicial falsehoods only got worse. CNN correspondent Drew Griffin reported that he was "on the trail" of the nursing home owners and had received information from someone who claimed to have seen the owners shopping in Mississippi. No fact checking, no second source—the report was simply that some unidentified, unknown person had seen the Manganos and they were on a shopping spree as they "fled" from authorities—but take heart, dear viewer: CNN and Griffin were "on their trail." It was total bullshit, of course, portraying Sal and Mabel as despicable people now on the run. But it was sensational. And that seemed to be all that mattered to Drew Griffin and Nancy Dis-Grace.

As the segment continued, the host flew into a rage:

Grace, screaming: Susan Candiotti (CNN) is joining us, bringing us the latest on St. Rita's Nursing Home, one of the absolute worst tragedies coming out of Katrina. And now I'm hearing that these two owners that made money off all these elderly nursing home citizens were out shopping—*shopping*!—after all these elderlies died. Some of them had managed to wheel their wheelchairs up to a window to try to get out—floating on mattresses."

She had a crazed, maniacal look on her face. She was having a ragegasm on live cable TV and she was obviously enjoying it in a perverted sort of way. If she wasn't on medication, she needed to be. If she was on medication, she needed to up the dosage.

Dis-Grace then brought in Steve Galladoro, whose father had drowned in St. Rita's, and confronted him with the appalling and untrue information that the owners had abandoned his father and were last seen shopping. For these kinds of segments, the producer and the on-air person are hoping and praying for a meltdown on live air as a loved one breaks down and cries. Great TV, right? Instead, Galladoro was given a live microphone to spread more false and highly prejudicial information about the Manganos.

> *Galladoro:* The last I heard they were spotted in Natchez, Mississippi. And then recently today I was in Baton Rouge for a meeting with four or five thousand St. Bernardians. And I was told that, you know, they had got wind that the owners are actually trying to leave the country.

Dis-Grace concluded the segment as a deranged former prosecutor would do, calling on authorities to institute negligent homicide charges and essentially predicting a guilty verdict, in a discussion with the defense lawyer on the panel:

> *Grace:* Lisa, it's not going to help the owners one bit that not only did they run away to safety, but now they're out shopping. You know, Lisa, in our country, you don't have to volunteer to help people. That's not a crime, not to be a volunteer. But once you take that money for taking care of these people and take on that duty, the law looks at you in a very different way.

I was livid. Once the attorney general's office learns what really happened, and the matter is resolved, I told myself, I'll sue the fork-tongued Dis-Grace for the false and defamatory venom she's spewing. I ran through the elements of proof on a defamation civil suit and thought, for a moment or two, about the damage award we would receive from a jury once they heard how utterly false and outrageous these allegations were. I was going to sue the bloody hell out of this woman and teach her a lesson in the process. As I climbed into my bunk bed and closed my eyes to try and get some sleep before tomorrow's big day, I saw the nursing home as described to me by the Manganos. The hurricane, the flood, the old folks on the roof clinging to life, those inside the building trapped and floating in a watery grave—these images appeared in my mind and were difficult to evict. They would re-appear, again and again, over the course of the next two years. No amount of sleeping pills or alcohol could dislodge or diminish these images. They would, most uncomfortably, be around for a while.

I woke up early the following morning after a terrible night's sleep. I was nervous and anxious about the coming day and rarely slept well under those circumstances. For breakfast, Andre and I went to a hotel across the street from his law office, right off College Drive and Interstate 10 in

the heart of Baton Rouge. I was mainlining coffee and preparing to eat a
hearty breakfast to combat the fatigue I felt from my previous night's futile
search for a co-counsel, Big Bad Bob. I gulped down a bunch of ice water to
combat alcohol dehydration, combined with plenty of orange juice (Vitamin
C) and some bananas (Potassium). This combination therapy was a time-
tested remedy for me when I had worked too hard the evening before. I
then attacked the buffet—a mound of scrambled eggs, grits, greasy bacon
and link sausage, and biscuits, which I covered in white gravy, and another
potassium infused banana. I was always a sucker for a breakfast buffet,
regardless of its quality or lack thereof. Andre and I chatted about the case
and he provided some insight into the personalities of some of the lawyers
in the A.G.'s office. I knew none of the players personally and he did, so I
paid attention, though not without asking the waitress if she had a couple
of Tylenol capsules. As we finished up, it was around 8 A.M. I wanted to
head downtown to be early for my 9 A.M. meeting with the Manganos. My
cell phone rang, which was odd because of the continuing communications
problems throughout southeast Louisiana. I didn't recognize the number on
caller ID, but it appeared to be from the Baton Rouge area code. I picked
up the call.

"Good morning, Jim, this is Fred Duhy with the attorney general's office,"
the caller said.

"Hey, Fred, how are you doing?" I answered, thinking he was calling to
confirm our meeting.

"Well, Jim, I've got bad news," he said slowly, "the meeting is off." He
paused for a second.

"Why is that?" I asked.

"Because I have in my hand an arrest warrant for thirty-four counts of
negligent homicide for Salvador and Mabel Mangano, your clients." An
uncomfortable and lengthy silence ensued. I broke the silence.

"Well, thanks for not piling on, Fred," I said. "We had a f—ing deal, man.
Your boss has been on TV saying he wants to find out what happened at St.
Rita's, and we are prepared to come in and tell you, and now you're going
to arrest us? That's bullshit, Fred, and you know it."

He shot back angrily, "Look, Jim, I'm the messenger here. This decision
came from the seventh floor."

"What's that seventh floor shit supposed to mean?" I asked. Andre,
listening in, whispered to me, "Foti's office is on the seventh floor. This came
straight from him." So Duhy's word to me, lawyer to lawyer, was broken by
his boss's direct intervention.

Though not apologetic, Duhy was cooperative as both of us tried to figure out how this new reality was going to play out. I was stunned at the betrayal but had to recover quickly. The Manganos, people I had just met, whom I had told everything would be okay, were headed to jail this very day. How was I going to tell them I had been horribly wrong? Would their confidence in me be so shaken that I would be fired within twenty-four hours of taking the case? And would they seek other counsel? With all they had been through, how could they possibly survive this latest emotional onslaught, I wondered. It was incredibly unfair and I could feel any control I thought I might have slipping through my hands, now trembling with anger. I was at the controls and we were headed for a crash landing.

"So, Fred," I said, "these thirty-four alleged homicides were supposedly committed in St. Bernard Parish, right? We're in East Baton Rouge Parish. How could you possibly have a valid arrest warrant when there's nobody in St. Bernard to issue one?" I asked, thinking I had him. "Easy," he said, "we found a St. Bernard Parish judge who is here in Baton Rouge. He was rescued after the flood and he's staying in town. Trust me, the warrant is valid." My one day of trusting him and his office had come to a screeching halt. "Who is the judge, where is he, what's his phone number, where is he staying, and I want a copy of the arrest warrant, *now*!" I demanded. He was surprisingly cooperative, giving me all the information I requested. He was going to fax a copy of the warrant to Andre's office across the street from where we were having breakfast. He provided the judge's name and contact information. I told him I'd get back to him after I read the papers. We rushed back to Andre's office, slipped in the back door, and before we could even get to the fax machine we heard it click on and begin spitting out the bad news. It was worse than I could have imagined.

There was an affidavit, a sworn statement, made by an investigator with the attorney general's office. He swore that the A.G.'s office had jurisdiction to investigate fraud and "abuse" committed against elderly recipients of Medicare- and Medicaid-funded care provided by the state and federal governments. All of these thirty-four victims were so situated. (The initial charges were raised to thirty-five counts when a final victim was found later outside the nursing home.) His affidavit went on to state that Sal and Mabel owned St. Rita's, that Mabel was the licensed administrator, and that all of these citizens had died on the premises, in St. Bernard Parish. Further, he swore that the parish had issued a mandatory evacuation order which the Manganos had failed to heed. Worse still, he swore to a conversation he had with St. Bernard Parish Coroner Dr. Bryan Bertucci, wherein Bertucci said he had called and spoken to Mabel before the storm hit and offered her buses and assistance to take her residents anywhere they wanted to go.

She refused the offer of help and ignored the order to evacuate, causing the deaths of thirty-five people.

When an officer of the law swears to certain facts discovered in an investigation, even if those facts contain hearsay or otherwise inadmissible evidence, those facts simply form the basis for a judge, reviewing them, to determine whether "probable cause" exists to have someone arrested. The "probable cause" determination to support an arrest is a far cry from proof at trial, beyond a reasonable doubt with legally admissible evidence, necessary to support a conviction. But this wasn't about a conviction; it was about an arrest—an extremely high-profile arrest which the attorney general himself clearly wanted. Hundreds of news cameras and every major network in the world were covering Katrina, and the tragedy at St. Rita's was front and center at that very moment. In ordering the Manganos' immediate arrest, it was as if Attorney General Foti, keenly aware of the coverage, and ignoring the opportunity to interview the targets of his investigation, looked into the assembled cameras of the world and said to all of them, "Mr. DeMille, I'm ready for my close-up." Whether he was, in fact, ready for his close up, would be determined on a national and international stage. The running time for the film would be almost two years from the exact day on which he declared his readiness and ordered the arrest of Sal and Mabel. A jury in West Feliciana Parish would be the judge of the Manganos' conduct and of me as their counselor. They would pass judgment on Foti as well, but ultimately his fate would be in the hands of the Louisiana electorate.

Chapter 10: Broken Promises

I rushed downtown to meet with the Manganos, bearing with me the terrible news. Traffic in Baton Rouge in the days and weeks after Katrina was mind boggling. Overnight Baton Rouge, previously the state's third largest city, had become Louisiana's largest. New Orleans was empty and some 200,000 residents had fled to the state capital, almost doubling its population. Every hotel room was occupied, every available apartment was rented, and a speculative housing boom had ensued, with people of means from New Orleans buying up houses that were for sale at a torrid pace. Prices rose accordingly. Put all these people on the road at the same time, any time of the day, and Baton Rouge was in perpetual gridlock. A drive that would normally take ten minutes took nearly forty. Accordingly, I was going to be late for the meeting that I had asked them to be on time for. Another broken promise, and I hated being late.

I entered the conference room at the law office and the family was already there. I shook hands with Sal, and Mabel got up from her conference room chair to give me a hug. These were touchy feely people and they were apparently comfortable with me after our marathon session of the previous day. I knew what they—and no one else—knew about the horror at St. Rita's, so we were members of a very exclusive club. Mabel spoke first, "So what's the agenda?" she asked.

"Mabel," I answered, "I've got bad news," copying what Duhy had said to me. "There's not going to be any meeting. They've issued an arrest warrant for you and Sal."

"What for?" she responded with a look of complete shock and surprise.

"The warrant charges the both of you with thirty-four counts of negligent homicide in connection with the deaths of your residents."

She almost collapsed into my arms, and I helped her sit back down in her chair. She began crying as she placed her forehead on her crossed hands folded on the conference room table. It was horrible. I had often been the bearer of bad news during the course of thirty years of practice, many more times than was my fair share. But I could not remember a moment worse than this one, nor more devastating to a recipient of the bad news, news that I carried around like a jailer's keys on a keychain. Sal could only shake his head back and forth in disbelief. The rest of the family was stunned and devastated. They had all endured the horror and the fury of Katrina. Any or all of them could have lost their lives in the flood. They were hurt and homeless. And now the government was poised to arrest the patriarch and matriarch of their clan, with the hope of convicting them of homicide and sending them to jail for the rest of their lives. How much more could these people be expected to endure, I wondered. I had arrived at my own personal breaking point in the Whataburger parking lot in Houston—and nobody was trying to put me, or a member of my family, in jail. I could not imagine their pain, confusion and bewilderment. But I knew it was up to me to stop their downward spiral and pull them out of their despair. I had no clue as to how I would accomplish that task.

Someone knocked at the conference room door, opened it, stuck her head in, and asked, "Is there a Jim Cobb in here?"

"That's me," I answered.

"I've got a phone call for you on the firm's land line."

Not wanting to take it, I asked, "Do you know who it is?"

"I believe he said his name was Bob Habans," she replied.

Jumping up out of my chair, I yelled, "I'll take it! Can you put it through to the empty private office down the hall?"

"Of course, Mr. Cobb, please wait for it to ring, then pick up. I'll go back to my desk and transfer it now," she said.

I raced down the short hall and got to the small, empty office before she got back to her desk. The phone rang and I picked it up before it completed the first full ring. "Hello," I said. "Jim, this is Bob Habans. I hear you've been looking for me."

"Well, yes, Bob, I have," I deadpanned. "I've got a little situation on my hands."

"What kind of situation?" he asked.

"I was just retained by a couple of clients yesterday and about two hours ago I learned that the government has issued a warrant for their arrest."

"What's the charge?" Bob deadpanned back.

"Just thirty-four counts . . . of homicide," I responded. "You busy right now?"

"Not really," he said, "I stayed in my house for Katrina and I got slammed and flooded. It was frightening; we lost everything we owned, but everybody's okay. I walked out in water up to my chest, so I've got a little time on my hands. What did you have in mind?"

"What city are you in? Where are you located?" I asked.

"I'm in Baton Rouge at my daughter's house." Finally, a lucky break: today, at least, I was not totally fortune's fool.

"Well, I could sure use some help," I said.

"Love to," was his response. "Let me get cleaned up and I'll see you in about an hour and a half." I told him our location and went back and told the Manganos that a criminal law specialist was on the way and that I had associated him on the case. I told them briefly about Bob, his experience, and his record of success and how we had worked together successfully on a negligent-homicide case involving multiple deaths. They appeared relieved but not nearly as relieved as I was. At this point in time, we were all in shock, and a new player with new questions and a fresh perspective was clearly what was needed.

While awaiting Bob's arrival, I worked the phone with the attorney general's office, beginning to negotiate a surrender and to discuss bail and how I could get Sal and Mabel out of jail once they were booked. I obtained local contact numbers for the St. Bernard judge who had signed the arrest warrant. I tried multiple times to reach him without success. I tried to call Houston, to tell Debbie and the kids what was happening. No answer. Telecommunication was still difficult, bordering on the impossible. Before the hour was up, Bob arrived and I met him at the front door, outside the conference room and out of the Manganos' presence. I brought him up to speed and informed him that my clients were the owners of the St. Rita's nursing home, where thirty-four residents had drowned. He was familiar with the case from press reports and was as disgusted as I was at how the attorney general had maligned and crucified these people on television without knowing the facts.

I was furious, I told him. I had made a deal to bring Sal and Mabel in today and to speak to members of Foti's staff about what really happened. I was convinced that if they heard what I had heard, there would be no charges. I was rambling on about Foti's office breaking our deal and how they were dirty, rotten M.F.s when I noticed Bob's eyes rolling in his head. Without saying a word, his rolling eyes communicated to me instantly what I should have already known. Eyes: "You were going to do *what?!* Bring them in and let them talk? Are you out of your mind? Never, ever let them talk to the heat, no matter what pre-conditions you set. When they say that anything a potential defendant says *can* and *will* be used against them in a court of law, they're not kidding! Do you know how many times people have been acquitted of the substantive charge in a case, only to be convicted of lying to the FBI or the authorities or whomever in connection with the investigation?" His rolling, communicative eyes had said a mouthful. I was done with my rage over the A.G.'s office breaking the deal to talk. Over the months ahead, I would find ways to use it to our advantage, again and again. With Bob on board, there would be no more exuberant rookie mistakes like the one I had almost made. I was bailed out by a predisposed prosecutor's rush to judgment and his burning desire to race to the microphones of a lynch-mob press to take the credit for "solving" the St. Rita's homicides and bringing these despicable perpetrators to justice.

I took Bob into the conference room, introduced him to the Manganos, and we all sat down to talk. Bob wanted to hear the story again for himself. His questions and emphasis would likely be different from mine, discovering additional information that he considered important. Given the buildup I had bestowed upon him and his imposing physical presence and obvious skill, Sal and Mabel took to him quickly. Bob asked me about the status of the arrest warrant. Had bail been set? Was there a surrender protocol, etc.? I responded that those were the subjects I was working on when he arrived. He suggested I get back to those matters while he further de-briefed the Manganos and prepared them for what was coming: their involuntary incarceration. At last, I thought, some help—an experienced co-pilot. We were headed for a crash landing, but at least Bob was in the cockpit with me and I'd have some company when we went into the ground, nose first.

I went back to the empty office to work the solitary phone in an attempt to reach the judge whose name appeared at the bottom of the piece of paper ordering Sal and Mabel's arrest and incarceration. I had no idea who this judge was and did not know what to expect. His name appeared to be Kirk Vaughn, but I wasn't sure from the signature. What I was sure of was that I had no experience with him and had never appeared before him in court on any matter. I assumed he was in favor of the Manganos' arrests because he had signed the warrant ordering them to jail for thirty-four counts of homicide. Given the charges and the sheer number of deaths, I was worried about what his attitude would be in establishing the criteria for their release. Would he require a huge cash bond for thirty-four counts of negligent homicide? Would he order a bond secured by the Manganos' property, now worthless and sitting beneath ten feet of water? Would he be influenced by media reports that Sal and Mabel were fugitive desperados, given to shopping sprees in the wake of their patients' deaths? I didn't have a clue as to what he would do or how I should approach him. Professionally, at least, I was unaccustomed to being clueless.

After more than a dozen failed attempts to reach him by phone, someone finally answered. "Judge Vaughn, please," I said. "This is he," came the response. He was well-spoken; a good omen I thought. "Judge, my name is Jim Cobb. I am an attorney and I represent Sal and Mabel Mangano." "I know who you are, Mr. Cobb," he responded, sounding ominous. "Why are you calling me?" he asked. We were not off to a good start.

"Well, sir, I understand you signed the arrest warrant for thirty-four counts of homicide against my clients and I was wondering if this was a convenient time for us to talk." "It is," he shot back. I pointed out to him that the affidavit supporting the arrest warrant contained numerous errors and misstatements of fact, and I started pointing them out.

"Look, Mr. Cobb, the investigator swore the facts he presented to me were true. Now I'm sure you and your clients have a different view of those facts, and who knows, you may be right, but that's not what I'm here for. I'm not going to vacate an arrest warrant I just signed based on a telephone conversation I'm having with you." A swing and a miss by me. Strike one.

"Your Honor, Mr. and Mrs. Mangano are lifelong residents of St. Bernard Parish, neither has ever been arrested, much less been convicted of a crime, any crime. In fact, they told me today that the last time either of them even got a traffic ticket was some twenty-five years ago. I had a deal with the attorney general's office in which we were supposed to meet with them this afternoon to answer all their questions regarding the tragic deaths at St. Rita's. And then today, I get a call breaking the agreement and stating they had a warrant for my clients' arrest. Judge, the A.G.'s office can't possibly know what happened at St. Rita's without talking to these people. Further, Attorney General Foti has been all over television saying he wants to talk to the Manganos about what happened. I arrange for that conversation, and he cancels the appointment and arrests them. That doesn't strike me as fair."

The judge interrupted me just as I was heating up the rhetoric. "Mr. Cobb, this wasn't my idea," he said. There was a long pause. The tone of his voice indicated to me that he didn't think much of the charges, but he had to sign the warrant based on the probable cause established in the affidavit, whether that affidavit was correct or not. I didn't know what to say and perhaps I was misinterpreting his words and tone. My instincts had already proven to be pretty bad, especially in the last twenty-four hours. He broke the silence. "What do you want, Mr. Cobb?"

"Under the circumstances, Your Honor, I would ask that my clients be released on their own recognizance, once the booking process is complete, without the necessity of posting bail or any bond whatsoever." I couldn't have asked for anything more. Being released on one's own recognizance

(ROR) means not having to put up any money or property in order to secure one's release from jail and appearance in court later. It was unprecedented to ask for an ROR in the face of seventy counts of homicide. There was another pause. The judge broke the silence once again.

"I don't have a problem with your request, Mr. Cobb. Get ahold of the A.G. and see if he has any objection. If not, you prepare the ROR Order and I'll sign it. Anything else, Mr. Cobb?" "No, sir, and thank you for taking the time for my call," I answered. "Mr. Cobb, I'm from St. Bernard Parish. All I've got left at this point is time. Good luck." And he was gone.

I contacted Duhy in the A.G.'s office and, as I suspected he was still feeling guilty about breaking our previous deal, he had no objection to the Manganos' release on their own recognizance. This was astonishing to me, and alerted me to the fact that perhaps there were members of Foti's staff who believed he had acted in haste and with a heavy hand. If, in fact, the government truly believed Sal and Mabel were guilty of thirty-four homicides, how do you let them go free without posting any bail whatsoever? The judge's, "this wasn't my idea," was still ringing in my head. Given his granting of an ROR, I concluded that he thought the case was a crock of shit thrown by a publicity-seeking politician—just as I did.

I rushed back to the conference room and asked Bob to step outside, interrupting his interview of Sal and Mabel. I told him we could get Sal and Mabel out ROR. "Jim, that's incredible. Terrific. You've earned more than a day's pay. Go lock it up with those assholes at the A.G.'s office before they change their mind. I'm in the middle of something I think could be important with Sal and Mabel, so you work on their release and I'll continue to work with them." At last some help, I thought. We were at the beginning of a war that was going to be fought on multiple fronts, and finding Bob allowed me to concentrate on one thing and only one thing—getting these two proud people who had never been to jail, out of jail, as efficiently and quickly as possible, minimizing the pain, humiliation, and embarrassment I knew they would surely feel while in the slammer. This is not a task easily accomplished on a regular day. Post-Katrina it became more difficult, bordering on impossible.

I commandeered a secretary in the office and cobbled together an order to be signed by Judge Vaughn, mandating the Manganos' immediate release from jail, on their own recognizance, on the charges of thirty-four counts of negligent homicide, without the necessity of posting bail. Months later, when I told lawyer friends who practice criminal law about this turn of events, they couldn't believe it. "How did you do it?" they asked. The short answer was, I don't know how I did it; I sort of talked my way into it and had a receptive judge. The importance of getting it done I did know. Obtaining a cash or property bond for Sal and Mabel in Baton Rouge amid the chaos that reigned there would have been difficult and time consuming. They would have had to spend several nights in jail, maybe a week. I sensed that would be the final straw for them emotionally. It was essential to get them in and out quickly, avoiding a stay of any length as guests of the East Baton Rouge Parish Sheriff's office. This elderly Italian grandma and grandpa were ill-equipped for incarceration, much less an extended stay.

I re-contacted the A.G.'s office in order to establish a timetable and to negotiate a surrender. I hated the word "surrender." We hadn't even been given the opportunity to explain events and already we were surrendering. The power of the prosecutor's office at this stage of any proceeding is virtually unchecked. If more citizens understood the magnitude of the power they grant through election, they might choose their prosecutors more wisely. I knew I was essentially powerless to affect what they wanted to do, so I resorted to a tactic I often employed. I barked orders and expressed outrage and threatened sanctions I couldn't likely produce. "Look, Fred," I said, "we're not going to turn this surrender into a media circus. I want it done in secret: no press and no perp walk!" During a "perp walk," the arresting officers parade the accused in handcuffs before television cameras and still photographers on the way into or out of jail. The image is indelible and further erodes the presumption of innocence, and it is usually well orchestrated by prosecutors, especially in high-profile cases. There was no higher profile case in America at this point than that of the soon-to-be-defendants in State of Louisiana versus Sal and Mabel Mangano. They were being portrayed as "public enemies" who had been tracked down and arrested by authorities for heinous crimes. It was bullshit, but that's the way the A.G. would play it in the hours, days, weeks, and months to come.

Duhy responded, "Look, I don't believe in all this media stuff. That's handled on the seventh floor by somebody else, as you know. Let's arrange a meeting between you and your clients and special agents from our office, no press, and we'll get them processed and booked and your ROR should roll them out fairly quickly." I detected more than a slight irritation in his voice precipitated by his boss's media manipulations. The A.G. was scorned as "Foti-op" by some of his professional staff, and I suspected Fred Duhy was a member of that group.

We were agreed. We would meet special agents in the gravel parking lot on the far side of the East Baton Rouge Parish Jail where we would surrender Sal and Mabel to their custody. Neither side would contact the media. The A.G.'s men would escort the Manganos into the facility for booking, photos, and fingerprinting, the usual routine. When processed, the ROR Order would be presented and they should be able to roll out in an hour, two at the most, depending on how busy it was at lock-up. It was simple and straightforward, and I hoped the state would live up to their end of the deal. I felt they would.

I returned to the conference room to tell Sal and Mabel that, yes, they really were going someplace neither of them had ever been before—jail. It would happen this very afternoon, with a secret rendezvous with agents from the A.G.'s office. I had a release order signed by the same judge who had ordered them arrested and they should be out in a couple of hours; Bob and I would be waiting for them. Mabel lowered her head and fought back tears. Sal's face betrayed a look of anger and confusion, like he wanted to tear someone's head off. I was hoping it wasn't mine. Tanner looked at me with disappointment and betrayal written on his face. He shook his head back and forth and left the room. My promise to him that his grandparents would be "okay" had gone up in smoke. I felt terrible. I had let everyone down and any faith the Manganos may have had in my ability to predict outcomes was gone.

Chapter 11: "Step Aside, Mr. Cobb"

We arrived at the rendezvous point in the gravel parking lot next to the East Baton Rouge Parish Jail. There were two large SUVs already there, black in color with tinted windows and police lights hidden in the grille of the vehicles. The lights were not flashing. There was no one else in sight, not even another vehicle in the parking lot. Bob pulled his car into the empty lot and parked. We were quickly joined by the two black SUVs who parked behind us. Six people, four men and two women, exited the SUVs as Bob and I got out of his vehicle. I told Sal and Mabel to stay inside. A person identifying himself as the lead agent introduced himself and extended his hand for me to shake. I did and everyone was introduced all around. It felt like the introduction of captains of opposing teams before the coin toss at a football game. Very crisp, very polite, very official. There were no lawyers in his group, only plain clothes agents, with visible guns and badges. The lead agent told me that he had been fully briefed by Fred Duhy and perfectly recounted the protocol and procedure we had agreed to. He was going to make this all happen as quickly and as smoothly as possible. I reminded the agent that I had an order, signed by the same judge who signed the arrest warrant, ordering Sal and Mabel's immediate release from jail. "That," he told me, "is in the jurisdiction of and the responsibility of the East Baton Rouge Parish Sheriff's Office, who runs the jail. We don't release them; we just put them in." I didn't like his tone or his attitude, but I knew he was right.

Bob and I returned to Sal and Mabel in the air conditioned vehicle. It was September 14, 2005, a mere sixteen days after Katrina struck, and it was still brutally hot outside at three in the afternoon. We had already prepared Sal and Mabel for their hopefully brief stay in jail. They knew to speak to no one, other than to provide biographical information. We had also informed the agents not to attempt any interview whatsoever with our clients, as they were now represented. They acknowledged our instructions and I did not think that anyone would try to obtain a statement from the Manganos while in custody. I turned around and looked at Sal and Mabel, sitting together in the back seat of Bob's car. They were holding hands and their faces were sad and confused—more sad than confused. Mabel was fighting back tears. I was the last to speak. "Be strong, Mabel. Don't let these pieces of shit see you cry. This should go quickly and smoothly, and Bob and I will be waiting right here for you when you come out. Okay? You ready?" Sal said, "Okay, let's go." Bob and I got out first and I opened the door for our clients, helping Mabel out of the car to make sure she was steady on her feet.

I approached the lead agent with Mabel on my arm and said, "Officer, this is Mr. and Mrs. Mangano. I understand you have a warrant for their arrest. May I see it, please?" He produced the warrant, a copy of which I had already read a dozen times. I was checking to see that his was the original of the copy which I had, but more importantly, I did it to piss him off and exercise the only control I could at this stage of the proceeding.

"The papers appear to be in order," I pronounced.

The agent barked back, "Step aside, Mr. Cobb." I did. The agent approached Sal and Mabel but this time there were no handshakes, no introductions, and no coin flips.

"Mr. Mangano, please step this way," he ordered, politely but forcefully. He and the other male agents took Sal in the direction of one of the vehicles. The two female agents stepped forward and instructed Mabel to accompany them to the other vehicle. She looked me in the eye, and I nodded in assent to the instruction she had been given and whispered, "It's okay, go ahead." She did. I stood no more than twenty feet from where the State of Louisiana was about to do its best to humiliate these elderly nursing home proprietors. They leaned Sal and Mabel on the hood of each vehicle and searched them, patting them down. "Is this absolutely necessary?" I asked. "Required procedure," he snapped back. Search complete, the agents then brought out the handcuffs. I looked at the lead agent and said, "Handcuffing a grandmother and a grandfather—homeless victims of Katrina. You ought to be ashamed of yourself. I promise you, I will have a piece of somebody's ass for what you've done here today. I only hope and pray it's yours." I was so angry I was almost shaking, wanting to punch somebody or something. That would have been a very bad idea as we were seriously outmanned and hopelessly outgunned. We would live to fight another day, I thought, as I watched Sal and Mabel disappear behind the concertina-wire-topped fence and into the building known as the parish jail.

Bob and I went back to his car to sit in the air conditioning. We were both dripping with sweat and seething with anger. There was silence for a good while as we stared at the prison. Bob spoke first: "It is political scapegoating at its worst. Maybe when things calm down, we can talk them out of this dumb prosecution."

"Not likely," I responded. "Evidently, they don't know what dumb is." We waited in the car. After an hour or so, I started checking with the guard every ten minutes, reminding him that the release order was presented to the sheriff's office at the same time Sal and Mabel walked in. They should be out by now, I argued.

"We're busy," he mumbled.

"Busy doing what?" I asked. "There are no cars in the parking lot. I've been staring continuously at the entrance gate for two hours and nobody's come or gone. Exactly how do you define busy?"

He ignored me. Given my state of mind at that moment, he made the right choice. At the three-hour mark, I sensed we were being intentionally jacked around. I insisted to the front-gate guard that I wanted to see his supervisor and that he and the sheriff's office were in violation of a court order to release the Manganos. "I want them out or I want an explanation as to why they're not out, or we will institute contempt proceedings against you and your office and seek damages for wrongful incarceration." It was bull, but he didn't know that. He summoned rank to the front gate. I started dealing with a captain.

I explained the situation again. He looked at a clipboard of papers, picked up a phone, and had a conversation with somebody "in the back." He then disappeared from view, promising to return with information. Another hour or so passed; Sal and Mabel were still in a cell someplace while an order commanding their release continued to be ignored. The captain finally returned. "I got it figured out," he said. This ought to be a good one, I thought. His figuring capabilities appeared to be quite limited. "The order you got?" "Yes," I answered. "It ain't no good."

"What do you mean, it ain't no good, captain?"

He answered, "It's signed by an out-of-town judge, St. Bernard Parish, I think. We don't have to follow his orders."

Trying to maintain composure, I explained, "Well, you followed his orders when you arrested them and put them in jail. Why can't you follow his very explicit order to release them immediately after booking? That would be right now, captain."

"Look, pal," he responded, "I'm just following orders. When you get a Baton Rouge judge to order me to release them, I will. It's now after 5 P.M., so good luck finding a judge. Your clients will probably have to spend the night."

We'd been lied to and hoodwinked again. The thought of Sal and Mabel having to overnight in jail was jarring and would break yet another promise I had made to them. "Captain, I am a member of the bar of this state and an officer of the court, and I'm not your pal, understand? I've got your name from your name tag. Now please provide me the name of your supervisor who ordered this, so that I spell his name correctly when we sue the living shit out of the both of you, as well as the sheriff's office, for false imprisonment and violation of my clients' civil rights. That won't be handled by one of your all-powerful Baton Rouge judges, pal, that's a federal civil rights lawsuit in federal court, for your information."

The threatened legal action rolled off his back like water off a duck. He then uttered the one word with the capacity to inspire me to violence: "Whatever," he said, as he turned his back on me and walked away. He had won the encounter; he knew it, and so did I.

I walked back the short distance to the parking lot where Bob was waiting in his car. He could see I was furious. "What happened?" he asked as I got into his car. I explained the situation to him and he paused to think about it for quite some time. After he processed the information, his head started to shake back and forth and the first words out of his mouth were: "Those rotten mother f—ers." He said each word slowly and quietly. "It's after 5 P.M. and as complicated a deal as this is, we're never going to get a state judge who knows nothing about the case to release two defendants, without bond, on the charge of thirty-four homicides. Do you know any state judges up here? I don't." Neither did I.

Both Bob's practice and mine were mostly conducted in federal courts in Louisiana and surrounding states. Neither of us even knew the names of Baton Rouge judges, much less how to contact any one of them after hours. Even if I could find someone to call, and an after-hours number, I imagined the conversation: "Hi, Judge X, my name is Jim Cobb. I'm a lawyer from New Orleans. Actually, I'm not from New Orleans anymore, my house was flooded in Katrina and I'm currently living in a hotel room in Houston on an interstate service road. I'm in Baton Rouge sleeping on the floor at a friend's house, a lawyer named Andre LaPlace, maybe you know him. Anyway, I've got these two clients in jail in lockup and I'd like you to release them, without bail, on their own recognizance. . . . What's the charge? Uh, um, thirty-four counts of negligent homicide. No, Judge, thirty-four counts of homicide against *each one* of them or a total of sixty-eight counts of homicide. Yes, I do want them released without posting bail and I don't know why you're chuckling, I don't find any of this amusing." I quickly concluded that Sal and Mabel were doomed to at least one night in jail, probably many more.

Just as that conclusion hit me, I noticed a black sedan turning onto the road that led to the gravel parking lot. The car was clearly exceeding the speed limit, right in front of the jail and the sheriff's office. It then turned into the dry, gravel lot, at a high rate of speed, its wheels spinning in the dirt and kicking up rocks and a cloud of brown dust. The vehicle was one of those relatively new, and therefore hot, Chrysler Hemi 300s. Its black exterior was complemented by tinted windows and special, shiny rims—the full package. It came to a screeching halt right behind Bob's car, skidding slightly and creating another dust storm. As the dust blew away, the car door opened and out stepped Andre, the lawyer/flop house proprietor. I stepped out to meet him.

He had on dark, wraparound sunglasses. Had there been background music as the dust dissipated around him, it would have been one of the themes from Clint Eastwood's spaghetti western period, dramatic and over the top. There were those who thought Andre looked a little like the king, Elvis Presley. I was not a member of that school of thought, except to remark on occasion that Andre's rotundity was comparable to the king's in his final days at Graceland.

"Dude, you are getting so hosed. You don't even know it. Foti is on live national television, on all the cable channels, announcing the arrest and slamming your people, hard. It's like a feeding frenzy. You need to get over there and punch back. It's about to be the prime time news hour. It's the only thing on television."

"They won't let Sal and Mabel out. They say they need a Baton Rouge judge to order the release," I said.

"I might be able to call somebody. Get in my car and let's jet to the EOC." The EOC—the Emergency Operations Center—was the Katrina command-post for state government and all other agencies. It was also where national and world media had set up shop. Bob nodded for me to go, saying he'd handle matters at the jail and try to figure a way to get them out. Andre blazed to the EOC like a man in a big car with a huge engine and no fear of getting a speeding ticket. We got there quickly. While en route, Andre was able to reach a Baton Rouge judge on his cell. He explained the situation and how we were getting jerked around. I suggested that the judge could issue an order, requiring the sheriff to follow the order of Judge Vaughn of St. Bernard for their release. In that way, if questioned, the Baton Rouge judge could say, "I didn't release them; Judge Vaughn's order did. I just made his order valid in this parish." Perfect. I knew we had it when Andre said, "Thank you, Your Honor," and hung up. "He's calling the jail now and ordering them to comply with your ROR," Andre said. I tried to reach Bob to tell him, but either his circuits or mine were overloaded. He'd figure it out soon enough and he was there to get Sal and Mabel out safely, hopefully without any press.

We arrived at the EOC. It was surrounded on three sides by several large, concrete parking lots. There were dozens of satellite trucks, tens of mobile-trailer production facilities, and tons of technical equipment and wires. It was all the national and international electronic media and dozens of local stations from Florida to California. The parking lot was full of local crews in trucks, the insignia on their doors advertising their call letters and their home city. There were certainly more media than emergency responders from what I could see as we cruised the parking lot. The lot was ringed with outdoor tents, under which the various news organizations were doing their interviews and live shots. This was the belly of the media beast that had been devouring Sal and Mabel for days, and the frenzy was palpable. I felt a twinge as my adrenal gland shifted into high gear. As we cruised the perimeter, some television lights were turned on under a tent just ahead of us. We pulled even with the tent and the lights. A cluster of camera people and production staff beamed lights in the direction of the EOC. I spotted the MSNBC insignia on the equipment trunks under the tent and around it. When some production people stepped aside, unblocking my view, by God, there was Chris Matthews and facing him, miked up, was Charles C. Foti Jr., the attorney general of the State of Louisiana. It appeared they were just beginning a live interview. "Stop here, Andre, I'm getting out." I jumped from the car and headed immediately in the direction of the bright television lights. The general and I were on a collision course and now, at last, we were at close quarters. My heart began to race as I slipped into the back of the tent unnoticed. I looked at the TV monitor to track what was going out to the nation, live, on MSNBC. Nobody knew it, but I was up next.

Chapter 12: Punching Back

The tent was approximately ten feet square. There were three or four production assistants standing behind a camera manned by an operator. There was a ton of electronic equipment with green and red lights flashing and modulating up and down. Chris Matthews was there, but he wasn't conducting the interview. He was reading papers in what looked like preparation for his show *Hardball with Chris Matthews*. The attorney general had an earpiece and a tiny lapel microphone on his shirt collar, and he was looking into the camera and speaking to someone who was obviously in his ear. There was no sound coming out of the monitor I was watching as the live segment was likely on a delay and sound would reverberate into the live shot. Everyone had headphones on, listening to the interview and sound levels.

I could barely hear what the attorney general was saying so I inched a little closer to the front of the tent. Now I could pick up on his self-serving blather: "I think in times of tragedy we have to act immediately to correct a wrong, and we did that in this case," he was saying. Exactly what wrong he was talking about I did not know. He fell silent for a moment, obviously fielding another question through the earpiece. I didn't know what the question was, but I clearly heard his answer: "The tragedy here was that thirty-four people died in a nursing home, abandoned, when they should have been evacuated."

I responded in a low voice in the back of the tent, to no one in particular: "He's full of shit." One of the staffers who didn't have a headset on heard me, and his head spun in my direction in an instant, as if it were on a swivel. I perceived that he thought I was a security risk and might interrupt the broadcast. "Who are you and why do you think he's full of shit?" he asked. "My name is Jim Cobb, I am an attorney, and I represent Sal and Mabel Mangano. And I don't just *think* he's full of shit, I *know* the attorney general is full of shit."

The staffer quickly picked up a headset with microphone attached, and started talking—either to someone in a production truck in the parking lot or someone in New York, I supposed. "Look, I got a guy here who says he's the lawyer for the Manganos and he says that what the A.G. is saying is bullshit. You want him?" There was a pause as he was obviously listening to some chatter and an answer.

He came back to me and said, "Look, we're live on MSNBC, someone in New York is conducting this interview with the attorney general. When he's done, are you prepared to go on the air, live, and respond?" he asked.

"That's why I'm here," I said with as much cool as I could muster. They went to a commercial break and there was more chatter between the staffer and New York.

"Have you spoken to anybody else yet, they want to know."

"No, I haven't, I just got here," I responded.

He turned slightly away from me hoping I wouldn't hear, and whispered into his microphone: "It's awesome, he hasn't spoken to anyone yet; we've got the exclusive." He listened for a minute and turned back to me, "You're on next. There are some more questions for the A.G., and then we'll go to a commercial break, hook you up, and you will answer Dan Abrams' questions."

"Can I move closer to the front so I can hear more clearly what he's saying?"

"Absolutely." The man escorted me to a place just off camera almost face to face with the attorney general. He looked at me with a puzzled expression on his face. I had met him over the years, casually, at various political functions. I doubted that he remembered me. Did he know who I was? Did he know why I was there? If not, he was about to find out.

He finished his segment, concluding and asserting that the Manganos had violated a mandatory evacuation order in the Parish and that this violation of law led directly to the horrible deaths of thirty-four senior citizens. The show went to a commercial and Foti's mug vanished from the monitor. I stepped forward. "Hello, Charlie, I'm Jim Cobb. I represent the Manganos."

I had extended my hand to shake his when some goon-like creature sporting a crew cut, a big belly, and a suit one size too small, karate-chopped my forearm. "He's on the air, step back," the goon grunted. He had a badge on his belt and a lump in his coat, barely disguising the handgun on his hip. He was, evidently, the A.G.'s bodyguard.

"Look at the monitor, asshole. They've gone to a commercial break and he's no longer on the air, and don't you ever touch me again or I'll have your badge, are we clear?" The bad start that I had already gotten off to with the arresting agents in the parking lot instantly got a lot worse. Foti slipped away, his hand unshaken. I was then moved into his spot by the production assistant, who hooked me up to an earpiece and placed a small lapel microphone on my yellow golf shirt collar. I was later told repeatedly that yellow was a bad choice of color for my first-ever live, national television interview. Some said I looked like a fat, old guy with jaundice. I could hear the director in my ear. I gave them my name again, and I listened to the live air of the commercial. I coached myself silently: stay cool, speak slowly, don't get flustered. "Ten seconds to air, Mr. Cobb, are you ready?" "I am," I said.

The production assistant counted down out loud, "Eight, seven, six, five, four . . ." at three he stopped counting out loud, and silently held up three fingers, then two, then one, and then pointed directly at me, indicating that the camera was on and the broadcast was live. In my ear, on-air anchor Abrams summarized what the A.G. had said in the previous segment, concluding: "Joining us now, live and exclusively, in his first interview since the arrest of the Manganos, is attorney James Cobb who represents Sal and Mabel Mangano. Mr. Cobb, were you able to hear our interview with Attorney General Foti?"

"Most of it," I answered.

"Do you have any response to what he said or to the charges leveled today against your clients?"

"I do," I responded, requiring Abrams to ask, "What's your response?"

I looked directly into the lens of the large camera with the small illuminated red light on top. It was no more than six feet away from me. Behind that lens, I knew there was an audience of millions of people, glued to their sets on this riveting story, just as I had been a few days earlier. I spoke slowly, forcefully, and with as much conviction as I could summon: "The attorney general of the State of Louisiana is one hundred percent, completely, totally, and unequivocally wrong! From what I just heard, there is not a single grain of truth in what he said. In arresting Mr. Sal and Miss Mabel, two innocent people, Mr. Foti has grossly abused his prosecutorial discretion. We had an appointment with his office today to explain what happened and answer all his questions. He canceled that appointment, giving no reason or explanation, and instead arrested Mr. and Mrs. Mangano. His action in this matter is outrageous, and he ought to be ashamed of himself."

I glanced away from the lens for a second and Foti was standing next to the camera, listening intently to every word I said. He was chewing on a large, unlit cigar, which dangled from his mouth, moving up and down slightly with each chewing motion. He squinted back at me through thick, silver-rimmed eyeglasses not nearly thick enough to hide his obvious displeasure with what I had just said. I thought back for an instant to the image of Sal and Mabel, spread-eagled on the hoods of police vehicles, just hours earlier. I was still furious. The attorney general had fired the first shot. My return fire developed into a full broadside, and, as each of his mistaken statements and assertions came up in the interview, I let him have it. He was standing no more than ten feet away from me—point blank range—next to the camera.

"Well, why weren't these residents evacuated and why did your clients abandon them?" Abrams asked, sounding perturbed with my previous answer. Based on media reports and the A.G.'s statements, he thought his pitch was a 100-miles-per-hour fastball that I would swing at and miss. The talking heads in the age of gotcha journalism love to embarrass the person being interviewed. But Abrams didn't know what I knew, and his 100-miles-per-hour fastball turned into a high, hanging curve ball meant to be knocked right out of the park.

"Dan, I'm so glad you asked this question," I responded. "Mr. Sal and Miss Mabel abandoned *no one*. They were there in the nursing home, when this unexpected wall of water hit them and their beloved residents. They weren't there by themselves, either. They stayed with their residents with the help of their own family members—their children and grandchildren, nieces and nephews, Mabel's brother and his wife. They were also there with staff members and the families of staff members who have always come to St. Rita's for twenty years for protection against storms and hurricanes. *They abandoned no one*. Mr. Sal and Miss Mabel swam out of the nursing home with residents literally on their backs. They saved more than fifty lives in the most courageous fashion I can imagine. They are heroes in my book, and somebody ought to be pinning a medal on them instead of arresting them for a crime they didn't commit. Mr. Foti might have learned all of this if he hadn't canceled the meeting in which we would have answered all his questions. Maybe this horrible mistake could have been avoided. As I said earlier, he ought to be ashamed of himself."

If stares could kill, I would have been a dead man at that very instant. Foti was staring me down, and he was visibly pissed. Livid is a better word to describe his demeanor. He was chewing furiously on that unlit cigar. It was moving up and down like a jackhammer. I noticed that there were a few more people in the tent listening to the interview than when I went on the air, and I wondered who they were.

Abrams shot back, "Why did your clients ignore a mandatory evacuation order, as the A.G. has said?"

I had to be careful with this one as I really didn't know the answer. Fortunately, a lack of knowledge was rarely an impediment to me speaking about anything, anytime, anywhere. "I have not seen a mandatory evacuation order issued by the civil authorities for St. Bernard Parish, Dan, have you?"

The TV guys hate when you ask *them* a question; it robs them of control and they generally don't have *any* answers. "Well, shouldn't your clients have seen it, Mr. Cobb?" Abrams was sounding as pissed as Foti looked.

"Whether or not a mandatory order to evacuate was issued will have to be learned in the discovery process, Dan, as you know. What I'm telling you is that if one was issued, and that's a big 'if' in my mind at this point in time, *no one* communicated that information to the Manganos. These are decent, law-abiding citizens. If Parish authorities, or the police, had ordered them to evacuate, they would have evacuated."

I had said too much and was way out on a limb, but it sufficed for the moment. What mattered was starting to change the public perception of Sal and Mabel. In raising legitimate questions and painting the A.G. as the bad guy, I hoped to cause the public to pause for a minute in this avalanche of bad publicity, and say to themselves: "Well, maybe there's another side to the story here." It would take a lot more than one interview to overcome the presumption of guilt that the attorney general had generated, with the media acting as his willing, enthusiastic accomplice.

The interview ended and I watched Foti turn his back on me in disgust and stomp off. He wasn't going to offer me the same handshake I offered him before his goon chopped my forearm. Accusing him of prejudging the case, not getting all the facts before making a decision, and arresting two innocent victims of Hurricane Katrina for a crime that they did not commit was an attack on his competence and fitness for office. He could not have been pleased that my attack took place on national television. As the production assistants unhooked me from the electronics, one of them said: "That was terrific, Mr. Cobb, great television. You represented your clients well." I assumed he knew what he was talking about and was encouraged by his comments.

Now some of the people who had come to the tent while I was on the air began to approach me. They turned out to be reporters or producers for other media outlets, print, broadcast, and electronic, and they all wanted me to come with them to their tents for live interviews. A spokesman and attorney for the Manganos had finally emerged, and he was fighting mad and punching back at the attorney general. Great television, as they say. Everyone wanted the story and I was more than happy to oblige them. I spent the rest of the day and long into the night doing one interview after another, refining the quickly constructed message I had improvised on MSNBC, but maintaining my sense of outrage. It felt good to be punching back on behalf of Sal and Mabel, and it allowed me temporarily to forget my station in life—homeless in Houston, with my family living in a hotel room and my comfortable world washed away in Katrina's floodwaters. It got personal between me and Charles Foti that very first day, and it remained personal, bitterly so, until almost exactly two years later, in September 2007, when there was a knock on a courtroom door in the quaint, old town of St. Francisville, Louisiana, and the sheriff yelled loudly and excitedly, "The jury has reached a verdict!"

Chapter 13: Media Madness

I got back to Andre's flop house late that evening. I was wiped out. It had been a tumultuous day, from the Manganos' surprise arrest to the attempts to have them released from jail, concluding with the rush to the EOC and the crush of interviews lasting late into the night. I hadn't spoken to Debbie and the kids all day. I reached them in the hotel room late, and they were already asleep. I told Deb to watch the news. She said they had already caught some of it. What did the kids say about it, I asked. "They said you looked old and tired," she replied. Unfortunately, they were correct on both counts.

Deb then reported disturbing news. Christopher was increasingly down, bordering on depressed. He hated going to school, had no friends, and was isolated and alone. School officials had called her in and recommended that she seek counseling for him as soon as possible. The fatigue I was feeling was immediately swamped by a tidal wave of guilt. Chris was asleep, so I couldn't talk to him right then, and anyway I wouldn't have known what to say. Thirteen is a tough time in any kid's life and instead of being there for him, I was off defending two people whom I had just met, and who the whole world presumed had negligently and carelessly killed thirty-five old people. I wondered, could my priorities have been any more screwed up than this? Should I turn around and race back to Houston?

I had multiple commitments beginning at 5 A.M. the next morning, as I was scheduled to do all the national morning shows: ABC's *Good Morning America*, NBC's *Today* show, CBS, FOX, etc. Having made an initial appearance and having begun the process of trying to undo the media-generated presumption of guilt, I couldn't just disappear. We decided fairly quickly that Debbie would get him to school in the morning and try to arrange an emergency appointment with a therapist right after school. Houston was teeming with Katrina evacuees and its healthcare resources were already stretched to the breaking point. Getting a quick appointment might prove impossible, emergency or not. This would not be the last time I would be forced to choose between my perceived obligations to Sal and Mabel and my crystal-clear obligations to my family. On pretty much each and every occasion, I put Sal and Mabel first. I was troubled by those decisions then and remain disturbed by them to this day.

I saw a news clip on CNN of Sal and Mabel leaving the parish jail in the dark, escorted by Bob. The media had obviously been tipped off by the attorney general's office and was waiting for them with camera lights and pesky, insensitive questions. Bob and I hadn't spoken since I left the jail and went to the EOC. I was glad they were out, and Bob handled the reporters' questions expertly. We had not rehearsed—or even discussed—how we would deal with the media. There had been no time. But Bob instinctively assumed the same outraged tone I had communicated in my interviews. It was comforting to learn that we were on the same page, even more so that Sal and Mabel had not spent the night in jail. I passed out in a chair after midnight and was awakened at 4:30 A.M. the next morning by Andre and a cup of coffee. "Get up, dude. The networks want you on site by 5 A.M. That's 6 Eastern time and they go live at 7 Eastern, 6 our time. Get your ass up, brother; it's show time!" He was obviously at least one cup of coffee ahead of me—he was way too enthusiastic for that hour of the day. I got up, got juiced on coffee, showered, dressed, and we were out of the door in fifteen minutes. I made sure not to wear yellow.

The entire day was a blur. Beginning at 6 A.M., I went from one stand-up interview to another, to another, and another. Whereas the A.G. had access to the EOC headquarters and the press room where he could conduct news conferences and reach dozens of media outlets at the same time, we were relegated to the parking lot, in the searing heat, schlepping from tent to tent. Andre assumed the role of scheduler and coordinator of my time. We did not plan it or even discuss it. It just happened.

Around mid-day, I found myself doing an interview with a local television station from Panama City, Florida. The more local the reporter, the dumber the questions were. Finally, I told Andre, "Look, nobody from Louisiana is going to see these kinds of interviews. Let's concentrate on Louisiana print and electronic media, where some potential juror, if it ever comes to that, might hear our side of the story." He agreed and we took a break.

Later that afternoon, the national print media convinced the authorities in the EOC to let them use the air-conditioned press room for a print-only interview with me. All of the big guns showed up—*New York Times, Washington Post, Los Angeles Times, Dallas Morning News, Houston Chronicle, USA Today*, the Associated Press, and many others. Very quickly the questions got a lot smarter and a lot harder to answer. Hadn't all the other nursing homes in St. Bernard Parish evacuated in advance of the storm? Why didn't St. Rita's? Was money a factor in the decision not to evacuate? If the St. Rita's patients were moved to another facility before the storm, wouldn't that receiving facility receive the revenue for all of the St. Rita's residents, not St. Rita's? Where was St. Rita's emergency plan and did the owners follow it? Why did the Manganos disappear after the flooding and why didn't they contact the authorities, knowing that thirty-five people had died in their facility? All of a sudden, I found myself longing for the TV reporter from Panama City, Florida: the guy with the perfect white teeth, the big hairdo, and the dumb, easy questions.

Andre, my "handler," was contacted in the parking lot by MSNBC staffers. They were putting together a one-hour live special for that evening, with expert commentators from around the country. Would I participate? Scheduled to appear was a criminal law professor and expert from Louisiana State University Law School, Alan Dershowitz from Harvard Law, host Dan Abrams, and me. Dershowitz had successfully obtained a new trial for Claus von Bülow and had gained an acquittal for this notorious defendant, a defendant who appeared guilty from afar. I was hopeful he would come down on my side of the issue. Sal and Mabel also appeared guilty from a distance and had seen their constitutional rights trampled on by an overzealous prosecutor and a sensationalist media. I wasn't sure what the support of a fancy-pants Harvard law professor would do for me, but I was desperate to get some support from somebody with national credibility. Dershowitz had plenty of that, but maybe not in the minds of Louisiana residents and potential jurors. We decided to do the show anyway and hope for the best.

We received one more invitation to do a live national special that night. After seeing me on MSNBC, producers for CNN's *Nancy Grace* show contacted Andre and said they were doing one hour on the "tragedy," with elder-care experts, prosecutors, defense lawyers, and the ubiquitous Ms. Grace. I had seen her before as I had clicked my way through cable news channels. I was never able to watch her for more than five minutes, as she always appeared to be several cc's shy of the medication she should have been taking to control her hysteria and paranoia. She had trashed the Manganos already and had reported as fact several highly prejudicial rumors that turned out to be pure, 100-percent fiction. Some of her "reporting" contained not even a sliver of truth. She did not bring any light to any issue she discussed, only hysterical heat. I didn't need things any hotter. I had been up since 4 A.M. and was likely to blow up on her show, which was scheduled to air at 9 P.M. We decided to decline the invitation and concentrate on MSNBC, and Andre told them no. Nancy's producers, it turns out, didn't like "no" as an answer and set in motion a series of events both devastating and psychologically destructive.

I was once again in the EOC parking lot, standing near the MSNBC tent, preparing to go on live national television. It was supposed to be a Professor Roberts from LSU, Dershowitz from Harvard, Abrams the host, and me. MSNBC had an unannounced trick up its sleeve. The show began with video footage from inside the nursing home. There was mud and destruction everywhere. Empty wheelchairs and patient beds were prominently featured as were fading, waterlogged pictures by children and grandchildren that hung on the walls of residents' rooms. It was a ghastly sight, knowing about the death and misery that had occurred on those premises. The producers then played taped footage of Foti, who asserted that the residents had died needlessly and negligently, and that Sal and Mabel were negligent murderers. With that as the setup, I expected Abrams to cut to me and ask me to explain my clients' position on the tragedy and how they were not criminally culpable. That's what they told me they were going to do in the pre-show interview. They lied.

Abrams' next words sent a chill down my spine: "Joining us now, live by telephone, is Steve Galladoro. Steve is a captain in the St. Bernard Parish Fire Department and a first responder who rescued dozens of people after the flood hit the parish. Steve's father was a resident at St. Rita's who died in the nursing home. Steve, on my behalf, and on behalf of all our viewers, please accept our condolences on your loss." The two of them engaged in a sad and moving conversation, while I sweated my ass off in an incredibly hot parking lot, with an earplug in my ear.

Galladoro related how his father had been a kind and gentle man, with numerous children and grandchildren. He had been put in St. Rita's after he fell at home and his family was told he needed twenty-four-hour care. He was eighty-four years old, and other than falling down, was in relatively good health. While they spoke, more video footage of the inside of St. Rita's was broadcast with the images of toppled wheelchairs in the mud and flipped over mattresses. Unexpectedly, Steve then relayed a conversation which he said he had with Sal Mangano, before the storm. Sal had promised that his father would be okay and that the nursing home had plans to evacuate and had buses, if necessary, Steve said. This was completely different from what the Manganos had told me. Finally, and most poignantly, he related how he had come to the nursing home the day after the tidal wave hit. There was still four or five feet of standing water in the facility and more than that throughout the parish. He had come to St. Rita's to find out about his dad. He said he came by boat and waded into the nursing home, in water almost up to his chest. As he moved through the home, he said he bumped into a floating object. It was a body. He pressed on in his search and several steps later, bumped into another floating object. It was another body. In shock, he decided to abandon his search because if he discovered his father among the floating corpses, it would have been too much to bear. Once back in his boat, he found the Manganos in the cluster of survivors at the Beauregard School, about a half a mile away. None of the staff would look him in the eye, he said. One of the LPNs finally told him what happened: "Mr. Steve, we couldn't save your dad," she said, before sobbing uncontrollably. The sight of these residents who survived and the knowledge that his father hadn't was more than he could stand. He looked for and found Sal and they had a conversation. The content of that conversation would become a significant piece of evidence in the trial two years later. Steve Galladoro would become a key prosecution witness

As Abrams wound down the interview, Galladoro cut back in: "Dan, can I say one more thing?" "Of course," Abrams replied. "I know you're going to have on your program James Cobb, the Manganos' attorney. I saw him on television yesterday and I know he's going to do an excellent job for his clients. I only wish the Manganos had done an excellent job for my father."

And with that, Abrams segued to yours truly: "Joining us now is James Cobb, the attorney for the Manganos. Mr. Cobb, do you have a response to Steve Galladoro's comments?" I felt like I had been set up. Without much chance to think, I responded instinctively: "Let me say first, Dan, to Steve Galladoro, who I don't know and have never met, I'm sorry for your loss. You have my sympathy and condolences, person to person. I know this has to be very hard on you and your family." I paused to catch my breath and try to gain some composure.

"As to the information Steve has related to your audience, those are not the facts as I understand them. St. Rita's would have evacuated had they been ordered to do so. Whether that order exists and whether it was communicated to the Manganos is something that will have to be determined in the discovery process, Dan, as you know." I felt like I had blunted the emotional assault of his moving interview. I continued with what had now become our pitch: the Manganos were good and decent people who were caught in an unprecedented, unexpected, and unpredicted flood; they were not criminals; they abandoned no one and were in the building saving lives when this horrible event happened.

After I had finished my explanation and pitch, Abrams swung to

Harvard's Dershowitz: "Alan, what's your take on all of this?"

He responded immediately and forcefully: "The defense attorney is exactly right. This conduct is not a crime. The prosecutor should have exercised his discretion and not charged these people with homicide. Before someone is subjected to the criminal law, can the government say that the defendant had a 'to be or not to be' moment, where he considered the consequences of his conduct and committed an act which is a crime? That is clearly not present in this case. They never should have been arrested." Finally! Somebody was on my side! It mattered not that he was an East Coast liberal from Harvard Law School. He was a major player on the legal profession's national stage, and I was encouraged by his comments and support. The interview lasted maybe thirty minutes longer with all the guests agreeing that it was going to be a very hard case—for both sides.

Steve Galladoro did not appear on camera for this special and was on the air by telephone only, so I never saw him and did not know what he looked like. The first time I would actually see him would be two years later, as I watched from a second-floor window as an extremely frail, bald man shuffled across the outdoor courtyard below the courtroom on his way to the witness stand. He had contracted cancer and showed the ravages of radiation and chemotherapy. He was thin and weak and walked with a cane. He appeared to be a dead man walking as he climbed the two steps into the witness box, slowly and in obvious pain. He would confront Sal again, this time as a witness for the prosecution. His story was gripping, compelling, and heartbreakingly sad. He was literally at death's door. How could we possibly cross-examine this first responder and hero who had saved so many lives, while we had lost the one life that mattered the most to him?

The show ended around 6 P.M. and I thought I was done for the day. I turned my cell phone back on after the cameras went off and was surprised to see that I had received a call. Turns out, it wasn't a call; it was actually a text message, a mode of communication I was using that week for the first time. Although voice communication on cell phones was still virtually impossible, text messages got through. They could be responded to, if I could figure out which button to push. I opened the message. It was from Debbie. It read: "emergency, call *asap.*" She never used this kind of language, never the dreaded word: *emergency.* Enough had already gone wrong in our lives; we were buried in bad news and there was more coming every day. What could this possibly be, I wondered, as I attempted to reach her by cell phone. I failed again and again and again. I couldn't raise her—the towers were down; the circuits were busy. We jumped in the car and raced to a land line on which I had sometimes been able to get through to her.

My thoughts and fears turned immediately to Christopher. Was he okay? Had he done something to himself? I recalled in my darkest hours looking out our hotel room window and the five-story parking lot out back, with rooftop parking and a very low ledge. I remembered thinking to myself if someone wanted to end it all, this would be a pretty easy and convenient place to do it. Had Chris looked out the same window and had the same thoughts? As an adult, when that kind of thinking takes over, you shake your head back and forth dismissively. It doesn't always work. In Katrina's aftermath, we began to hear unconfirmed reports of suicides by lawyers, doctors, cops, and business people. Those reports, in many instances, turned out to be tragically true. In the best of times, some of us hang on to sanity by a thread. Katrina tore at those threads.

Using the land line, I called Debbie's cell phone: all circuits were busy. I tried the hotel room. No answer. I called the school and received another recording about their business hours and when they would reopen the next day. I was descending into sheer panic. I crudely texted Deb the land line phone number and told her to call me *asap*. My mind wandered for the thirty minutes or so before the phone rang. I imagined the worst and then began looking for less ghastly outcomes—a mere car accident, perhaps. Those thirty minutes were an eternity, but the phone finally rang. "Debbie, is that you? Is Christopher okay?" She said he was fine. "Is everyone else okay?" "Yes," she said, "what's got into you?" "Your text said there was an emergency!" It was amazing how I could shift from relief to anger in a split second, denying myself that moment of relief which minutes earlier I had been longing for. My anger was about to get a whole lot worse.

Debbie explained that she had received a panicked phone call from her mother, Dawn, in upstate New York. Dawn, a woman who was not exactly media savvy and lived in Watertown, New York, had been contacted by CNN. She had been grilled by some producer who asked if she was related to Jim Cobb, a lawyer in New Orleans. She responded that he was her son-in-law, whereupon the producer told her that there was someone, a "handler," in Baton Rouge who was preventing the *Nancy Grace* show from talking to her son-in-law. The network was going on air this very evening with a major one-hour special on the St. Rita's homicide case. It would be a huge, devastating mistake if her son-in-law didn't participate. They didn't know how to contact me, and it was an "emergency" that they reach me immediately. Did she know how to find me?

Debbie's mom then began trying to contact her, running into the same frustrating telecommunication problems I had. She was worried and upset and panicked. The *Nancy Grace* show had called her and told her that her son-in-law was making a terrible mistake in not appearing on their show. She was not media savvy, so of course, she believed them. Hence, her frantic attempts to reach her daughter and Debbie's frantic attempts to reach me. The "emergency" designation in Debbie's text was the invention of Grace's producers.

I explained the situation to Debbie and told her why we weren't doing the show and she agreed with the decision. Her mom had been concerned, and so was she, that I was making some terrible, life-altering mistake, as the producer had portrayed it, and it would be visible to the entire world on cable television. They were upset. Christopher had overheard the conversation and he was upset that his dad was potentially screwing up on national television. And I had been placed in a state of panic as I contemplated what I assumed was the latest calamity to befall our family. I hung up the phone relieved but furious at the schmucks from cable TV.

This was not a heart-healthy existence I was living. My emotional state had gone from an hour's worth of panic and imagining the worst, to a brief sense of relief, to a raging fury and anger at whoever was responsible for this latest bump in the Cobb family's road.

I related the story to Andre, who was offended at being described as my "handler." Adding insult to injury, the unknown producer was telling the world that he was doing a terrible job as my "handler." Andre thought about the story for a minute and said, "Let's go find this asshole and confront him." My thoughts exactly!

We climbed into Andre's jet black Elvis-mobile and drove over to the EOC. We got out of the car and started searching for the CNN trailer. Finding it, we entered and ran into some clown with a headset on one ear and a cell phone clapped to the other. He must be important, I thought. Two phones at the same time. "Is the *Nancy Grace* show producer here?" I asked.

"Who are you?" he asked in response. I hated people who answered questions with questions.

"My name is Jim Cobb and I understand somebody with her show is looking for me," I said. He disappeared into the back of the trailer and I could dimly hear an animated discussion.

A young woman appeared. "Are you Jim Cobb?" she asked.

"That's what I just told the other guy," I said.

"Great," she said. "Glad we found you; let me get somebody on the phone in New York with the show." I let slide the remark that "they found me," when the exact opposite was true. I was becoming more annoyed by the second.

Finally, I was placed on a call with a "segment producer" in New York.

"Thank goodness we found you," she said. "We've got this big one-hour special planned for tonight and you need to be there to represent the Manganos. We're going to have a number of guests, experts in elder care, some lawyers . . ." I cut her off.

"Look, lady," I said, "please don't tell me where I need to be and what I need to do. Why are your people calling my family and telling them that being on your show is an emergency?"

A little taken aback, she responded, "Well, you've got some handler down there who cut us off and obviously isn't telling you how important this is and our message wasn't getting through to you."

"It got through," I said. "Doing your show is not my definition of an emergency. There are people dying down here. Don't you know that? Now, that's an emergency. You've upset me, my wife, and kids for no reason whatsoever. Tell your crazy boss that I wouldn't appear on her dumb f—ing show if it was the last television show on earth. And never call me or my family again or I'll sue the shit out of you for invasion of privacy and intentional infliction of emotional distress." It was bullshit, but it sounded great and she sounded just dumb enough to believe it. I slammed the phone down, hanging up on the New York producer, turned to the CNN staffer in the trailer, her mouth wide open in shock, and said, "Have a nice day." We stormed out of the building almost slamming the door and never heard from Nancy Grace or her show again. I felt much better.

We watched her special later that night and it was her usual diet of hysteria, paranoia, and speculation. It was anti-Mangano to be sure, but I figured we would weed out any potential juror who saw that show or any of her shows for that matter. Any potential juror who was a regular viewer of the Grace show was never going to make it onto a jury—not one I was selecting, anyway. Grace's show appealed to small and closed-minded people—minds unburdened by facts, reason, or logic. In this respect, her viewers had a lot in common with the host.

Baton Rouge was getting crazier and more crowded. I needed to get back to Houston to lay hands on my family and to begin the work of conducting an investigation and planning a defense. Without much thought or deliberation, I had climbed onto the back of this Bengal tiger of a case. Once aboard, getting off a tiger's back gracefully and without grievous injury is not really an option.

Chapter 14: Cocktails and Chianti

Interstate 10 was still packed in both directions, with emergency gear going one way and shell-shocked families the other. As I looked upon the bewildered passengers headed in my direction, it struck me that I was looking into a mirror. This is how I must appear, for I was in the same sunken boat they were. Stupidly, I thought, I had just loaded additional and dangerous cargo into my already unstable craft—undertaking the defense of the most hated couple in America in the highest profile case in the nation. That kind of weight could sink *any* boat, I thought, certainly mine. I was disgusted to have caught myself once again wallowing in self-pity. I yelled out loud: *"Snap out of it!"* I needed to focus on what had to be done to investigate and prepare a defense. My mind temporarily back on track, my head began to spin with a "to do" list.

First and foremost, I had to locate and lock up the testimony of witnesses to the tragedy, employees who were there when the murderous water came. Various media outlets had already located some employees, and the ones who were talking had nothing nice to say about the Manganos. Some orderlies and licensed practical nurses (LPNs) who were talking spoke about how obsessed with money and cheap the Manganos were. The media finished the thought with the chilling idea that maybe, just maybe, they had failed to evacuate because it would cost too much and there would be a loss of revenue going forward. This innuendo gave life to a horrible conclusion—the Manganos had allowed these innocent elderly to die because they valued money more than the lives of their residents. It was a theory that the government would happily seize upon as a critical element of their case—a motive. I had to get to the bottom line on this theory, and I had to do it quickly.

Above all, I wanted to interview middle-management types from St. Rita's—the director of nursing, the assistant director, and anyone else who might have been consulted about the decision not to evacuate. I needed to get to these people first, before the A.G. and his intimidating goons with guns and badges put words in their mouths. If anybody was going to put words in their mouths, it was going to be me! Truth is rarely absolute in a lawsuit, whether civil or criminal. Often, outcomes turn on who gets to the "truth" first, locks it up, and then best defends that truth to the bitter end. The best, most believable "truth" comes from disinterested witnesses—people who have no stake in the outcome, no skin in the game. If this case were to proceed to trial, Sal and Mabel had plenty of skin in the game. They were facing jail terms that would last for the rest of their lives. Because they had so much at stake, a jury would likely view their version of "the truth" with great skepticism. I needed disinterested, nothing-to-gain witnesses who were not under the threat of jail. But where were they?

Simply finding people, much less persuading them to talk, was a huge challenge amid post-Katrina chaos. After Sal and Mabel were arrested, every health care worker in the flood zone became skittish about talking to anybody about anything. Twenty-plus bodies of dead patients were discovered in an uptown New Orleans hospital, and weeks after Sal and Mabel's arrest, a loving and courageous New Orleans doctor and two nurses were arrested and handcuffed in front of their families and charged with the murders of these patients. Foti had struck again. Amid this state-sponsored hysteria and attempted scapegoating, witnesses were hard to come by and even harder to convince to get involved. Everyone was running scared and no one wanted to talk to a lawyer like me who, as most ordinary folk believed, was in the case just for himself.

Government investigators had more advantages than guns and badges. They possessed three awesome powers that I did not. First, they had the power of subpoena. If I found a witness and wanted to talk to him or her and was refused, I was done. I couldn't make an individual talk to me. The government, upon finding the same reluctant witness, could say, "Fine, pal, you don't want to talk to us? Here's a subpoena compelling your attendance in our offices and we'll talk there. Maybe that will loosen your tongue!"

Second, the government could, and often did, threaten prosecution of the uncooperative witness. This usually scares the shit out of ordinary people and allows words to be put into their mouths by the guys with the guns and the badges. Those words, once uttered, are hard to shake, for any change in statement or testimony can result in a charge of perjury.

Finally, and most powerfully, the government can grant immunity from prosecution to a witness who has some really damaging things to say about a defendant. The agents imply that the witness has some exposure to criminal prosecution, but if the witness will just "tell the truth" about the defendants, he or she will get immunity from prosecution for the nonexistent misdeeds. The government's quiver was full of arrows, now all trained on Sal and Mabel. I, on the other hand, had the force of my gentle ways and kind personality. Boy, were Sal and Mabel in trouble, I thought, if they had to rely on me to be the nice guy! I was hopelessly outgunned on this front, which is why I had to get to the witnesses first and lock up their favorable testimony, if any even existed. The clock was ticking.

I eased off Interstate 10 and onto I-610, which loops around Houston. I exited at Westheimer and pulled into the Sheraton Suites parking lot, avoiding the Galleria traffic. The hotel reception desk was still a madhouse, much as it had been a week earlier. Dozens of people were still looking for a place to stay, kids were running wild in the lobby, and the hotel staff members appeared to be at their collective breaking point. I avoided the crush of people and went straight to the elevator. A sign had been posted above the "up" button for the elevators. There was a red cross on the sign and it read, "All Louisiana residents please report to the front desk immediately." I just knew this was going to be bad. I once again feared that they were kicking us out of the hotel. I went back to the madhouse to stand in yet another line and receive the dreaded news.

When I finally reached the front of the line, the receptionist asked for my room number and driver's license. Confirming my state of residence, she announced to me: "Mr. Cobb, the American Red Cross has designated this hotel as an official Red Cross shelter. Your room fees and taxes will be paid by the Red Cross for two weeks. You are still responsible for all incidental charges. Do you have any questions?" I was stunned by the unexpected good news.

"What's the room rate I'm paying now?" I asked.

"$149.95 per day," she answered.

"Could you do me a favor," I asked, "Do you have a calculator?"

"Yes, sir, I do," she responded.

"Could you divide $149.95 by $7.25 for me?" She did it quickly and came back with the answer of 20.6. "Thanks," I said, as I turned away to head back to the elevators.

She called me back, "Sir, could I ask you why you asked me to calculate those numbers? What does it mean?"

"Sure," I said. "You guys charge $7.25 for a martini in your bar. I wanted to know how many I could drink per day for free now that my room rate is being picked up by the Red Cross. Thanks."

She shook her head and laughed, "You people from Louisiana are funny," she said.

"I wasn't joking," I replied. I gave her a wink and left her to ponder whether anyone could actually drink twenty martinis a day.

Upstairs, the group was almost as glad to see me as I was to see them. Collette's lot in life had improved dramatically. Debbie had persisted and pleaded with the coach of the club soccer team in the area to let her try out. Several of the girls in her class were on the team, and Collette was really good—a prolific scorer who never saw a shot she didn't like. The coach was reluctant at first. The team was already formed; their season had begun—and anyway, how long was she even going to be staying at St. Mark's? But then he relented, and in Collette's first game she scored all three goals and the team won for the first time all season. Overnight, she emerged as a class favorite. Soccer parents began joking that they needed to buy us a house so she would stick around. I shot back, "Please do! I'm entertaining all offers." We were invited over to people's homes based on Collette's celebrity and things got a little better for us and a lot better for her. But eleven-year-old girls were a lot more open and friendly than the thirteen-year-old boys in Christopher's class. He was pretty much all alone in this new place, isolated on an island of anonymity.

Without a soccer club or some other focus, Christopher had become totally fascinated with the St. Rita's case in my absence. He had always been interested in politics and the media, and now his dad was a major player in the middle of a legal/political media circus. He wanted to know everything, especially about the media personalities I had run into and what they were like off camera. Who was I talking to? Are there any other appearances scheduled? What shows was I planning to do and why? Of course, I didn't have answers to any of his questions, as this entire drama was unscripted and unplanned. But I did stumble upon a response that made his eyes light up. "I don't know," I said. "What do you think?" I could almost see the gears begin to turn in his head. I asked him to go on the Internet to check out the various shows that still wanted me to appear. What were their "numbers"? Which shows had the most viewers? Which shows were the most watched in Louisiana, etc. He tackled the mission with a vengeance; he constantly asked questions and was full of ideas. With something to focus on, to feel part of, Chris's despondency gave way to determination and grit. I lectured him often, as I did my law students, averring that the strongest steel is always forged in the hottest fire: if he could come through this personal catastrophe intact and emerge from the darkness, there would be no challenge in life going forward that he could not overcome. But we had to fight each and every day.

Debbie needed a little bucking up as well, I gallantly decided. She had been holding down the fort alone. While I sashayed around in Baton Rouge legal circles trying to restart my career, she had endured walls too close, kids too loud and often at each other's throats, and a dog crying at the door longing to go outside. Not that I lacked torments of my own: dealing with the attorney general, fighting for Sal and Mabel, and coping with the locust swarm of world media. But these had been somebody else's problems, external to our family's struggle for sanity and survival, until I signed on to defend the Manganos. It was a choice I made without so much as consulting my wife, much less obtaining her approval. *Mea culpa.* Making momentous, life-changing decisions without so much as consulting one's spouse could be characterized as selfish and self-centered. Happiness does not flow from such decisions like juice from a good melon.

I decided to make it up to Debbie, bit by bit. Returning one night from Baton Rouge to our hotel-room hovel, I suggested we go out to dinner without the kids. They could order room service, which was always fine with them.

I picked an Italian place, Debbie's favorite kind of food, close to the Galleria. We couldn't stay away too long; one of the kids' disagreements might flare into a duel waged with room-service steak knives. We arrived at the restaurant and were delighted with the news that we'd have to wait at the bar for fifteen to twenty minutes. Debbie was then in her cosmopolitan phase—a too easy, down-the-hatch concoction of chilled vodka with splashes of cranberry juice, triple sec, and a lime twist, served straight up. It was a pretty drink, and pretty potent, especially for a petite woman, five-foot-two with eyes of blue. She knocked back two. I had three drinks of my own. The usual: Bombay Sapphire, rocks. At the table, we ordered a Caesar salad—split it, please. One of us got lasagna, the other spaghetti Bolognese. Two tomato-based sauces, I thought, how about a nice bottle of Chianti— thus more or less guaranteeing that I would be DUI for the drive back to the hotel. Over dinner, we caught up on each other's problems. Debbie's daily routine was brutal; the kids argued incessantly and Christopher was a constant worry. On the legal front, I was coming to the hazy conclusion that I was in over my head and could, at any moment, be embarrassed on an international stage, courtesy of the media. Money, school, our destroyed home back in New Orleans, and friends with whom we had lost contact— there wasn't much good to talk about. "Give me a cognac and the check," I told the young waiter. "We've had enough fun tonight."

I don't know what precipitated the explosion, but suddenly we were in a huge fight, right there in the restaurant. A large quantity of alcohol had lubricated the silo doors as the missiles were readied for a thermonuclear exchange. On the short drive back down Westheimer to the hotel, the radiation level became toxic.

To punctuate some heated remark, as we tooled along in the left lane at thirty-five miles an hour, I saw fit to throw the car into a 90-degree right turn that took us across two-lanes of brake-popping traffic and up onto the curb. We came to rest in a driveway, partially blocking the sidewalk. I jammed the shift into park, opened the driver's side door, and stepped out, slamming the door so hard the car rocked back and forth. I then strode down Westheimer, gallantly leaving my wife to cope with the worst parking job in the history of Houston. I knew I had to get out of the confines of that argument chamber or something terrible would have happened. A hasty retreat was my only option.

I walked around for an hour or so in pedestrian-unfriendly Houston. What Debbie did, where she went, and how she got there, began to cross my mind and so I started my walk of shame back to the hotel—if only I could figure out where it was. On the advice of a homeless panhandler I asked for directions, I reversed course. The irony of asking a homeless person how to get home was not lost on me. My plan was to slink back into our room and slip into bed unnoticed, no easy task given that we were a foursome who shared limited space with a restless dog, but somehow I succeeded. And World War III gave way to deep sleep.

The next morning we ran the daily gauntlet: one bathroom, no place to make breakfast, Houston traffic, and arrival at a school the kids loathed. Not knowing where my car was, and not wanting to ask, I used Debbie's. I returned to the room, took a shower, and got ready to go to work. The armistice had degenerated into a "no talk" zone. Finally, I broke the silence. "Where's my car and car keys?" "Your keys are on top of the television and your car is somewhere in the parking garage." I grabbed the keys, strode purposefully to the five-story garage, and began a floor-by-floor search for my green BMW. Was it possible she had given me a bum steer, as a final act of revenge? Finally, there it was, on the roof, broiling in the morning sun. Had she deliberately bypassed the numerous sheltered spaces in order to punish me for my sins with a steering wheel too hot to touch? No matter. I had found my car in one piece and in time to still make a meeting downtown. I placed the key in the ignition and turned it fully to the right. In place of German engineering roaring to life, I heard the dreaded *wrrr, wrrr, wrr* sound with which a car proclaims its battery totally dead. A glance at the dashboard confirmed that Debbie had left the lights on all night. On purpose? To drive me nuts? Either way, I now had to find someone to give me a jump start in the heat of a Houston summer morning. By the time this mission was accomplished, I was soaked in sweat and obsessed with fantasies of exquisite revenge. I let them go. The dead battery, I decided, was karma: a sign from the gods. I had been an ass the previous evening and was now paying a cosmic price for my transgressions. The Italian restaurant wasn't too bad. For some reason we never again returned to it.

Chapter 15: "Hi Diane, This Is Chris"

As media feeding frenzies go, the post-Katrina version lasted longer than most. America's attention span is astonishingly short, and the media and the public move on quickly to the next car wreck or atrocity *du jour*. Katrina was different. There were just so many stories—stories of loss and death, broken families, economic catastrophe, and personal tragedy. First among these was the St. Rita's story, which combined every element of the larger narrative. How could these helpless old people have been allowed to die their horrible deaths? More importantly, who does society blame for such an unspeakable tragedy? Surely, it is someone's fault, for every bad thing that happens in America is somebody's fault—*somebody else's* fault. Accordingly, I was much in demand in the weeks and months following the storm, with Sal and Mabel only more so.

All the morning shows were still after us for the "exclusive" interview with the Manganos, the one that would expose what *really* happened and why. Larry King and Paula Zahn wanted it and competed against one another even though they were with the same cable network. Happily, Nancy Grace and her people didn't even call. All of the shows used the same tactics; I was besieged by calls from staffers—producers, segment producers, writers, etc.—all of whom made their pitch. I set ground rules: I wanted preapproval of all questions. I might allow the Manganos to talk about themselves and their life and family, what actually happened inside the home when the flood hit, how they risked their own lives to save their residents, and how broken hearted they were because they couldn't save them all. I would not allow any questions about why they did not evacuate, whether they followed their emergency plan, or what their discussions were with parish authorities and family members in advance of the flood. In other words, anything touching on their allegedly criminal conduct was off-limits. The staffers would then go back to the on-air talent and either obtain acquiescence to my conditions or propose their own. It was a very fluid back and forth negotiation, with every show trying to navigate the tightrope wire that separates a scoop from forfeiture of its journalistic integrity.

I started receiving surprising and unexpected phone calls.

"May I speak to Jim Cobb?"

"This is he," I said.

"Hi, Jim, this is Larry King, my guy tells me we are close to a deal on having you and your clients appear exclusively on my show. I think it's an important story and, from what I've been told, everything we've heard about them in the media is wrong. I'd like to help make it right."

Wow, I thought, he is really smooth. It's not about his show and ratings, and his obtaining the most sought-after exclusive in the country; it is about helping out Sal and Mabel. Yeah, right. He was, however, very persuasive. The questions he pitched were decidedly slower and more hittable than some other interviewers', and that was a factor I had to take into account.

"Hi, Jim, this is Matt Lauer. . . ." "Hi, Mr. Cobb, this is Paula Zahn…" "Hi, Jim, this is Brian Williams." It went on and on—heady stuff!

We soon ran out of Red Cross benefits at the Sheraton shelter and moved into an apartment near the Galleria. Our wet home in New Orleans was a 4,000-square-foot, two-story brick house, where everyone had a bedroom and private bath. Our new apartment was 750 square feet, two bedrooms, one bath, four people, a dog, and a kitchen not big enough for two people at

Ninety days before trial was to begin, the author posed with NBC's Brian Williams at Tulane graduation where he was the commencement speaker. Always the reporter, Williams still lobbied for the exclusive with Sal and Mabel.

the same time. We would be there for the foreseeable future, but how long that was we had no idea. It was better than a hotel room, but the extremely close quarters brought challenges of their own. Christopher and Collette shared a bedroom for the first time in their lives as well as the bathroom. Chris and I made frequent trips to the out-of-doors when the girls were in the bathroom and nature's call could not go unheeded.

I was in the apartment one morning when I received yet another call, seeking an "exclusive" with Sal and Mabel. "Hello, Jim, this is Diane Sawyer with *Good Morning America*. I know you've been speaking with Santina and Monica on our staff, and this is a story we really want to do. I understand that most of what is out there in the public domain is inaccurate, and your clients' side needs to be told. We'll do that."

She was persuasive and genuine, and I had been told by Stephen Jones (defender of Timothy McVeigh) that she was a woman who kept her word. Chris was at home with me. I put my hand over the phone and whispered, "It's Diane Sawyer, be quiet, please." He complied immediately and began pacing around the living room, eavesdropping as I talked into the phone. We danced the same dance I had danced with the others, and she ended by promising to be fair to Sal and Mabel.

"Diane, could you do me a favor?" I asked as the conversation wound down.

"If I can, sure," she said.

"I've got a thirteen-year-old son who's having a hard time, as we all are. Could you say hello to him?"

"I'd be happy to," she replied.

I walked over to Chris, who was lurking in the micro-kitchen, and handed him the phone. "Diane Sawyer wants to talk to you."

Without skipping a beat, he took the mobile phone from me, put the receiver to his ear and said, "Hi, Diane, this is Chris," whereupon he walked the three or four steps to his bedroom and closed the door. I did not follow. He did not emerge for at least fifteen minutes, a longer time than I had spent on the phone with Sawyer during the business portion of our call. Eventually he emerged from his room and handed me the phone.

"She's very nice," he said.

Curiosity was killing me. "So what did you guys talk about?"

"Dad," he responded matter of factly, "that's kind of between me and Diane, don't you think?"

So much for that! But I couldn't help being curious about a conversation that, I would later come to understand, had changed Christopher's life. Some weeks later, I was in New York to do a live *Fox & Friends* show, at

Fox's expense. I brought along Debbie, who needed a New York City visit as badly as any human ever needed one. Sal and Mabel still had not spoken to any one of their many TV suitors, because I had concluded that the risks were greater than the rewards. But as their second fiddle, I was still talking and in-demand. I had stayed in close touch with Monica and Santina of *Good Morning America,* along with other network guest getters, and from time to time they called me with one of their myriad questions about all things Katrina. When I mentioned that we would be in New York for Fox, they insisted on taking us to lunch with Diane, their treat. Of course we accepted the generous invitation.

Lunch was arranged at Café des Artistes, off Central Park West. It was frequented by media types, movie stars, and, of course, artists and musicians. Neither Deb nor I had ever been. Done with Fox, we arrived right on time and were met by Santina and Monica. Diane was in a meeting and running late, but she would be joining us, they said. The restaurant was sumptuous—very Manhattan. Once settled at a table in the rear, Santina and Monica wanted to know everything about our lives, our family, and the daily challenges we were facing. The three women got along famously, and I was soon relegated to drinking martinis while waiting for Diane, a chore I had no problem executing.

As the ladies went on and on, occasionally throwing a sympathy question in my direction, I noticed a tall woman walk in wearing a scarf and dark sunglasses. It was Diane Sawyer, trying to be inconspicuous and failing spectacularly. Heads turned as she was led through the main dining room to our table. Removing her sunglasses, she offered her hand, and I said, "Diane, we're from New Orleans and since Katrina, we don't shake hands. We hug," whereupon she gave both of us warm ones. She, too, wanted to know everything and peppered us with questions, the first of which was, "How's Christopher?"

We reported that he was "hanging in there and was jealous when we told him we were having lunch with you. He said to say hi."

"Well, please give him my very best and tell him I enjoy our chats," she said. I was puzzled but let her remark slide by, uncertain what she meant. We spent about an hour together, which went by in the blink of an eye. As always, she pressed for the exclusive, sympathetic to the unjustified beating the Manganos had taken in the press. She wanted to know how Sal and Mabel were holding up and what our plans were for the future. "We really don't know what we're going to do" was our most frequent response.

As our time together drew to a close, I had to ask: "Diane, that first time you called, when I asked you to say hi to our son, what did you guys talk about for fifteen minutes?"

She only revealed that she had sensed Christopher's loneliness. From there she digressed quickly to the aftermath of the conversation: how it had set her to thinking about all the children of Katrina and what effect this disaster would have on their lives—"educationally, socially, and psychologically." This interest prompted her to do a special on "Children of the Storm," on ABC's *20/20* as well as on *Good Morning America*. So Chris, it turned out, had had something to do with a major programming initiative on network TV.

She had given Chris her email address, and he had written to her in the intervening months. She responded as her schedule allowed, and they had become e-pals, providing Chris a bridge over troubled waters. What Diane did not reveal in any detail, then or ever, was the content of that first fifteen-minute conversation. I guess she shared Christopher's view that it was none of my business.

Months later, as a reward for surviving a very rough year, I took Chris to New York on a guys-only blowout. It was his first trip to the Big Apple. The most special moment for him was being Diane's guest for a behind-the-camera view of *GMA*, live from Times Square. Chris was transported from the streets of Times Square to an eighth-grader's version of heaven. We had picked a good day. There with us, walking the studio's back corridors,

A rose between two thorns. Diane Sawyer with Chris and the author. New Orleans 2007.

were George Clooney and Pres. Jimmy Carter with his Secret Service detail. When the show ended, Chris met Diane in person for the first time and was smitten. It would have been hard not to be smitten with a razor-sharp newswoman and former Junior Miss Kentucky, who had taken the time to get to know him.

Diane Sawyer never got the exclusive with the Manganos. Nobody did. In the end, the risk of exposing them in an interview outweighed any possible reward, no matter what ground rules I attempted to put in place. But Chris stayed in touch with Diane and she with him. We would be her guests again when *GMA* came to New Orleans for a town hall meeting with John Edwards during the 2008 presidential campaign. As Diane invited questions from the audience, she called on Chris who asked Edwards a cogent and thoughtful question about Social Security, Medicare, and Medicaid. I about had a heart attack until the question was successfully completed. Katrina all but faded from memory as Chris emerged from under the clouds of a storm-tossed time in his life to ask an articulate question of a presidential candidate under the bright lights of a national TV show.

Chapter 16: Saved by a Loaf of Bread

Media aside, priority number one after meeting Sal and Mabel became tracking down key witnesses and employees of St. Rita's. There was only one problem—none of them were in Houston. None of them were in St. Bernard either. There was *nobody* in flooded and destroyed St. Bernard Parish. After their arrest and release, Sal and Mabel fled to Mississippi to stay with friends and to be as far away from the media and St. Bernard as possible. I had instructed them to lay low and talk to no one about the case, not even friends or family. Mabel had obtained a cell phone and I contacted her to get her help in finding the people I needed to talk to. Within a day or so, she had located Diane C., a registered nurse and St. Rita's director of nursing (DON). She also found Thelma L., a licensed practical nurse and the assistant director of nursing (ADON). These were the people effectively in charge of patient care. Their recollection of events and decision-making could be critically important.

Diane was in a hotel room somewhere in Georgia. I tried, unsuccessfully, to reach her a half-dozen times. A man finally answered the phone in her room. I identified myself as the Manganos' attorney and asked if I could please speak to Diane C. "She's not here."

"Do you know when she'll be back?" I asked.

"No."

"May I ask with whom I am speaking?"

"This is her son, and she really doesn't want to talk to anybody, okay?" With that he hung up on me.

Off to a very bad start, I wondered if the state investigators had already gotten to her and whether they suggested that she not speak to me, or anyone else on behalf of the Manganos. All I could do was continue to call back in the hope that Diane would pick up the phone, not her son. I called back a couple of hours later and got sonny boy again. Of course, he told me that Diane wasn't in. This time, I left my phone number before her son hung up on me once again.

I reached Thelma on the first try. She was in her brother's house in Dallas, one stop away on the Southwest Airlines bus-like airplane from Houston's Hobby Airport. We spoke briefly.

I asked how she was doing and she said, "I'm not sleeping very well." I knew why.

I told her I was working for the Manganos and wanted to interview her. "Sure," she said, "I just sit here in front of the TV all day, alone, come see me."

I found her response odd and sad at the same time. I told her I'd get back to her with travel arrangements as soon as I could. I continued to try to reach Diane as I preferred to talk to the head nurse first, before talking to her assistant. If there were some conflicting facts in their stories, I could tell Thelma, "That's not what Diane told me," hoping she would adopt her supervisor's recollection if it were favorable to the Manganos.

Trying to reach Diane again, I got her son, who by then was clearly running interference for his mother. "Look, Mr. Cobb, you have no idea what my mother has been through. She is shaken and depressed and I think she's still in shock. I don't want her bothered by nobody and I don't want her going over what happened with you or anybody else."

"I understand," I said, "and I do have some idea of what she's been through. When she feels ready to talk, please have her call me."

I asked him whether the attorney general's office had attempted to contact her, and he said no. Carefully, I explained to him what his mother's rights were as a witness. She was not obligated to speak with anyone—me, the attorney general, the police, anyone. I could not tell her not to speak to the other side, nor should they tell her not to speak to me. It was totally her choice. If she were to be contacted and wanted to have a lawyer present to protect her interests, I would help her find someone appropriate, and St. Rita's would pay the lawyer's fee.

"That lawyer would be totally for your mom, protecting her, not St. Rita's, at no cost to her. Do you understand me?" Finally, I had struck the right cord.

"I do," he said. "I appreciate that. Good-bye." Click. He was a man of few words. I was already offering to spend Sal and Mabel's money without obtaining their authority, something lawyers are not supposed to do. The situation was, in my view, an emergency and I needed to do something to break through sonny boy's barricade. If the attorney general's office got to Diane first, and if she in her shock and depression panicked, she could say things that would be fatal to Sal and Mabel's defense. I had to break through first.

Approximately one hour after sonny's hang up, my phone rang. "May I speak to Jim Cobb?" the female voice asked.

"This is he," I responded.

"Mr. Cobb, this is Diane C. from St. Rita's. I understand you've been looking for me."

"I have, Diane. Thanks so much for returning my call. And please call me Jim."

I was relieved that I had finally made contact with this potentially critical witness, and I was aware that I better not blow this opportunity to get Diane on our side and keep her there. "Diane, I've spent hours and hours talking to Sal and Mabel and others who were in the nursing home when the flood hit. So I don't need to go over any of those details with you now, if you don't feel like talking about it."

"I can't talk about it now," she said. "The memories are too fresh and painful. I haven't slept in days."

"No problem," I said. "I understand and appreciate your feelings. We don't have to talk about any of that stuff now. Only when you're ready, okay?"

"Good," she responded, obviously relieved that some lawyer she had never met was not going to take her through the most painful experience in her life in excruciating, painstaking detail.

"There are some things I want to go over with you, in case you're contacted by the A.G.'s office or the police. Would that be okay?"

"It sure would," was her forceful reply. I then covered with her directly the points I had raised with her son.

"No one, not even the police, can make you talk to them voluntarily if you don't feel like talking. Just like you told me you don't want to talk about it, you can say the same thing to them, and one would hope that they would respect your wishes, just as I have. You understand?"

"I do," she said.

"Do you watch any of those TV police shows?" I asked.

"I watch *Law and Order*," she said.

"Perfect," I said. "You know how the police tell suspects they have the right to remain silent, anything you say can and will be used against you in a court of law, you have the right to an attorney, etc.? Well they mean all of that and plenty of folks have gotten in trouble when they waived their protection against self-incrimination guaranteed all citizens under the Fifth Amendment to our Constitution. Do you understand?"

"I do," she said. "And Mr. Cobb, I'm scared. I saw they arrested Sal and Mabel and put them in jail. I saw them walking out of the jail in Baton Rouge when they were released and felt horrible for them. I can't believe the A.G. arrested them without even talking to them, as you said in one of your interviews. What if they decide to come after me, Mr. Cobb, what should I do?"

"That's a great question, Diane. Since I already represent Sal and Mabel, I would have a conflict of interest in advising you, and our rules of ethics prohibit me from doing so anyway. I can help you find a really good criminal lawyer in Louisiana who would have your interests and only your interests at heart and he could advise you. Since your exposure, if any, arises out of your employment at St. Rita's, the company could pay your lawyer, so you would have no expense. Would you like me to try and help you do that?"

"Please!" came her immediate and excited reply. *Bingo!* I thought. Unlike my almost colossal error in offering Sal and Mabel up to the A.G.'s office for an interview, no decent criminal lawyer would ever allow Diane to be interrogated by Foti's gang, especially in the legal hysteria that currently ruled the day. The urge for creating scapegoats became virtually irresistible for authorities. A doctor and a number of nurses were under investigation for euthanasia and three were eventually arrested and charged with second-degree murder for their actions in a hospital in uptown New Orleans. Doctors, nurses, and health care professionals were under assault throughout the region.

"Okay, Diane, I'll go to work on that for you. In the meantime, if you have any questions, or just want to talk, here is all of my contact information. You can call me any time, day or night, okay?"

"Okay," she said, "and thanks. I feel a little better. Please tell Sal and Mabel I'm so sorry for what's happened to them and that I'm praying for them."

"I will," I said, "I'm sure they'll appreciate that. Goodbye."

I took a deep breath and exhaled a huge sigh of relief. I felt confident that she would resist any pressure from the A.G.'s office to point a finger at Sal and Mabel. This was especially true once we found her competent counsel upon whom she could rely. And she was afraid that maybe she would be next up in the prosecutor's crosshairs. That fear promoted silence, and silence was good for us, at least at this point. Two years later when the trial began, Diane would be called as a witness for the prosecution.

I turned my attention back to Thelma, and since she wanted to talk and was close to Houston, I decided to travel to her and do the interview in person, which is better than a phone call for getting a sense of how a potential witness might perform on the stand. I made my own travel arrangements—no secretary or travel agent like the old days. I had forgotten how difficult it could sometimes be dealing with airline reservations and car rental companies. It also caused me to confront an issue which so far I had ignored in representing Sal and Mabel—money.

I started charging expenses incurred in their representation to my credit card, a card so hot with new charges it threatened to burst into flames at any moment. Money owed by clients was rarely an issue in my usual practice of defending corporations and insurance companies. Although many of them were slow pay, almost none of them were *no* pay. As a firm, we collected 95 percent of what we billed. This was rarely the case when representing individuals. In fact, the 5 percent of uncollected fees our firm experienced was mostly owed by private individuals. As I started charging hundreds and thousands of dollars in expenses to defend the Manganos, I was reminded of an old law school professor's admonition. This professor was not an academic. He was a real lawyer: a former prosecutor, then a crusty criminal court judge, and then a defense attorney.

"When it comes to representing people charged with a crime," he said, "there's only one method of payment. I used to tell them, 'I don't get out of this chair until your money hits the table.' Always get a retainer up front and work off that money in your trust account. Never allow the criminal client to owe you money; instead, you should owe them an accounting of the more than adequate money they've already given you. Always stay ahead of them or you'll never get fully paid."

Other than quoting the Manganos an hourly rate for my time, which I discounted to them by 20 percent, we had no money discussions and I had no retainer. I had violated the cardinal rule of criminal defense work. I had started spending my money, when I should have been spending theirs. "Book me the cheapest flight and least expensive rental car you have," I told the reservationist. Soon, I would engage the Manganos in a serious money conversation, but that had to wait, cardinal rule violation or not. I booked my trip to Dallas for the very next day.

I fought Houston traffic the next morning on my way to Hobby Airport. I've never understood how Houston can have so much traffic, going in opposite directions, at all times of the day or night, rush hour or not. The pilot announced that we had landed at Dallas Love Field, the same place JFK landed on that fateful November day in 1963, I thought to myself. As I walked to the rental car counter, I had a flashback. As word spread that someone had opened fire on the Kennedy motorcade, our entire Catholic school had been summoned to St. Dominic Church to pray the rosary in hopes that the nation's first Catholic president would survive the shooting. When word came that he had died, I was instructed to lower the schoolyard flag to half-mast as I was the sixth grader with flag duty that week. I remember walking slowly and somberly to the flagpole in driving rain. Once there, I followed protocol I had memorized, lowering the flag fully, then raising it back to the top of the pole, and then lowering it to half-mast and tying it off. As I turned to go back inside the school building, I could see my classmates looking out the windows at the solitary ceremony I had just performed. I walked slowly and as ceremoniously as a sixth grader could walk, ignoring the rain, doing my duty, and getting completely soaked.

"Driver's license and credit card," the counter attendant ordered, snapping me out of my reminiscence. As I put the plastic on the counter, I remember thinking to myself, man, I need to stop combining sleeping pills with alcohol at night—an occasional event which was now becoming routine.

I remember neither the make nor model of the cheapest car available from the cheapest car rental place at Love Field. I do remember that when I closed the door to take off, it sounded like the inside of a flimsy tin can and the engine had all the oomph of a lawnmower. Thelma had given me directions from the airport saying it would take ten to fifteen minutes to reach her brother's house. Her directions were faulty. It took thirty.

The house was among many others that looked just like it: a single-story, blond-brick structure that dated to the late 1950s. It had a small side yard surrounded by a sagging hurricane fence. I knocked on the front door. A voice from inside: "Are you Mr. Cobb?" "Yes, it's me, Thelma." She opened the door, I shook her hand, and she let me in. The house was dimly lit and relatively dark at 10:00 in the morning. I could hear the air conditioning units laboring against the Dallas morning heat. She invited me to the kitchen for a cup of coffee and we sat down at the kitchen table. She told me there was no one else at home; her brother was at work. The television was on in the small, adjacent den, blaring cable news.

She wanted to know how Sal and Mabel were doing and her concern appeared genuine and heartfelt. I told her they were holding up as well as could be expected but were devastated by what they had been through, including their arrest.

"I'm devastated too," she interrupted.

"Are you okay talking about what happened?" I asked.

"Yeah, I guess so," she replied softly.

I started off by telling her that I lived in Lakeview, almost as famous for its flooding as St. Bernard Parish. Our house went under and we lost everything, I told her. "Me too," she nodded. There was a kinship among flood victims, regardless of where they were from, and I didn't want her to think I was some slick, New Orleans lawyer who had escaped harm. She warmed up a little.

We talked for several hours and she largely confirmed what Sal and Mabel had said about St. Rita's hurricane preparedness. They had plenty of supplies, food, water, diapers, medicine, and fuel for generators. It was everything they needed to survive for two weeks or more, with no help from the outside—in a non-flooded world.

"But what were you all still doing there?" I asked. "Who was watching the weather?"

She replied quickly and a bit defensively: "I was. I watched the weather on TV so much that they called me 'Bob Breck' at the nursing home." (Bob Breck is a weather man on the local Fox affiliate in New Orleans. Some of his previous hurricane forecasts had proved unreliable, but Breck maintained a large and loyal following and Thelma was one of his disciples.)

"Didn't you see how bad they were saying Katrina was going to be?" I asked.

"Of course I did. Everybody knew how bad they were predicting it would be. Sal and Mabel knew it too. You couldn't miss it," she said somewhat testily.

I moved on to a related issue: "Tell me about the decision-making process you all used to determine whether you were going to stay or evacuate, how did that work?"

"There wasn't no process," she said. "Sal and Mabel made all the decisions. I mean, we all talked about stuff, but it wasn't like we sat around a table and voted on anything. Sal and Mabel were the owners and Mabel was the administrator; it was their call. You know, I'd been there for years and we never, ever evacuated before, and everything turned out fine. Just this time . . ." Her voice trailed off, and I dropped the subject.

"You know, I shouldn't even be here," she said softly, staring down at her clasped hands on the kitchen table.

"No, I don't know anything about that. What do you mean?" I responded.

I thought I had heard it all, about that terrible morning inside St. Rita's as raging flood waters claimed the lives of thirty-five loved ones, gone too soon. I hadn't. Thelma described the powerful impact of the leading wave, its force knocking her off her feet and sending her sprawling some thirty feet down the nursing-home corridor. Some of the residents had been sitting in their wheelchairs in the windowless interior halls to avoid flying glass. These unfortunates were toppled first. Some struggled to regain their upright position and get back in a wheelchair. Too weak to do so, most of them drowned where they fell. Thelma, the Manganos, and other staff struggled frantically to pick people up and get them on a mattress in the hope that the mattress would float, and the water would level off and stop rising. Some residents, more physically capable than others, could cooperate with their rescuers. In the end, it came down to the survival of the fittest.

At some point, Thelma realized that the water was continuing to rise and was now approaching her upper body. She was, perhaps, 5'3" tall and all of a sudden began to fear for her own safety. But there was no safe place to go. In a matter of minutes, she was transformed from rescuer to someone in need of rescue. The water swept over her head and she searched desperately for something to hold on to that was floating. A piece of furniture provided temporary buoyancy, but the water continued to rise, reaching a level of 8 to 10 feet in fifteen minutes. It was now higher than the tops of the doors, trapping her inside.

Most of the others who had survived the initial onslaught had somehow managed to get outside and were now on the roof, but Thelma was not alone inside. Four other souls were clinging to pieces of floating furniture, she discovered; one of them was Diane, her supervisor, the director of nursing. They floated next to each other, joining forces in their struggle for survival. It was strangely quiet and dark and both women had no idea what to do, except hope and pray for rescue. But who would rescue them, they wondered, as they floated in the dark. Did anyone even know they were still alive? After what Thelma estimated was a couple of hours, she was totally spent.

A diabetic, Thelma had not eaten since an early breakfast and her blood sugar was completely out of whack. "I can't make it," she said, clinging to Diane. "I can't hold on any longer," whereupon she slowly slipped off their furniture raft and into the water that now covered the nursing station. Diane grabbed her by her hair and shoulders and pulled her back, saying, "You're not going anywhere." Diane hung onto Thelma, giving her the support she needed. About five minutes later, a plastic container floated right in front of them. Diane grabbed it. It contained a loaf of bread that was meant to be eaten with the red beans and rice at lunch. Diane opened it and fed Thelma a couple of slices of bread, providing the nourishment she needed to re-balance her blood sugar level and supply her with some energy. The plastic container, Thelma believed, was a gift from God, intended to help her survive after she had given up hope. She hung on.

Hours later, they heard the sound of an outboard motor and men calling out, "Is anybody in there?" They screamed in unison, "Help, Help, we're in here!" Shortly thereafter, they could hear the sound of people walking on the roof overhead. They continued to call out. The next thing they heard was a ferocious banging. Sal and others had come back to the building with makeshift tools—a fireplace poker, hammers, and a crowbar—and were cutting a hole in the metal roof. Diane, Thelma, and three others were pulled out of the building, placed in a boat, and taken to the Beauregard School. They had been saved, thanks to Sal's tenacity and ingenuity, and a floating plastic container holding a loaf of white bread.

There was no way, I figured, that Thelma was going to turn on those who had saved her life. She was loyal and grateful to be alive. I explained all her rights to her in case the authorities should call or track her down. I asked if she wanted her own lawyer, to protect her interest in any interviews, and she sensibly said she did. The company would pay her lawyer, I said, and she responded with relief. "Thank Gawd, cause I sure can't afford one right now," she said. We parted as friends and I gave her a big hug at the front door. "I'm glad you're still here, Thelma," I said. "Me, too!" she chuckled. I climbed into my bicycle with doors and retraced my route back to Houston. It had, I thought, been a couple of good days for the defense.

Chapter 17: Gone Too Soon

A couple of good days does not a recovery make, however. The suffocating reality was that progress on one front always was countered by crashing and burning on another. One step forward, three, four, or five steps back was the order of the day in the fall of 2005. Having locked up (I hoped) Diane and Thelma's favorable testimony, I reengaged with my insurance company in an effort to get the proceeds for my ruined home. This should be easy, I thought. Our house had five feet of standing water in it for two weeks. Surely the flood policy I had paid premiums on for ten years would be honored quickly and fully. The maximum one could receive under the National Flood Insurance Program was $250,000. Some insurance companies were issuing checks for full policy limits based upon the zip code in which the property was located. No inspection, no bureaucracy, no bullshit: here's your $250,000. These enlightened companies were in the extreme minority.

My insurance company, the despicable Allstate, took a different path. I battled with their adjusters and home-office personnel for months attempting to obtain what was rightly mine. My big mistake, several weeks after the hurricane, was to have slipped back into New Orleans and attempted to start work on the house. The idiot adjuster's moronic rationale for denying me full policy limits can be summarized as follows. "You see, Mr. Cobb, your problem is you got in your house early. You knocked out flooded sheetrock and stopped the mold from spreading. You mitigated your damages and that's why you don't have a total loss and why I can't pay you full policy limits." I could feel my fists closing and clenching as this joker with a clipboard and an Allstate hat and T-shirt tried to tell me about insurance law, a specialty of mine for thirty years. He was, of course, totally wrong. Miraculously, I avoided planting my fist in his Neanderthal-like forehead. Ultimately, I prevailed, but it took months and the threat of a lawsuit and was at all times an infuriating, exhausting, debilitating ordeal. It robbed us of the energy we needed for other, more difficult crises. One of them was about to happen.

Debbie continued fighting her own battles in our multi-front war. The Texas education and health departments had caught up with our kids, who were newly enrolled in Texas schools as were tens of thousands of Louisiana children, by late September. They wanted to see health records, proof of shots and inoculations. As with everything else, Debbie had been having great difficulty reaching our pediatrician, Dr. Kent T.

Dr. Kent was a character. He was a second-generation pediatrician, and his son, finishing up a residency in pediatrics, was about to carry the legacy forward into a third generation. Kent was a jokester, a prankster, and a pied piper in uptown New Orleans. He had been present with me in the delivery room when both our children were born and that special bond was unforgettable to me. On the rare occasion when he needed legal advice, he would turn to me, and I gladly obliged him without charge. He was a friend, who was a doctor, who happened to take care of our children. When I showed up in his office with a sick kid, he would spend twenty minutes in the examining room with us, even though his office was packed with runny noses, sick and crying babies, and impatient parents. He avoided over-medication, making him, in that respect, old school. With kids out of earshot, his jokes were usually off color and politically incorrect. You couldn't help but love the guy. He was tireless in his devotion to his patients and their parents.

Debbie reported one evening that she had finally reached him. She said he sounded terrible. "Is he depressed?" I asked. Her answer to my question was jarring. "He doesn't even sound like the same person over the phone. You need to call him." Debbie related parts of their conversation. His office was destroyed. He had no flood insurance on the building, which he owned. It was located on Napoleon Avenue across from Southern Baptist Hospital, the place where a doctor and nurses had been arrested for second-degree murder by euthanasia. His home had flooded and was partially destroyed. All his patients, all the kids who followed and loved this pied piper, were gone. He had no business; he had no future. "He went on and on about losing his garden, especially his Japanese magnolias, which had died in the flood waters. He told me he had planted them as saplings and cared for them for more than twenty years, and how perfect and beautiful they were when in bloom. And now, they were dead. His voice was very strange. Like I said, he didn't sound like the same person. You need to call him," Debbie told me. "Okay, okay," I said, "I'll call him tomorrow." I had problems enough of my own.

I made the obligatory phone call the next day and reached Kent's voicemail. "Hi, Kent, it's Jim Cobb. I'm in Houston. Thanks for looking for the kids' medical records. Give me a call when you get a chance." In hindsight, it was a pretty uninspiring message for someone who was as down as Debbie said he was. I should have called him again and again, but I was too busy, I thought, fighting my own personal demons. He never returned my call.

I did receive a call three or four days later from another New Orleans physician, Dr. Brobson Lutz. Lutz was a character in his own right. He was a board-certified specialist in internal medicine and had done a stint in public health as the director of the New Orleans Health Department. He served under former mayor "Dutch" Morial, the city's first black mayor. Lutz was a TV commentator on health issues, taking calls from the viewing audience on Monday mornings. His answers to some of these crazy callers were often amusing on multiple levels. I had hired him as an expert witness in a number of insurance cases and with his pronounced Alabama drawl (or, perhaps, despite it), he was animated and effective on the stand.

"Jee-yum," Lutz began, making my name duosyllabic.

"Hey, Brobson, what's up?" I asked, hopeful for one of his many stories about inept hospital administrators or dumb and crooked politicians. He had plenty of material to choose from in both categories, but this was not an occasion for mirth.

"Did you hear about Kent?" he asked.

"Hear what? Debbie just spoke to him the other day."

"He committed suicide yesterday." I was speechless. There was a long, long silence between us and I can't remember who spoke first or who said what. I can only remember the details he shared and the pain I felt upon hearing them.

Kent was obviously depressed after the storm and there were people, including doctors, who were reaching out to him. He had come down with intense back pain, for which he was taking medication. The fog these drugs create in a sound mind is well documented. But his case may have been complicated by something terrible that had occurred some fifteen years earlier. A neighbor had committed suicide at home—a gun to the head—and too distraught to do it themselves, others in the community had asked Kent, a medical professional, to clean up the splattered blood and brain tissue. As always with Kent, he said yes and did the miserable job, alone. When I asked how Kent had ended his own life, Lutz said he had hanged himself, which is not a very good way to go and most unusual among professionals who commit suicide.

"Why did he do that?" I asked.

"I heard he left a note for his family saying he didn't want to leave them a mess," came Lutz's reply.

Completely devastated, I shared the news with Debbie, who was in ut-
ter disbelief. Days later, the required medical records arrived in the mail.
Sending them must have been one of the last things Kent did. We fought
back tears, sitting on the couch, our mouths wide open, our minds trying to
comprehend this latest blow. Quickly, we had to go on defense for the kids.
We could not let them see us like this or they would know right away that
something terrible had happened. One day, we would have to confront the
tragedy with them, but that day wasn't today, or any time soon.

Lutz called days later with information on funeral arrangements. Most
everything was still closed down in New Orleans, and visitation was going
to be "at some *eye-talian* funeral home on Veterans Highway," he said, referring to a suburban shopping strip that had not flooded. I traveled from
Houston, thinking about our latest loss for most of the six-hour transit. I
made arrangements to attend with my law partner, Susan Henning. Prior to
joining our firm, she had been general counsel to Baptist Hospital. She had
known Kent forever and was intimately familiar with all his pranks and
shenanigans around the hospital. She, too, was crushed. "How much more
can we all take?" she wondered aloud.

We arrived at the funeral home, named Lamana Panno Fallo, at dusk.
There was a line of people out the front door and into the parking lot. We
took our place at the end of the line and, very quickly, there were as many
people behind us as ahead of us. The line moved slowly, giving us time to
think about what to say. Once in the funeral home, we saw the place had
been festooned with the cards and pictures and well-wishes from the children
he treated. Christmas cards, birthday cards, birth photos, party photos, first
communion photos—every imaginable kind lined the room. It gave us something to ponder as we approached the visitation room, with its open casket
and Kent's wife and children lined up dutifully to receive condolences. As we
moved up, I was struck numb by the sight of my family's Christmas card to
Kent from the previous year, a photo of Chris and Collette staring up at me.
I bit my lip hard, trying to keep it together. I don't remember what I said to
the family, just that everyone's eyes were puffy and red and filled with tears.
I glanced at Kent in his open casket, thinking for a second, "Kent, how could
you do this to all of us?" I bowed my head, made the sign of the cross, and we
were gone. A youthful, vibrant fifty-eight years old when he died, Kent was as
much a casualty as any of the 1,600 people in Katrina's official death toll—a
toll from which hundreds like him were omitted. My considerable anger at
those who would point the finger of blame at a victim, any victim, continued
to grow and fester. I found myself vowing to get even with those responsible
for Kent's premature death, if I could just figure out who they were.

Chapter 18: "I Love You, Grandpa"

As we watched in real time, on live television, the city of New Orleans flood to its citizens' rooftops, we were sick to our stomachs. The most spectacular of these "levee breaches" was the floodwall failure at the 17th Street Outfall Canal, less than a mile from our front door, the one that washed five feet of smelly, oily, toxic water over the ground floor of our humble abode. We watched in complete disbelief as army helicopters hovered over the breach, dropping huge sandbags into a gaping hole. I remember wondering helplessly, "Is this the best we can do?" There was obviously no contingency plan in place. This wasn't the United State of America; this was some third-world country, with people running around in circles, like chickens with their heads cut off. It was pathetic as well as deeply destructive of human life and of what we had built together as a family over the past ten years. When the holes were finally plugged, the long process of pumping out the flooded city began. It took weeks, and stories of lawlessness and looting abounded—some of them myths, some not. I had two immediate missions and the official nature of one made the second possible. The bodies of the deceased had been removed from St. Rita's, but the facility was still an active crime scene, and as counsel for those charged with homicide, I had a right—and a need—to visit the scene of the "crime." There is no substitute for actually being there. I had to make my own inspection and get a feel for the topography of the place and anything else that might prove helpful.

I obtained a pass to enter the destroyed city at the end of September. "If you're going," Debbie said, "go to our house and get us some clothes, and our china, silver, crystal, artwork, paintings, anything of value. Get it out of there before somebody steals everything!"

I prevailed upon a client of mine, the head of a tugboat company, to lend me some of his men, trucks, and tools. We met on the north shore of Lake Pontchartrain for our trip into the necropolis that New Orleans had become. Stopped at various checkpoints along the way by National Guard troops with automatic weapons, we got ourselves past all the roadblocks with my pass. As we traversed the non-flooded portions of neighboring Jefferson Parish, all seemed normal. When we crossed over the 17th Street Canal Bridge into New Orleans, it was as if we had landed on the moon. The green grass and trees of Jefferson were instantly replaced by the color gray. There was no green visible anywhere. There was a layer of gray mud in the streets, on lawns, and in houses. There was no sound whatsoever. No birds, no animals, no cars, and no air conditioning compressors cycling on and off against the incredible heat. There was no life to be seen, anywhere. I was reminded of pictures of Hiroshima and Nagasaki after the atomic bombs. Crossing the Bucktown bridge (another name for the 17th Street Canal Bridge), we had passed from the land of the living into the land of the dead. The street in front of my house was unrecognizable. No one spoke as we took in the bizarre surroundings, mouths wide open in total disbelief.

We approached my front door and I unlocked it, attempting to gain entry. The door unlocked but couldn't be moved. I peered through the beveled sidelights. The Brazilian cherry floors, which we had installed only a month earlier, were now black, without a shade of red to be found anywhere, and so warped they looked like corrugated tin. The back door was equally immobilized. I broke glass to climb inside then ripped up the flooring with my bare hands until the door could be opened wide enough to let us all in. Our home was a tomb of mud, water, destruction, and wall-climbing mold. The four of us looked around in total disbelief. There was little to be saved or salvaged. I stepped back outside. Our small, formerly blue pool was filled with toxic water and was black as night, a vile-smelling breeding ground for swarms of mosquitoes that now owned New Orleans. I leaned against a crooked wooden fence and completely lost it, once again. The tough, tugboat guys didn't see me, I hoped. Composing myself, I returned to the house. At least we hadn't been ripped off. Like pirates on a treasure hunt, we quickly grabbed anything of value and placed it in the trucks. There was no deadline for ending our visit, but we all acted like thieves on borrowed time, even though everything we were taking was mine. Subconsciously, we all needed to get out of this land of the dead, which I had once called home. We packed up the loot and made our getaway.

On our way out of Deadwood, we pulled over at the Bucktown bridge and stopped. I wanted to inspect the monster canal breach now plugged with sandbags dropped from helicopters. It had destroyed our neighborhood and all my family's first-floor possessions. All our photographs, the memories of a lifetime, were stored downstairs in a wall unit filled with water. As I stood

The unimaginable. Chris helps to throw out all of his, and our, possessions in the street in front of our home. Thirteen year olds should probably be spared this experience.

on the bridge, facing west, placid Lake Pontchartrain was to my right (north) and the gaping hole to my left (south). My head on a swivel, I looked back and forth at the lake and the hole. Something wasn't adding up. The official explanation for the area-wide flooding was that Katrina was a monster, a storm of such strength that it happens only once in several centuries. The Army Corps of Engineers' contention was that Katrina's powerful storm surge had simply overtopped a flood defense built to congressional specs. In the contest between man and Mother Nature's fury, eventually nature was always the winner, or so said the Corps.

But this killer hole was located well within the canal's interior, more than three hundred yards from the lake's edge and any direct pounding the storm surge might have delivered. And one side of the canal had failed, but not the other. Jefferson Parish was green and dry because the levee wall had collapsed on *our* side of the canal, not theirs. If the breach was due to storm surge, why didn't the levee break on both sides? I chalked it up to luck: our bad luck, their good luck—an explanation that would prove laughably insufficient. Before getting back in the truck, I walked to the earthen levees girdling Lake Pontchartrain itself. They stood tall, unbroken and undamaged, as far as my eyes could see. How is it that this killer, Category 5 storm surge had no effect on these miles and miles of levees, but caused failure three hundred yards inland in some chicken-shit drainage canal? I had tons of questions, but no answers. At least not yet.

New Orleans is a city slightly below sea level and surrounded by all kinds of levee structures. There are the Mississippi River levees protecting the city on its south. The Lake Pontchartrain levees protect the city on its north. Multiple drainage canal structures flanked by floodwalls serve to remove rainwater and deposit it in Lake Pontchartrain. There is probably no city in America more dependent on levees and floodwalls than New Orleans, and several of the floodwalls had failed.

The tugboat, bayou boys took off with the china, silver, and artwork and headed down Bayou Lafourche into the heart of Louisiana's rough-and-tumble Cajun country. Our possessions of value would be stored in a conference room in Galliano, Louisiana, for more than a year. Occasionally, I would get a phone call, asking, "Hey Cobb, how much you want for this picture with a glass of wine and some strawberries on it? I'll give you $50." I didn't have the heart to tell them it cost me more than one hundred times their $50 offer. The good ol' boys would have mocked me unbearably. "Man, what kind of dumb ass pays that kind of money for a picture of strawberries and a glass of wine? You must be a lawyer," I could hear them cackle. Instead, I said it now had sentimental value, so I'd be keeping it.

I spent the night on the west bank of the Mississippi River, a part of New Orleans that hadn't gone under. The next morning, I would make the trek to St. Bernard Parish alone, to visit the alleged crime scene and to walk the halls where almost three dozen senior citizens lost their lives. Nothing could prepare me for what I was about to see.

To reach St. Rita's, I drove through New Orleans' now infamous Lower 9th Ward, where the floodwalls also failed and hundreds of African Americans clung to life on rooftops and in trees. This was the scene of the spectacular Coast Guard helicopter rescues that transfixed TV watchers around the world. As I crossed from Orleans into St. Bernard Parish, the scenery only worsened. Carefully, I made my way deep into the parish and searched for St. Rita's. It was past the main commercial area of St. Bernard, on an improved road that ultimately led to Delacroix Island and the Gulf of Mexico. I turned into the parking area and noticed dozens of huge, toppled trees. In the mud next to the home were a dozen or more flipped-over cars and trucks. Sal Sr. told me that when the tidal wave hit, cars were picked up and carried like toys. They moved two hundred yards and more, such was the force of the initial wall of water. Against this kind of force, the elderly residents of St. Rita's never stood a chance.

As I entered the 30,000 square-foot building, I felt like I was entering a muddy mausoleum. The furniture in my home had floated around and

The inside of St. Rita's after the storm. Many of the residents were in wheelchairs when the water came. Courtesy of CBS News, from *48 Hours: No Way Out* (02/02/08).

moved a bit from where we had left it. The inside of St. Rita's was quite different. It was as if someone had picked up the entire building, filled it with water and mud, shook it violently as if mixing a cocktail, and then dropped the building back on its concrete foundation. There was no sense of place or order anywhere. Walls had blown out from the force of the water. Rotting furniture had been left in configurations that might have been suggested by an interior decorator gone mad. The inside of the building was like a train wreck with water, mud, and mold thrown in. I wore a breathing mask, boots, gloves, and a hazmat suit. It was hot as hell.

I moved down what I sensed had once been hallways and entered residents' rooms, most of them doubles. Cards and pictures carried memories too sorrowful to contemplate: "Happy Birthday, Grandma!" "I love you, Grandpa!" "Merry Christmas, Nonnie." These were the mementos that connected the residents to the outside world and to their families. The human loss became suddenly all too real for me. The St. Rita's case was no longer a matter of "thirty-five counts of negligent homicide." These were people with names and faces and families who loved them. I went through as many rooms as possible, making a mental note to have someone return to box up the cards and children's drawings and place these memories somewhere for safe keeping. Perhaps we could return these mementos to the families one day, as an expression of our sadness and condolences. It was a naïve thought on my part: the family members would prove inconsolable, riddled with guilt that their loved ones had died, drowned, when maybe they should have picked their relatives up. That guilt turned into anger and a hatred of the Manganos that also extended to their lawyer. "How can you defend people like that?" I was asked more than once. Sal and Mabel felt it. I did too.

The inspection of St. Rita's and the surrounding property confirmed that something of tremendous force had struck the home and the immediate area. Once again, the government's explanation—that the levees were simply "overtopped" by storm surge higher than they were built to withstand— began to look like bullshit to me. And I wasn't the lone ranger in this belief.

Soon multiple investigations, led by nationally recognized forensic scientists, would fan out all across southeast Louisiana, searching for the truth of what happened and why. Maybe their findings would prove useful to the defense of an elderly couple against thirty-five counts of negligent homicide. At this point, I could only hope so.

Chapter 19: A Promise, Not a Threat

September slipped into October and October became November in the blink of sleeping-pill-blurred eyes. Ordinarily, Thanksgiving was my favorite holiday of the year. I would take a couple of days off work, gather the finest ingredients available, and cook a meal for family, some friends, and a few others who had no place else to go. Our number ranged from twelve to eighteen guests and it was a gourmet production. No frozen butterball, bowling ball, pop-up-timer turkeys for me—we used fresh, free-range Amish birds, brined for twenty-four hours in salt, sugar, and spices and cooked to perfection. The white meat was moist and flavorful, the skin was golden brown, to die for. My oyster dressing was, quite simply, the best that any guest had ever eaten. I made a huge pot of it every year and delivered small casserole dishes of it to select friends on Thanksgiving morn, as our bird roasted slowly in the oven. It became a tradition. Debbie's desserts were off the hook—chocolate cream pie with homemade whipped cream, key lime pie made with fresh-squeezed key lime juice, homemade pecan pie, served warm, with a scoop of Häagen Dazs vanilla ice cream on top, gently melting, creating a pool of cream and sugar on each and every plate. It was the culinary highlight of my year and it was a big deal.

Thanksgiving 2005 was anything but a big deal. It was an expensive, unsatisfying annoyance. We ate in a hotel restaurant, one which we had been told was "quite good." It was horrible. Overcooked turkey and vegetables, lumpy mashed potatoes, and gravy right out of a can: Houston haute cuisine. Cut off from family and friends, and unable to renew our annual tradition, we were reminded of how far we had fallen. We put the best face on it we could, went back to the apartment, and watched rented movies.

The St. Rita's media firestorm slowly began to burn itself out. We were off the front page. I reconnected with Ron Goux, the Nursing Home Association president, who had gotten me into this mess to begin with. He had the same idea I did. With the heat off and the media gone, wouldn't this be an opportune time to approach the attorney general's office, in private, and attempt to talk them out of this misguided prosecution-turned-persecution? "Let me make some inquiries, and I'll get back to you," Goux said. A lonely and sparse Christmas passed without much joy in the Cobb household. We survived and plodded on, moving back to the New Orleans area by way of a tiny suburban apartment on an interstate service road behind a shopping center. It appeared we would be stuck on service-road living for the foreseeable future. The kids' school had reopened and they desperately wanted to come home and be with their friends. Their lives were correspondingly improved. But it wasn't like before. We weren't home, and had no earthly idea when, or if, we ever would be.

A few weeks after the move, Ron Goux got back in touch with me. He had actually met with Foti himself, pleading with him to drop the charges against Sal and Mabel, two people Ron knew very well. He was also personally familiar with the home itself and the high quality of care it provided. He assured Foti that these two people cared for and loved their residents, they weren't criminals, and they shouldn't be subjected to the criminal law. The family members of the victims had all filed civil suits for money damages and it was in this forum, Ron argued, where the case should be decided, not the criminal courts. Foti refused to budge, but he said he and his top staff would take a meeting with the Manganos' attorneys and allow us the opportunity to change his mind. "You're on, kid," Ron told me, "impress the hell out of them and talk them out of this bullshit."

Goux rarely put all his eggs in one basket. He clued me in to another angle he was pursuing. Foti's top assistant, the first assistant attorney general, was also Foti's cousin. Turns out that in Louisiana, the first assistant attorney general is allowed to have a private practice on the side and keep whatever fees it generates. Conflict of interest, anyone? The appearance of impropriety? The state's number two in its department of justice was moonlighting. Turns out further that this first assistant cousin's firm back in Lafayette did some liability defense work for none other than the Louisiana Nursing Home Association, defending malpractice and other kinds of claims. This cousin's firm worked for the very association Goux headed and of which Sal and Mabel were members. I was not privy to the conversation, but I was certain that the Foti cousin would be strongly motivated to advise the A.G. to drop the case. The cousin would be at our meeting, I was told. "He should be a friendly ear," Ron said with a wink and a nod.

I contacted Bob Habans, the man I had tapped as co-counsel, and brought him up to speed on developments. Bob was always cautious and distrusted government and prosecutors. I suggested that we present the A.G.'s office with a hard-hitting argument, essentially showing them all our cards, telling them what we were going to do, and why we were going to kick their ass and win the case. He offered a warning: "Criminal trials"—which he did— "are not like civil trials"—which I did. "There is no discovery to speak of; it's trial by ambush and the element of surprise often carries the day. It's a gunfight at high noon in the center of town. I'd rather not show them our strengths or our weaknesses. F— 'em, we'll mow 'em down in court and they won't know what hit them," he deadpanned.

I was still reeling from the embarrassment of having erroneously told Sal and Mabel that everything would be okay—that no one would charge them with any crime once their compelling story was heard. I hadn't really been proven wrong, as the A.G. ordered their arrest before hearing their story. Now, Ron Goux was telling me to have a meeting with Foti, his cousin, and others, and that at least somebody in the room was going to be on my side. He liked my chances.

In addition, I was becoming more and more concerned about whether Sal and Mabel could survive this ordeal. Sal's blood pressure was up, way up. The dollar cost of going forward, if we couldn't talk the A.G. out of a prosecution, was likely to be astronomical. Some kind of deal, any kind of deal, at this early stage might prove to be in their long-term best interest. I decided to hold the meeting and go for broke. It was an extraordinarily high-risk strategy to show the other side all our cards without them showing theirs. I remained convinced that once they found out what we were going to do to them, they would throw in their unseen cards and fold. I couldn't be wrong this many times in a row, I thought; surely the odds were in my favor. Or had I consumed way too much personal-confidence Kool-Aid?

Regardless of what I'd been drinking, I had not been idle. I had a comprehensive brief on the legal definition of negligent homicide in Louisiana, and its conclusion favored our common-sense argument. St. Rita's wasn't the only institution required to have an Emergency Operations Plan (EOP) for hurricanes—the state of Louisiana had one too. That five hundred page plan, the important parts of which I had almost memorized, contained a trove of detail that could be cited to prove that the state had critically failed to fulfill its own responsibilities, failures that doomed the residents of St. Rita's. The coroner of St. Bernard Parish, Dr. Bertucci, had been deposed in the civil wrongful death cases and his testimony was eye-poppingly helpful to us. Finally, the entire power structure of the state had been called on the carpet during U.S. Senate and House hearings. A disgraced White House had joined the blame game by accusing Louisiana's governor of incompetence—

not a charge that Governor Blanco could effortlessly refute. She and others had testified at length, and the transcripts were of tremendous value to us, I thought. And so, in defiance of Habans' advice, I decided to hold nothing back, show them all our cards, and make all our arguments, in the hope that they would see the light. And we did it not just orally, but in writing, in the form of a brochure we left with them after the meeting.

The cover was an aerial photograph of collapsed levees in St. Bernard Parish, with water pouring over them. The caption to the photo was Governor Blanco's sworn testimony before Congress:

> What happened to us this year, however, can only be described as a catastrophe of Biblical proportions. We in Louisiana know hurricanes and hurricanes know us. We would not be here today if the levees had not failed. (Governor Blanco testimony, House Select Committee Hearing, 109th Cong., *Hurricane Katrina: Preparedness and Response by the State of Louisiana,* December 14, 2005.)

Levee failure was the key and if this explanation (excuse) was good enough to get the governor off the hook, why wasn't it good enough for Sal and Mabel?

Governor Blanco, left, takes the oath before the U.S. Senate in its Katrina hearings. Courtesy of CBS News, from *48 Hours: No Way Out* (02/02/08).

Because we were dealing with the Medicare/Medicaid Fraud and Abuse unit of the A.G.'s office, we decided to include a complete education on the negligent homicide statute, a law which none of the special prosecutors likely knew anything about. Negligent Homicide is a strange and unique legal hybrid. Most criminal statutes require the state to prove "criminal intent," *i.e.*, that the defendant intended to commit the crime charged. Not so with negligent homicide. This made it easy for the government: they could argue that, sure, Sal and Mabel didn't "intend" to kill their residents, but their negligence caused the deaths anyway. Criminal negligence was defined as "gross negligence" or "recklessness," and gross negligence was defined as reckless disregard for one's own safety, or the safety of others, coupled with a "willful indifference" to the consequences liable to follow.

The "leading" case of negligent homicide in the state was a Louisiana Supreme Court ruling that had been handed down a quarter-century earlier. It contained magic language that we thought would exonerate the Manganos. In *State v. Moak*, Mr. Moak pulled off the road to avoid a car coming right at him in his lane. After pulling off the road, he hit a ditch and his vehicle came into contact with a twelve-year-old boy, killing him. The state charged him with negligent

St. Bernard Coroner Bryan Bertucci, right, supervising the recovery of bodies from St. Rita's. Courtesy of CBS News, from *48 Hours: No Way Out* (02/02/08).

homicide and he was convicted. The Supreme Court reversed his conviction, setting him free. The language they used was golden for us and compelled the conclusion, it seemed to us, that Sal and Mabel should also go free:

> Although the testimony at trial revealed that the defendant did not reapply his brakes once his car hit the ditch, *the wrong choice of action* (if it was wrong) *in an emergency does not meet the test of criminal negligence.* The facts at best show only ordinary negligence.(*State v. Moak,* 387 So. 2nd 1108 (1980). Emphasis added.)

Bingo! Game, set, and match. I thought Katrina was obviously an emergency of the first order, and this rock solid case stood for the proposition that making the wrong choice in an emergency (sheltering in place instead of evacuating) could not, as a matter of law, meet the test of criminal negligence. I believed our position was unassailable. It hardly gets clearer than this in the law. Even if the state could obtain a conviction, highly doubtful, we would reverse it on appeal. We included the case in our packet of materials to the A.G. along with some other bombshells, and set the meeting to determine Sal and Mabel's fate. I was supremely confident, bordering on cocky. Insufferably confident would also suffice as descriptive of my state of mind. Foti and his henchmen were about to get a full dose of me.

The meeting was arranged for the seventh floor of the Louisiana Department of Justice building in Baton Rouge. This was the same seventh floor from which the orders had been issued to cancel the agreed-upon meeting with the Manganos and, instead, arrest them on thirty-five counts of negligent homicide. I was told the meeting would take place in the A.G.'s "personal" conference room on the building's top floor. The building itself was new and impressive. The exterior was neoclassical, and the taxpayers of Louisiana had obviously spent lots of money building this temple to Lady Justice. The irony that this magnificent edifice was now inhabited by a minister of justice who was a jailer, not a lawyer, was not lost on either of us as Bob and I climbed the steps. It was a clear, cool day late in the winter of 2006.

We made our way through layers of security and exited the elevators on the seventh floor. There we faced a glass partition etched in bold letters with the words: "Attorney General, State of Louisiana." We passed through large, mahogany doors emblazoned with the great Seal of the State of Louisiana, Department of Justice.

A receptionist greeted us before we could announce ourselves: "Mr. Cobb, Mr. Habans?" she asked.

"Yes, ma'am," I answered.

"Please have a seat. General Foti is expecting you."

As we sat, I thought to myself, "Boy, I bet he loves being called General Foti." Through an election against a pathetic Republican opponent in a then largely Democratic state, Foti had ascended from the rank of sheriff of a local parish jail to a general of justice for an entire state.

Based on his televised performances in the run-up to the Manganos' arrests and those of the doctor and nurses charged with euthanizing patients at Memorial Hospital, it was clear that the "general" was enjoying his new platform. He was full of himself and, just as clearly, full of shit. In my mind, he was abusing the power of his office. I resolved to treat him with respect, but I wasn't going to address him as "General Foti," and I wasn't going to kiss his ass. Maybe he and his staff had the home-field advantage, but we had the facts and the law on our side. When they listened to our presentation, I believed we would also have the advantage of surprise.

"Mr. Cobb, Mr. Habans, would you please come this way." The receptionist led us to a windowless conference room. Already assembled in the room were five men with stern looks on their faces. They did not appear to be enthusiastic at the prospect of this meeting. Fred Duhy was there, and so we met face to face for the first time. He introduced a member of his division who assisted him in Medicare/Medicaid fraud and abuse cases. The first assistant, Foti's cousin, was there along with an assistant to the assistant. Finally, there was the lead investigator who had signed the affidavit establishing probable cause that resulted in the Manganos' arrest. There were handshakes and introductions around the table, and once again, it felt like team captains meeting at the center of the field for the coin toss before the big game. Regardless of the result of the coin toss, I expected we would be kicking off and the A.G.'s men receiving. But there was no A.G. present. Foti wasn't there.

The first cousin explained that the "general" was busy but would be joining us shortly. Some Katrina small talk ensued. In response to questions, I told them my home in Lakeview had been destroyed. Bob offered that he, too, was flooded out and had not evacuated in advance of the storm. Residents of Baton Rouge and beyond, none of the A.G.'s men had suffered any losses in Katrina whatsoever. Clearly, we were the angrier, hungrier team before kickoff. Just then, the door opened and in walked the man himself, Atty. Gen. Charlie Foti. Some of his men twisted in their seats as if they were about to rise. Bob and I were glued to our seats. Foti waved his hand, dismissively, muttering, "Just keep your seats," and he sat down at the head of the long table. Bob and I were on his left, facing his team across the wooden expanse. Once again, no handshake was exchanged between me and the general.

Fred Duhy spoke first. "Well, Mr. Cobb, it's your meeting," he said. Showtime, I thought. I leaned over and unsnapped the latches on my briefcase. The sound broke what was already becoming an uncomfortable silence. I reached deep into the large case and pulled out multiple copies of our presentation brochures, our battle plan for defending Sal and Mabel. And here I was turning over our plan of attack and defense to the enemy. I thought I noticed Bob's eyes rolling ever so slightly. Too late to turn back now, I thought, "half a league, half a league, half a league onward."

"Gentlemen," I began, "if you take a look at the cover page, it is an aerial photograph of the collapsed levee in St. Bernard Parish, with water pouring into the parish. This is the water, and the source of the water, that killed the residents of St. Rita's. Sal and Mabel Mangano had nothing to do with the building of this levee." The already silent room grew even quieter as the general and his staff perused the photograph. "The quote below the photo is from Governor Blanco's sworn testimony before the U.S. House on December 14, 2005. She concluded this portion of her testimony with the following sentence: 'We would not be here today if the levees had not failed.'

"We know exactly how the Governor felt, as she was called on the national carpet to explain her state's failures. By the way, we wouldn't be here either, today, and Sal and Mabel would not have been arrested if the federal levees had not failed." The silence became deafening. As all the general's men contemplated the obvious jury appeal of this opening salvo, I perceived that they were rocked back on their heels. I pressed the attack: "into the valley of Death rode the six hundred."

The first page inside the booklet was a beautiful, color photograph of Sal and Mabel in happier times. They were on a cruise ship, dressed to the nines, standing at the bottom of a large, curving, wooden staircase reminiscent of the one where Leonardo DiCaprio and Kate Winslet met in the movie *Titanic*. The A.G.'s men had only seen Sal and Mabel in their mug shot photos, where they appeared disheveled and confused, looking like two characters out of a *Sopranos* episode. They positively *looked* guilty. Mug shots are never flattering, even for the beautiful people. Just ask Nick Nolte, Mel Gibson, Paris Hilton, and a host of others. I wanted the A.G. to know that these two were real people, who weren't just a photo in a mug shot. Subliminally, I wanted them to know that Sal and Mabel cleaned up real nice and would make a compelling, sympathetic appearance in front of a jury. In this photo, they looked kind and gentle, and certainly *not guilty*. I then gave a thumbnail biographical sketch of these two people, who had begun their lives in rural poverty, but through hard work and persistence had lived the American dream of prosperity and success. They were the heads of a large, devoted family, a family with a long record of military and community service. "They are not criminals," I said, "and they abandoned no one at the nursing home. They stood their post . . ."

Duhy interrupted me, for he knew I was on a roll, and the expression on the lethargic Foti's face suggested growing impatience with my storytelling and advocacy. "They shouldn't have been at their post. They should have evacuated," Duhy said forcefully.

"That's easy for you to say, Fred," I responded. "Hindsight is always 20/20, and you weren't there."

"I was in St. Bernard Parish before the storm," Duhy said. "My eighty-five-year-old father lived in his home and I went down to pick him up and make him leave. And it was hard because he wanted to stay in his house. I literally had to drag him out, as he didn't want to leave." His voice cracked with emotion; his hands trembled with anger and anxiety. It was a bizarre response, but it revealed that he was emotionally and personally involved in the case, never a good combination when what's needed is the application of reason. He was pissed and it was personal. I pressed on and got back on message.

"Sal and Mabel weren't there alone," I said, "they stayed with their residents with the help of their own flesh and blood. Their children and grandchildren were there, as were Mabel's brother and his wife. It was all a family affair."

This was a planned segue into the legal standard and definition of negligent homicide. Reading from the case law, I told them that negligent homicide was the killing of a human being by criminal negligence, and the "gross negligence" that is its predicate is the reckless disregard for one's own safety or the safety of others and a willful indifference to the consequence liable to follow. "Do you really believe that Sal and Mabel were willfully indifferent to the lives of their own children and grandchildren?" I asked. "Of course not. The idea is preposterous and a jury's not going to believe it either, based on the legal definition of the crime," I said. Out of the corner of my eye, I could see the General squirming in his seat. I tossed the ball to Bob and he ran with it for a while.

He reviewed *State v. Moak* in great detail, explaining that making the wrong decision in an emergency cannot, as a matter of law, constitute criminal negligence and will not support a negligent homicide conviction. He went further. "Part of the statute contemplates a willful indifference to the consequences *liable* to follow," he deadpanned in his deepest baritone voice. "No one, and I mean no one, could have imagined the consequences liable to follow in St. Bernard Parish. In fact, the parish authorities are on record as saying the flood that hit St. Bernard was 'unimaginable.' Their word, not mine. As such, the requirement of the negligent homicide statute cannot be met." He was too big and intimidating for anyone in the room to take exception to his argument. None did.

The next section of our presentation put us on increasingly thin ice, farther and farther away from shore, in water way over my head. What the hell, I thought, we're only going to get the chance to do this once. I had included in the materials a transcript of selected portions of Congress's Katrina hearings. The witness was Johnny Bradberry, secretary of the Louisiana Department of Transportation and Development (DOTD), and his exchange with Sen. Susan Collins (R-Maine) was highlighted in the materials. It was, in my view, a game changer:

> [Sen. Collins] Mr. Secretary, the state of Louisiana's emergency operations plan clearly designates your department, the DOTD, as the primary agency responsible for developing plans and procedures to, quote "mobilize transportation to support emergency evacuation for at risk populations."
>
> During an interview with this committee's investigators, you conceded that the department had, quote, "done nothing to fulfill this responsibility. We put no plans in place to do any of this," end quote.
>
> The plan is very clear that your department did have the responsibility. How is it that the department did not carry out such a clearly designated and important duty?
>
> [Mr. Bradberry] Yes, Madam Chairman. Admittedly, I'll state that in April 2005, I did indeed sign the plan that said that we would accept this responsibility for Emergency Safety Function (ESF) function number 1 . . . I signed it. And I'll admit to that. We had done nothing to fulfill this responsibility.

"At-risk populations," as used by Senator Collins in her question, was defined in the state EOP to include "all nursing home patients."

"Thus, gentlemen," I argued, "we have evidence of a state official, who admitted under oath, that he and his department were responsible for the evacuation of nursing home patients. Yet he did nothing to fulfill that responsibility. Absolutely nothing." I let the words sink in.

"That responsibility was not his by chance," I continued. "He signed the state EOP acknowledging his responsibility and accepting it. Of course, Mr. Foti is aware of this, because *he signed off on it, too*." I turned towards Foti and was stunned to see his eyelids drooping as though he were about to doze off. The General had not said a word in the meeting to that point, and appeared totally disengaged. I decided to fire a last blast, in the hope of waking him up. I directed my remarks to Duhy.

"Fred, you are aware that the state EOP signed by all department heads, and by Governor Blanco, is in the form of an Executive Order, and becomes the law of the state of Louisiana, a violation of which constitutes a violation of law. If you want to charge somebody with negligent homicide, I suggest you start with Secretary Bradberry, who had the *legal obligation* for the evacuation of nursing home patients and did nothing."

"That's ridiculous," Duhy shot back. "He wasn't in charge of those patients."

"No, he wasn't," I said. "He was *only* in charge of their safe evacuation. How do you think he did? Look in the back of the booklet at tab 8, please. Louisiana Revised Statutes, Title 14, Section 134, Malfeasance in Office. It reads:

Malfeasance in Office is committed when any officer or public employee shall: Intentionally refuse or fail to perform any duty lawfully required of him as such officer or employee.

"Secretary Bradberry is guilty of Malfeasance in Office, based upon his own sworn testimony before the United States Senate." I took a deep breath and let the next broadside fly.

"And Attorney General Foti commits Malfeasance in Office if he looks the other way and doesn't charge the secretary with the crime he has already admitted committing, and even you guys can win that case; he's admitted it under oath."

Duhy was fuming and responded loudly, "Is that some sort of veiled threat against the attorney general of the State of Louisiana?" It sounded odd for him to refer in the third person to someone present in the room, but it was clearly an attempt to leap to Foti's defense.

I paused, thinking carefully of his words and the legal implication of his suggestion that I was threatening the state's chief legal officer. I spoke much more carefully and softly than he did.

"No, Fred, I don't think there's anything veiled about it at all."

We were at the end of any meaningful discussion with these guys. I closed by saying that under all the circumstances, dropping the charges against Sal and Mabel was the right thing to do. I offered to read any statement to the press that the A.G.'s public relations' people drafted, praising the attorney general for doing the right thing. And no, I wouldn't file a claim of malfeasance in office against the secretary. "But, if we have to try this thing," I warned, "we will subpoena and call as a witness every official in state government whose fingerprints are all over the deaths at St. Rita's. That includes the governor, Secretary Bradberry, and the attorney general of the State of Louisiana. That's not a veiled threat. It's a promise."

I implored all present to consider our arguments and the evidence we would submit at trial. There was no good reason to put the Manganos and the people of Louisiana through a trial that would be painful for everyone. "It's time to move on and stop the blame game," I said. "There is a way, politically, for this office to spin its way out of this situation and I will be a willing participant in providing political cover if the charges against Sal and Mabel are dropped. We look forward to hearing from you guys, and thanks for having this meeting," I concluded.

On the issue of a negotiated settlement, or dropping the charges, we never heard from them again. On the eve of trial, more than a year and a half later, I received a call from prosecutors offering a plea-bargain deal. The decision to accept or reject their offer was entirely up to Sal and Mabel. Their answer, and in particular the language Sal used, would surprise even me.

Chapter 20: Barbarians at the Gate

I had, of course, obtained Sal and Mabel's approval, in advance of the high-risk meeting with the A.G. and his men. They wanted to exhaust every possibility to make this living nightmare go away. When I told the Manganos that showing the other side all our cards, our defenses, and plan of attack carried some risk, their answer—a refrain throughout the case—was: "Whatever you think is best, Jim." This places a special kind of pressure on the decision maker. Guess wrong and defendants who have placed such trust in you wind up in jail for the rest of their lives. This was new to me. Past clients had almost always been sophisticated and frequent consumers of legal services—corporate types, insurance managers, and claims adjusters. More often than not, they had their own ideas about how things should come out, what risks they were willing to take, and under what circumstances. Right or wrong, these kinds of decisions only involved money—sometimes very large sums of money—but no wrong decision sent someone off to jail. I began to be more circumspect and cautious in outlining our options to Sal and Mabel on any given issue. My caution was the by-product of previous errors and the rising stakes as Foti bet his political future on a big prosecutorial victory. And besides, a good lawyer always leaves himself an escape hatch. Their complete and total reliance on my judgment was more unnerving than it was flattering. They had, quite literally, placed their lives and freedom in my hands. No wonder I couldn't sleep.

Life outside the St. Rita's case went on. The Manganos, the Cobbs, an entire city, and hundreds of thousands of people struggled just to make it through each day. Sal and Mabel's struggle would have been the same as everyone else's, but for that pesky little matter: they were charged with thirty-five counts of negligent homicide each. They had lost their business and means of future income. And all of the family members had lost their homes. Where were they going to live? How were they going to live? And—I

151

had to wonder—where were they going to find the money to finance their defense? By now, thirty-four of the thirty-five families whose loved ones had drowned in their beds and wheelchairs had filed civil suits for wrongful death and were asking for damages. There were only thirty-four wrongful death suits, because the thirty-fifth victim had no relatives who could sue on her behalf. In their civil suits, the family members only had to prove ordinary negligence or a deviation from the standard of care in order to prevail and recover money damages against Sal and Mabel. And unlike a criminal case, the family members' burden of proof was only by a "mere preponderance" of the evidence. They didn't have to prove their case "beyond a reasonable doubt," the very high standard applicable to the criminal case. As a practical matter, were the Manganos to lose the criminal trial, they would have no legitimate defense in the civil cases and would lose them all rather easily.

Another twelve residents who survived the flood, saved by the Manganos as they swam out of the nursing home with these very people on their backs, now filed suit against Sal and Mabel and St. Rita's for personal injuries, mental anguish, and post-traumatic stress disorder. Talk about ingratitude! But the legal feeding frenzy had already begun, and anyone with any sort of claim, legitimate or not, was filing suit against everyone in sight for any and all Katrina damages. It was a plaintiff lawyers' paradise, an orgy for ambulance chasers, and an environment target-rich with defendants and insurance companies. Many of them deserved to be sued. The court systems— state and federal—would be clogged with these claims for years to come.

"Can they make us pay, personally?" was Mabel's immediate question. St. Rita's was a member of the Louisiana Nursing Home Association Malpractice and General Liability Trust Fund, a voluntary organization that had procured re-insurance in London. This fund was supposed to protect them from lawsuits like the ones that were filed against the Manganos and St. Rita's, but there was a major problem: the total limit of the insurance was $1 million. Whoever bought the policy had not anticipated that thirty-five residents would die in one event and that the nursing home would be blamed. Thus, they had not purchased "excess" coverage above $1 million, a woefully inadequate amount to defend and cover thirty-four wrongful death suits and twelve claims for personal injury filed in the same policy year. I did some math quickly. If we just threw in the towel and offered the million dollars for each of the forty-six cases, it would amount to $21,739.13 per claimant, be it for wrongful death or personal injury—a sum likely to be deemed woefully inadequate, if not downright insulting. Families who truly believed that Sal and Mabel had murdered their mothers, fathers, grandmothers, and grandfathers would never accept it.

"Yes, Mabel, when the $1 million in insurance coverage is exhausted, the families will come after you and Sal for everything you own. They will allege that you have personal liability for the fact that you made the decision to stay."

As with all things Katrina, just when one thought things couldn't get any worse, they invariably did. I received a frantic call from Mabel. She reported that she had just received a certified letter from the attorney for the liability fund and its insurers. Certified letters from attorneys rarely bring good news. We arranged to meet for lunch in the kitchen of René Bistrot, a restaurant ruined in the flood but now partially repaired. The kitchen was separated from the sparse dining room by a thick piece of plastic sheeting running from floor to ceiling. We sat at the "chef's table," on the kitchen side of the plastic curtain, where we could speak in private, beyond the gaze of a public preoccupied with the notorious Mabel Mangano's hair and general demeanor. Chef René, a borderline French anarchist, was sympathetic to the Manganos' plight as designated scapegoats of a government blaming everyone but themselves for the tragedy. He was also the best cook in town. Sal and Mabel ordered the duck to be split. I ordered René's signature chicken dish, *poulet grand mère,* an aromatic concoction of roasted chicken swimming in bacon, potatoes, mushrooms, and pearl onions. I was parched and it was hot in the kitchen, so I ordered a Bombay Sapphire, rocks. Now I was ready to read the letter.

I took a gulp of the chilled juniper juice and opened it. I recognized the format and the language immediately, as I had either authored or received this kind of letter dozens of times. It was what's called a "reservation of rights" letter, in which the liability fund and its re-insurers reserved the right to deny the Manganos any coverage whatsoever under the policy. Because they had been arrested and charged with alleged criminal conduct, the insurer stated that, should they be convicted of a crime, the underwriters would deny coverage, for one cannot insure against criminal or intentional conduct. Thus, the paltry $1 million in coverage could become $0.00.

"I'll have another Bombay, chef," I said. *"Quelle surprise,"* came his immediate response, as the refill magically and swiftly appeared.

Sal and Mabel took on their all-too-familiar deer-in-the-headlights look as I attempted to explain the letter's ramifications. I was lead defense counsel in all the lawsuits filed against them. I had been hired to defend the Manganos by the same fund and insurers that were now prepared to deny them coverage. Mabel got right to the point: "Whose side are you on, Jim?"

It was a good question, asked at precisely the right time. I explained that even if their insurer denied them coverage, they still owed St. Rita's a defense, and the insurer had to pay for that defense. "Mabel," I said, "I'm on y'all's side, and I'll remain there for as long as you want me. I am ethically required to give my complete, undivided loyalty to you, regardless of who's paying me. And that's what I pledge to do. And besides, I don't really give a shit about some nameless, faceless underwriter at Lloyd's of London. I care about you guys."

A long silence ensued broken by Sal, who said, "That's good enough for me, Mr. Jim. Now what do we do?"

"How about dessert?" I asked. They didn't smile, although I meant for the remark to be funny. Given the circumstances, it was no small wonder that their sense of humor had been numbed.

"No thanks," they both said in unison.

"Let me think this over and I'll send this asshole lawyer a nasty gram, telling him if they deny you coverage, we will sue the hell out of them for arbitrary, capricious, and bad faith claims handling. This is the time they're supposed to step up and provide you the coverage you've been paying for, for years. They shouldn't be searching for an excuse to weasel out of the contract of insurance. But, of course, that's what *all* the insurance companies are doing. Mine tried the same game with me, until I threatened to sue them and they finally paid up. So let me handle this and you guys don't worry about it. Remember, we've got bigger fish to fry in the criminal case, so let's not lose sight of that. Okay?"

"Okay," said Mabel. Sal proclaimed his luncheon duck the best he had ever eaten and thanked me for getting us seats at the chef's table. They had been treated respectfully and well by Chef René and seemed to feel a bit better after my pep talk. The short, Italian couple, now approaching fifty years of marriage, walked out of the kitchen holding hands. René and I watched them walk down the long, shiny hallway, the sliding glass doors automatically opening as they approached, and then closing behind them as they disappeared from view.

"Those are good people," said René. "I can't believe that asshole Foti charged them with murder. It's so unfair. Can you save them?"

"I don't know, chef," I responded. "I just don't know."

"Tasting?" the chef asked. "Tasting" was a euphemism the chef used to describe wine drinking, usually in large quantities. As a Frenchman and a master chef, he was constantly "tasting," searching for just the right wine to be paired with his unique cuisine. We retired to his plastic kitchen and promptly knocked off a bottle of Chablis, *premier cru*. Our "tasting" concluded, I made the same trek to the parking lot. Waiting for the attendant to bring down my car, I was haunted by René's question, "Can you save them?" Given the reservation-of-rights letter and the Manganos' dwindling bank account, saving them from incarceration for life meant devising a strategy to save them financially, as well.

Step one was to draft a response (a nasty gram) to the Trust and to Lloyds of London. My letter was directed to the lawyer who had written Sal and Mabel. He was the Nursing Home Trust's regular lawyer, the man who had actually set up the trust and drafted its originating documents. He had already been looking over my shoulder and backseat driving my defense of the civil claims, much to my chagrin. It was my view that he believed *he* should have been defending the thirty-four wrongful death and twelve personal injury cases filed against St. Rita's. It was, far and away, the largest, most complex claim that had ever been filed impacting the trust, his brainchild and baby. It also represented a tremendous billing opportunity for his law firm, an opportunity lost when I was hired as lead counsel instead of him. While outwardly affable and quick to offer help and support, he also had a stiletto pressed against my back, one he would be happy to shove deep should anything go wrong. And given the magnitude of the case and the terrible facts of the thirty-five wrongful deaths, something was bound to go wrong.

I was a firm believer in Gen. George S. Patton's creed that the best defense is an all-out offensive. In strong language, I pointed out that his entire letter and the position of the trust and underwriters was completely misguided. The Manganos had not been charged with an *intentional* criminal act. They had been charged with negligent homicide, which by definition is *not* an intentional act. "People buy insurance for negligent acts whether they are driving a car or producing a product," I continued. "The Manganos' decision to shelter in place, as opposed to evacuating, was negligent, according to all the wrongful death suits filed against them. None of these lawsuits alleged an intentional act; therefore, the trust and policy you represent must respond. Please inform your clients that failure to do so will necessitate a suit against them for all damages sustained, including punitive damages, as a result of their proposed denial of coverage. Finally, Sal and Mabel have been good and valued members of the association: dues paying active members for years. On their behalf, I do not appreciate the groups you represent kicking them when they're down. Please communicate our displeasure and objection to the course of conduct you propose. We had expected more, especially from people who said they were our friends."

I never heard from him again on the issue of denial of coverage.

Step two: Given the pitifully small amount of insurance covering St. Rita's for negligence, and the threat of a denial of coverage issued by underwriters, I had to do something to protect Sal and Mabel's assets from seizure by the wrongful death claimants when the day of reckoning came. That day would surely come; the plaintiffs' lawyers were like a pack of hungry dogs, chasing an exhausted fox. I could not kid myself. Eventually, we would be found responsible for civil negligence and Sal and Mabel would owe money damages. Owing money damages was a far more attractive option than incarceration for life, but I needed an asset protection specialist, an attorney who could be discreet and who was familiar with corporate law, IRS regulations, real estate, bankruptcy, and family trusts. As a litigator, my knowledge of these subjects could easily fit inside a jigger glass of rye whiskey, with plenty of room left over to make a respectable Sazerac, a New Orleans tradition.

I turned to a trusted friend and advisor, a golfing partner and buddy, and a fellow wino, Albert Ajubita. He had a master's in tax law, had worked as an attorney at the IRS, and was one of the area's leading business lawyers. He had also worked previously with Bob Habans on criminal tax cases with great success and was a team player who would fit in. He believed that Sal and Mabel were being scapegoated by Foti and wanted to help. I arranged a meeting with the Manganos to try to plan a defense of all they had acquired in their business careers, for all of their worldly possessions were now at risk. The barbarians of avarice were at their gates, threatening to storm their castle and clean them out. We needed to find a way to put important assets beyond their reach.

Turns out the nursing home business had been good to the Manganos. Very good. Because every family member worked in the business for minimal salaries, and because they did everything themselves—maintenance, plumbing, repairs, roofing, you name it—the home had been very, very profitable. They plowed these profits back into the business, but they had begun a savings program years earlier. They placed their savings in a most conservative, low-yield instrument—an annuity. Turns out annuities were the perfect instrument for our purposes, because, as a matter of law, they are beyond the reach of creditors. Albert made some recommendations and some things were moved around corporately and personally. I am not qualified to describe all the legal maneuvers Albert masterminded, but he assured me we would soon be able to repel the barbarians at the gate. I had to buy him some time to put the plan in place for it had to be done carefully and methodically.

Step three: I had been flailing around for some time, searching for a way to go on the offensive. We were on the defensive with the A.G.'s office, but there was nothing we could do about that. All the plaintiffs' lawyers in the wrongful death cases were pressing the attack, wanting to pursue discovery and push the case along. They also wanted money we didn't have. They wanted to take Sal and Mabel's sworn depositions in the civil cases, which could imperil their Fifth Amendment right against self-incrimination in the criminal case. A judge might even order them to give the depositions. We were under assault from all directions, fighting a two-front war, which is rarely a recipe for success. We needed a game changer, something that would allow us to go on the offensive, while at the same time buying us some time and breathing space.

By now, the evidence was mounting that the flooding of St. Bernard and New Orleans was the result of levee failure and collapse, not Katrina. Massive class action lawsuits had already been filed in federal court claiming all the damages were the fault of the ineptitude of the U.S. Army Corps of Engineers. A horde of plaintiffs' lawyers—masters of disaster—salivated over the prospect of fees proportional to the billions of dollars of damage done by what the lawyers were now calling "the Federal flood." A one-third fee on billions is an awful lot of money.

The vision of the strategy we would use came to me, margarita in hand, at a cheesy Mexican restaurant in the shopping center next door to our service road apartment. It was stumbling distance from the apartment and I had become something of a regular at happy hour, where the margaritas were affordably strong, and the warm chips and spicy salsa were free. As I hit the door on this particular day, the bartender began mixing my usual without asking what I wanted. That's the moment when you know you're a regular, and that feeling of belonging was welcome even at a Mexican restaurant facing an interstate service road. "I saw you on TV news last night," he said, presenting me with the wonderful mescal libation. I had done some forgettable local interview on the latest St. Rita's developments. "Yeah, man," he said. "I'm from St. Bernard and my parents lost everything too. They ought to leave your people alone. Everybody f—ed up." Ah, I thought, a friendly ear and a philosopher who also mixed a killer margarita. Life was good on this happy hour.

He did the talking and I did the listening, the inverse of the usual bartender/bar patron relationship. He told me how it wasn't just the Corps who screwed up, everybody did. "The Parish was supposed to maintain those levees," he said, "and I know they didn't."

"Really?" I asked. "How do you know that?"

"I had a buddy from high school who worked for the levee district," he continued, "and all he ever did was go to work, smoke dope, and drive a tractor cuttin' grass. Ain't nobody inspected those levees like they were supposed to. Everybody was either sittin' on their ass or smokin' weed. Somebody ought to sue all them people," he concluded.

"Hit me with my free one," I responded.

"I got you covered, brother," he answered, cementing our newly invigorated relationship.

The bar got busy and so did he, giving me the quiet time I always sought at my neighborhood joint. All the massive class actions filed thus far had targeted the Army Corps and the federal government, the only entity with pockets deep enough to respond to a potential judgment of billions and billions of dollars. But what about everybody else who screwed up, I thought, from the governor on down to the stoned tractor driver who went to high school with my newly found brother? If Sal and Mabel were going to be held to account, why not make everyone at every level account for their actions, too?

The legal vehicle we would employ is known as a Third-Party Demand. All the wrongful death claimants had simply sued St. Rita's and Sal and Mabel. Those were the only parties they needed. But a defendant like St. Rita's can file a pleading that contends, "I'm not responsible for this; somebody else is!"

We drafted and filed Third-Party Demands against everyone who we believed, in good faith and after sufficient investigation, played a part in the St. Rita's tragedy. We sued the U.S. Government in the form of the U.S. Army Corps of Engineers. We filed suit against Governor Blanco, Secretary Bradberry, St. Bernard Parish President Junior Rodriguez, the St. Bernard Levee District, and numerous others we believed were implicated. This maneuver had the effect of throwing a smoke bomb into the middle of the wrongful death cases. I love throwing smoke bombs. Reluctantly, I decided to leave the stoned grass cutter out of our third party lawsuits. My bartender would be disappointed.

The U.S. Government, predictably, filed a Notice of Removal of all the cases to the U.S. District Court for the Eastern District of Louisiana in New Orleans, immediately kicking the cases out of state court. The federal government always takes the position that the only place where it can be sued is federal court—which was precisely our strategic goal. Plus, the whole case was shut down for months, as all these new defendants had to get lawyers, do an investigation, and file pleadings. The government and all the public officials we sued claimed "sovereign immunity," an outdated doctrine that had its foundation in the notion that a mere peasant or ordinary citizen can't sue the king! This was the same position the federal government was taking in the massive class action cases alleging billions of dollars of property damage. It would take time to sort out all the legal issues raised as a result of our Third-Party Demand. Time, in this case, was our ally.

The filing of the demand received widespread media coverage, locally and nationally. The *National Law Journal,* the country's most respected and widely read paper about lawyers and the law, carried a photograph of me at the press conference announcing the suits and termed the maneuver a "stunning development." For the first time, someone (the Mangano defense) was saying that the government's negligence didn't just flood the region and destroy people's homes. We charged that through gross negligence and incompetence, the federal and state governments had killed the thirty-five residents at St. Rita's, citizens of the United States of America. It was an explosive charge, which made me more enemies in high places. I had never aspired to win personality contests, and this latest broadside ensured that I would remain winless for the foreseeable future. The filing of the Third-Party Demands also gave me a platform from which to start hammering away at what would become our theme at the criminal trial. That theme was simple: the Manganos didn't kill the residents, whom they loved and cared for, *they* did! The *they,* of course, was a widely despised governmental establishment, whose incompetence ran from George W. Bush through Kathleen Blanco and all the way down to Cheech and Chong, mixing marijuana smoke with diesel fumes as they mowed the levees. Finally, we were on the offensive and I liked our populist, anti-government, little-guy-against-the-big-guy message. Whether that message would resonate with a jury in either the civil or the criminal cases remained to be seen.

Chapter 21: Army Corps: "It's Our Fault"

Meanwhile, on the home front, we were stuck in an oxygen-depleted dead zone and going nowhere fast. The inertia had a corrosive effect on our initiative and drive. Occasionally, I would sit around all day, without moving, glued to mindless television. I first became a fan of, then addicted to, the *Jerry Springer Show*. I confess. I began to plan my non-existent work day around Springer. Of all the things to be addicted to, Springer wasn't so bad, I thought. After all, Jerry and I had a lot in common. We were both Tulane University graduates and both recognized the absurdity of the world around us. I was insanely jealous that Jerry was getting paid for his insight and I wasn't. I'm still a fan, but no longer build my day around his show.

On those rare occasions when some minimal forward progress was detectable—a partial insurance payment, with the bank finally agreeing not to take all our insurance proceeds, leaving us on the street with a gutted, uninhabitable home—there was always the inevitable speed bump to knock our life's front-end alignment out of whack.

Although I appreciated my service-road Mexican joint's two-for-one margaritas, the special was only good Mondays through Thursdays. Fridays saw full-fare Cuervo and my drinking bill doubled on those days. Given a choice between preserving shrinking cash and drinking without regard to it, drinking won every time. And so it was that an expensive Friday night led to a Saturday morning hangover—and to a major break in the St. Rita's case on June 3, 2006. Awakened by an incredibly dry, lime-flavored mouth and a throbbing head, I stumbled out of the apartment and into the dark around 5 A.M. I was headed to the curb to steal somebody's newspaper and find out what Katrina atrocity or murder had been committed in the previous twenty-four hours.

Scantily clad in tighty-whities and a two-sizes-too-small T-shirt that exposed a midriff several thousand sit-ups shy of six-pack abs, I must have been a sight. I thought I'd get to the curb in the early dark and make a clean getaway. But as I bent down to cop the copy, I heard a raspy voice in the dark. *"Hola, abogado!"* In the direction of the sound, I could see the lit end of a cigarette grow brighter as the speaker inhaled. The voice, while not menacing, was certainly discomfiting. He'd probably had too much tequila the previous night just as I had and was now topping things off with tobacco. *"Hola,"* I responded, beating a hasty retreat—filched paper in hand—in the direction of our hovel. "How 'bout that?" I thought to myself, "busted by an illegal alien." I was confident he wouldn't be calling the authorities.

In our coffin-sized kitchen I flipped the pilfered paper on the counter, upside down, and stumbled into coffee-prep mode. I was shoveling ground coffee with unsteady hands, when I glanced at the *Times-Picayune* and noticed a small headline: "Corps Admits Katrina Mistakes."

I looked again to be sure I wasn't dreaming this up, but there it was—a small one-column headline below the fold on the right hand side of the front page on the least-read newspaper day of the week, Saturday. The government knew how and when to release unfavorable information so that the fewest citizens possible would see it. The piece began with this sentence: "A contrite U.S. Army Corps of Engineers took responsibility yesterday for the flooding of New Orleans by Hurricane Katrina and said the levees had failed because they were built in a disjointed fashion using outdated data." The first quote in the article came from the Corps head, Lt. Gen. Carl Strock. "This is the first time that the Corps has had to stand up and say 'We've had a catastrophic failure,'" said Strock. The article went on to say that the agency had issued a six thousand-page report. The final Strock sound bite was incredible: "For this failure, we are responsible to the American people." *Holy shit,* I thought, the commanding general has fallen on his sword on the front page of the *Times-Picayune*. This had to be a game changer, I thought, for Sal and Mabel. The story went on to say that the $19.7 million report included details of the engineering and design failures that allowed the storm surge to overwhelm New Orleans' levees and floodwalls on August 29, 2005. Nearly 1,600 U.S. citizens had died in the flooding—thirty-five of them at St. Rita's. Surely the Corps' *mea culpa* deserved more coverage than this! No matter, I thought, I'm going to put it to use first thing Monday morning.

And so it happened, forty-eight hours later, that I found myself charging to the office to confect a letter to the attorney general of the great State of Louisiana. I actually looked forward to going to work that day, a feeling not experienced since Katrina. I wrote several drafts of differing lengths, some incredibly detailed, others shorter and to the point. I finally decided on the one reproduced below in its entirety:

June 5, 2006

Honorable Charles Foti
Attorney General
State of Louisiana

Dear Attorney General Foti,

I understand you are looking for those responsible for the tragic deaths of the thirty-five residents of St. Rita's Nursing Home, lost in Katrina's flood waters. I found them for you. They have admitted their responsibility. In legal circles, this is known as an "admission against interest," and is fully admissible at trial.

The U.S. Army Corps of Engineers has admitted that the flooding was caused by their negligence in the design, engineering and construction of a flood prevention system which failed catastrophically **"on their watch."** Further, the commanding general of the Corps has stated, "We are responsible to the American people." You might be interested in learning how I discovered those truly responsible for this tragedy. Our discovery was not the result of great detective or investigative work on our part. Instead, this admission of responsibility can be found on the front page of this past Saturday's Times Picayune, a copy of which I enclose herein for your easy reference.

Once again, we call upon you to drop the charges against Mr. and Mrs. Mangano in a prosecution that can now only be seen as unfair, unfounded and abusive.

Sincerely yours,
James A. Cobb, Jr.

It was a mash note to which I never received a response. The prosecutor's silence was ominous. We knew not what they were planning or doing. Our back-channel lines of communication had been cut off, no doubt due to the stormy meeting we had in their offices. My letter now surely added fuel to that fire. The Corps' admission had been made on the first day of the 2006 hurricane season, the first since Katrina. The entire state was incredibly anxious and fearful. Would we get another storm? In their weakened state, could any of the remaining levees survive? What did the future hold for Sal and Mabel? And what about us—where were we going to live, and what were we going to live on? Such anxiety could only be met with one course of action—*road trip*! Let's get the hell out of here, I said to Debbie and the kids. Escape, at the very least, delays the malignant inevitable. The four of us fled to the Rocky Mountains of Colorado's Roaring Fork Valley. Some idiotic bank had sent me a new credit card, Chase Blue, I believe. The card promised a super-low introductory interest rate. Since I'd blown through all my other cards, maxing them out, I activated this new one and off we went to paradise for the most needed vacation in human history.

Debbie and I had been going to Colorado for almost twenty years. We mostly skied Snowmass and Aspen mountains and spent many a Mardi Gras away from the New Orleans madness in the beauty and solitude of clear, blue skies towering over mountains covered in eight feet of snow. As awe inspiring as the winters were for us denizens of the Deep South, the summers were even better. While New Orleans drooped in 95-degree days and 100-percent humidity, mile-high Colorado held the prospect of bone-dry sunshine and temperatures that peaked at 75 before dropping back into the 40s at night. We hiked, biked, golfed, swam, exercised, played tennis, and were restored. We didn't hang out in phony, expensive Aspen. We preferred down-valley cowboy towns with names like Basalt, El Jebel, and Carbondale. At the end of our trip, we drove to Marble, where the four of us took a horseback trip to the top of the world, ate lunch in a field of wildflowers, and then went back down the mountain on precarious trails. Concentrating on not falling off a horse on the edge of a cliff makes other troubles disappear. It was exhilarating and stunningly beautiful, and we bonded again as a family—we were the only cowboys on the ride.

Getting into the car for the drive back, I was reminded why I didn't go horseback riding more often. Every muscle in my body was sore, my back ached, and I could barely sit straight on my dilapidated butt. But it was a good kind of soreness, in which we all shared. I was about to get a lot sorer.

As we cleared the mountains and came into the outskirts of Carbondale, my cell phone service was reestablished. Within minutes it rang. I wondered who in hell had the nerve to bother me on such a perfect day. It was Mabel. Apologizing profusely for calling me on my vacation, she was her usual considerate self.

"Mabel," I said, "you can call me anytime, anywhere." I had a flashback to her being placed in handcuffs and hauled off to jail. "What's up?" I asked.

"Well," she said sheepishly, "I just got a letter from Charlie Foti, and I thought I should call." My cool, calm, Rocky Mountain high was instantly snuffed. I exploded.

"You got *what*? What did it say?" When a party is represented by a lawyer, the lawyer on the other side is prohibited from communicating with the client directly and *must* only communicate through counsel. It is an ethical rule that real lawyers take very seriously. This is especially true in a criminal case.

Mabel heard the instant edge in my voice. "The letter is a fundraising letter,

Chris and Collette on the slopes in Basalt, Colorado, 2006.

Debbie on the Roaring Fork Club golf course, Basalt, 2006.

addressed specifically to me, asking me to make a campaign contribution to his re-election campaign. What should I do?"

I went off. "It is highly unethical for him to contact you, Mabel. This is especially so given the fact that he arrested you and charged you with homicide. For him to contact you and ask you for money is outrageous. Keep that letter, take it to my office, and give it to my bookkeeper. Tell him to put it in our safe."

I went on and on. The letter was at minimum an impropriety; or you could call it a shakedown, an effort to extort cash from a defendant. When I got done ranting, Mabel said, "I don't really understand all that, Jim. So . . . how much money should I send him?"

Poor thing, I thought, she doesn't get it. "We're not sending him any money!" I exclaimed. "He'll take your money, and then indict you, saying he's incorruptible, even charging his own campaign contributors with homicide. Don't send that asshole a dime. I don't know what all the implications of this improper solicitation are," I said, "but it's a big deal, Mabel. If I can, I intend to break it off in his ass."

Forgetting who was in the car, I glanced in the rearview mirror and noticed Christopher and Collette paying rapt attention to my every word, their eyes and mouths wide open, astonished at their dad's instantaneous transformation from Dr. Jekyll to Mr. Foul Mouth. I probably could have done without the "break it off in his ass" comment for both Mabel and the kids, but it was too late. I imagined Collette asking, "Dad, what does it mean to break something off in somebody's ass?" Oh well, another unintentional infliction of emotional distress on my offspring. Time to end the conversation with Mabel, I thought, before I committed some other atrocity.

"I'll call you when I get back in town, Mabel," I said. The rest of the ride back to Basalt was quiet. I turned on a country music station and let my mind wander. This *was* a big, stupid deal, and I was going to bust the A.G. if I could.

When I got back to my office, there was some icing on the Charlie Foti campaign-solicitation cake. As I read through my mail, I came across an envelope that had as its return address, "Foti campaign." I ripped the envelope open and there was a letter addressed to me asking *me* to contribute to Foti's re-election campaign fund. The typed salutation read "Dear Mr. Cobb," but someone had drawn a line through it and written "Dear Jim," by hand. Incredible. He's not just soliciting a criminal defendant with charges pending, but also that defendant's lawyer. Was this extortion or stupidity or both? It didn't matter. Months later these communications would be at the heart of a Motion to Disqualify Foti's office from handling the case. It was, in fact, a very big deal. Big enough to cause us to win or lose the case.

There began to be a flood of publications, films, and documentaries about "the flood." National Geographic, the National Science Foundation, PBS's award-winning series *Frontline*, and others turned their attention to what really happened and why. My office staff acquired every publication or documentary and I devoured them all, highlighting passages I thought helpful and taking tablets full of notes as I viewed the investigative reports. My internet research skills were woefully inadequate so I took to visiting Barnes and Noble at least once a week. There I could peruse their vast selection of periodicals, look for new book titles related to Katrina, and have a cup of coffee and a blueberry muffin at the Starbucks franchise right in the bookstore. It was a great, quiet, reflective place to hang out. On one such visit I noticed a clerk setting up a table in the Louisiana section, with a couple of boxes of what appeared to be new books about to be put out for the first time. One book stood upright in a cradle, looking right at me. Even with my failing eyesight, I could make out its title in bold reddish-brown letters: *The Storm*. I was drawn to the table like a moth to flame.

I picked up one of the newly unpacked books and turned to its back cover, looking for blurbs and endorsements. There were none. There was, however, one paragraph with no identified author. The type was bold and printed in white ink on a midnight-black jacket:

> It was a natural disaster—but magnified enormously by government's crushing incompetence in both preparation and response. The storm leveled the Mississippi Gulf Coast, but man-made problems destroyed New Orleans. The catastrophic flooding there should never have happened. Properly designed and constructed levees would have protected the city. Instead, they collapsed. Never in American history was a natural disaster so fatally coupled with the systemic failure of our government to protect and serve the people. The result is the national tragedy known forever as simply Katrina.

This author was singing from our hymnal. I immediately bought the book, rushed home, and read the three hundred pages in one sitting. With highlighter in hand, I read *The Storm* more carefully than any textbook I had ever studied, either as an undergraduate or law student.

The book's author was Ivor van Heerden, on the faculty at Louisiana State University and a co-founder and deputy director of the LSU Hurricane Center. Van Heerden had been one of the scientists on the Corps' case from jump street. He had been all over the TV news, local and national, and was articulate and focused. Born in Johannesburg, South Africa, he spoke English with a slight trace of his Afrikaner roots. He had a PhD in marine sciences and, although a professor of civil and environmental engineering at LSU, he wasn't a professionally licensed engineer. This one lacking credential would prove problematic later on.

I didn't read the book; I inhaled and devoured it. The book was incredibly detailed and appeared to me to be scientifically sound. It contained maps, storm-surge modeling data, time lines, and simple, easily understood drawings illustrating the book's conclusions. In whole and in part it was a stinging indictment of the Corps and others, and it tracked the theory of our defense.

The book stated emphatically that if the only sources of water in New Orleans had been the rainfall from Katrina (seven to ten inches) and some minor, predicted over toppings and breaches, the flooding would have been relatively insignificant. My eyes widened and my mouth opened as I read the following paragraph:

> According to our latest calculations, 88 percent of the flooding in the Orleans Metro Bowl, by volume, was due to the breaches on the London Avenue and 17th Street Canals. In Orleans East, 69 percent of the flood was due to breaches. In the St. Bernard Bowl, 92 percent of the flooding was the result of levee failure. (*The Storm*, 95)

The intrepid South African, Ivor van Heerden, in a boat on the MRGO, 2007. Courtesy of CBS News, from *48 Hours: No Way Out* (02/02/08).

My mind began to whir. There were ten feet of water in the nursing home as a result of the flood. If 92 percent of that water came from levee breaches caused by the Corps' now admitted negligence, that meant St. Rita's would have had less than one foot of water, not the ten feet it got when the levees failed. I grabbed a twelve-inch ruler and placed it on the ground next to where I was sitting, measuring the distance from the floor to the end of the ruler. The twelve-inch ruler came to the middle of my calf, well below my knees. The closing argument formed in my imagination instantly: "Ladies and gentlemen of the jury, you've just heard Professor van Heerden's testimony. In his expert opinion, the flooding at St. Rita's *but* for the levee breaches would have been less than one foot . . . significantly below anyone sitting in their wheelchair or lying in their bed. Some ankles and calves may have gotten wet, but no one would have drowned if the government had delivered on its promise of sound, sturdy levees . . ." and so on and so forth. My imagination ran wild with the prospects.

Van Heerden was employed by the State of Louisiana, the very same state now going after the Manganos. His testimony, *if* we could establish its relevance and admissibility, could turn the day. There would be many battles fought in the run-up to trial as to whether and how much of van Heerden's conclusions could be heard by the jury. I knew that battle was coming and would be hard-fought by the state. There was an even more important battle about this hoped-for testimony, one which I did not anticipate and could not imagine. That battle was Ivor van Heerden's battle with himself and his conscience.

Chapter 22: The Hammer Falls

Early in the summer of 2006, we began to hear drumbeats in the distance, heralding the onset of all-out war. The case had been quiet for some time and we were hopeful, given the Army Corps of Engineers' front page admission, that the charges against Sal and Mabel would quietly disappear. Our hopes disappeared like a puff of smoke in a strong wind. Mabel called to tell me some of her employees had been contacted by the A.G.'s men wanting to interview them. They were petrified. They had seen St. Rita's matriarch and patriarch laid low, humiliated on an international stage, hauled off to jail in handcuffs, and vilified and demonized by a press corps longing for a villain and scapegoat. This tragic story needed a tidy, media friendly ending. "Greedy Nursing Home Owners Found Guilty!" is the headline they all longed to write. "Family Members of Victims Feel Closure" would be the sidebar story. "Thirty-Five Innocent Elderly Avenged by Guilty Verdict," would be Nancy Dis-Grace's take. We intended to write our own ending, if only we could figure out how.

I contacted Bob and he swung into action, securing separate, private counsel for those with whom the attorney general wanted to speak. The A.G.'s list included family members—Little Sal, his wife T.J., and others who were present on the day the thirty-five died. Our concern, of course, was that if these witnesses went in unrepresented, they could say something they thought innocent about the event, but this comment would be viewed, or distorted, very differently by prosecutors. Without counsel, any witness can be led, unknowingly, into becoming a cooperating witness for the government. Changing their stories could lead to the threat of perjury or obstruction of justice charges, a tool frequently abused by prosecutors ravenous for evidence to use against a defendant.

Bob had been down this road many times before. In our business, it's known as everyone "lawyering up" and he knew who to call and how to make the referrals. The lawyers he contacted would never consider letting their clients talk to the government without first obtaining immunity, something the government rarely doled out. Only lawyers and the government could take a simple concept known as immunity—freedom from prosecution no matter what one says—and slice it and dice it into unrecognizable portions. There was "use immunity," "transactional immunity," "full immunity," and who knew what else. Without a full and absolute grant of immunity, Bob's lawyer buddies would keep their clients as silent as stone. And if Foti's people badgered them further, the clients would take the stand and plead the Fifth, refusing to testify on grounds that it might incriminate them, as protected by the Fifth Amendment. If nobody's talking, then no one is saying anything bad about us, is the general idea. In any event, the wheels of justice had been set in motion against us once again.

Through contacts in the St. Bernard Parish courthouse, we learned that the A.G.'s office was having trouble empaneling a grand jury to consider the St. Rita's case. There were hardly enough people back in the parish to respond to jury summonses, much less to allow for the fair composition of a grand jury. The parish was still devastated and only a brave few had moved back home. As subpoenas went out to prospective grand jurors, more than 50 percent of them were returned, marked by the sheriff, "unable to serve." This failure to constitute fairly a grand jury, both diverse and representative of a non-existent community, created a possible issue for us on appeal. It was an esoteric item and we recognized the issue as an extreme longshot. I felt we had to do something to de-rail the indictment express. We decided to play the only card we had left.

It was late August 2006, the one year anniversary of Katrina. A week or two before the grand jury was scheduled to meet, I filed a Motion to Recuse and Disqualify Foti and his office from handling the case. Our motion was based on his over-the-top, impermissible press comments, designed to destroy the presumption of innocence. It was also evidence of his bias and prejudice against the Manganos. The second part of the motion revealed publicly, for the first time, the fact that he had solicited the defendants and their lawyer for campaign contributions while he considered whether or not to proceed against them. This created the appearance of impropriety and maybe constituted an outright shakedown, requiring his disqualification. We hoped that a fair-minded, independent prosecutor would be appointed by the Louisiana Supreme Court, and that he or she would decide to drop the charges.

The Supreme Court had appointed a retired, veteran judge from New Orleans to handle the matter after the D.A. and the judges in St. Bernard

Parish recused themselves from this white-hot, emotional case. Judge Jerome Winsberg would preside over the grand jury, our pre-trial motions, and the case in chief. The motion to disqualify Foti drew much attention from the press, as we intended. Winsberg, a no nonsense judge (except in private), quickly scheduled a hearing and oral argument for the following Tuesday. I had called a news conference to discuss the motion and our incendiary allegations against Foti, for the Friday before the Tuesday hearing. The state lawyers got wind of our plans and initiated a telephone conference call with the judge right before the press conference was to start. With all the parties and the judge on the line, the A.G.'s men argued that I should be silenced until after the motion was heard. I countered that the First Amendment gave me the right to speak and that I found it incredibly hypocritical that an office, which had illegally bludgeoned the Manganos in the press, now wanted to silence my response.

The judge was circumspect. "Look, Mr. Cobb," he said, "I'm not going to order you to cancel the news conference. There is no motion or request for a gag order in this case in front of me at this point in time," he said softly. "I'm *asking* you not to hold the news conference." That put me in a trick bag. We were instantly on the defensive at a time when we were looking forward to a strong news cycle at Foti's expense.

"I'll think about it, Judge," I said.

His retort, as he hung up on me, was doubly curt: "Good," he said, "I'm sure you'll do the right thing."

I was already in my car headed to the hotel conference; the assembled press was awaiting my arrival. I hated missing an opportunity to stick it to the A.G., but I was equally concerned about not giving the judge the opportunity to stick it to me. I was conflicted. I huddled with associates and quickly decided to bow to the judge's request. He would be making a lot more critical decisions in the case in the coming months, and I didn't want our relationship to begin on a sour note. But neither did I want to lose credibility with the assembled media.

There were a half dozen or so TV cameras in the room and their lights went on as I entered. Print media, radio, and others perked up. It was show time. I approached the microphones at the lectern: "We have extra copies of the pleadings we have filed in the record for those of you that don't have them," I began. "It will save you a trip to the courthouse." I urged them to read the pleadings carefully. They accurately reflected our position and arguments in this most serious matter before the court.

"I have just finished a conference call with representatives of the A.G.'s office and Judge Winsberg," I said. "The government doesn't want me to hold

Judge Jerome Winsberg, appointed by the Louisiana Supreme Court to handle the red-hot St. Rita's case.

this conference or answer your questions. Judge Winsberg has requested, not ordered, that I cancel this conference. I am going to honor the judge's request and hope to see all of you next Tuesday when the matter will be argued in open court. After that, I hope to be able to speak with all of you."

There was an audible groan from those assembled. It wasn't just that the reporters were concerned with freedom of expression or their right to cover this story. Their cameras were already set up, they had a story line and a block of time scheduled for the evening newscasts, and this unexpected development interfered with their plans. As I attempted to exit the room, I was peppered with questions. The operators shifted their cameras from tripods onto their shoulders and followed me out into the street, as the story now became "no news conference." I was trying to make a dignified exit, but retreats are rarely dignified, and I was muzzled. The visuals made it seem like I had something to hide, as opposed to the other side, whose whining to the judge had put me in this position in the first place. I was voluntarily speechless and therefore helpless to effect a different outcome. We had a bad day when we should have had a very good one. Within a week, there were more bad days for us; one of them was the *worst* day for Sal and Mabel since their residents had drowned at St. Rita's.

At the hearing on the Motion to Recuse and Disqualify Foti and his office, the A.G.'s men took the laughable position that our motion was premature. They argued that a grand jury "might" decide against indicting the Manganos, in which case there would be no need to hear the motion. While technically correct, the argument was practically and logically facetious. The A.G. knew full well that the manner in which he chose to present the evidence to the grand jury would determine its outcome. Grand juries are the tool of the prosecutor's office, not some fair and independent adjudicator of facts. If the A.G.'s office was presenting the case, the prosecutors were going to present it in such a fashion as to guarantee indictments. This they already knew. One of the things the public hates about lawyers and the law is that "technicalities" appear to prevail over truth and substance. My much ballyhooed motion was swiftly and ignominiously denied. At the pretrial phase, we were now defenseless, at the mercy of an unscrupulous, politically motivated prosecutor.

Proof of the A.G.'s duplicity in his contention that the grand jury "might" decide not to indict the Manganos was soon amply available. The A.G.'s men never called a live witness who was actually at St. Rita's on the day the thirty-five lost their lives. The only witnesses called before the grand jury were investigators from the A.G.'s office who detailed the results of their investigation. None of these investigators had any firsthand knowledge of the alleged "homicides." Unlike in a real trial, even hearsay evidence is admissible in front of a grand jury, along with speculation, conjecture, and guessing. No evidence was presented by us; we were not even invited to attend—Bob would have insisted, of course, that we *not* attend, and rightly so, for the outcome was already predetermined and there was nothing we could do to stop it. Anything we said could, and would, be used against us.

I was sitting at home, late on a weekday afternoon, having devoured all the day's Springer reruns, when my mindless channel surfing was interrupted by a local anchor announcing breaking news: "A grand jury in St. Bernard (Parish) has just returned a multi-count indictment against Sal and Mabel Mangano, the owners and operators of the St. Rita's Nursing Home where dozens of residents drowned in Katrina's floodwaters. There may be more than one hundred counts in the indictment and Eyewitness News will bring you all the details beginning with our 5:00 P.M. newscast. We understand that many of the charges are for homicide. Tune in at 5 P.M. for details." Even though I knew it was coming, I was numbed nonetheless. I sat in silence awaiting the details that would come with the late-afternoon broadcast.

Five o'clock arrived and my worst fears were realized. All three of the local network affiliates led with the story as did the national cable networks. In the version I watched, a reporter stood in front of the parish courthouse to describe grand jurors solemnly filing into the presence of Judge Winsberg. Both Sal and Mabel had been charged separately with thirty-five counts of negligent homicide and twenty-four counts of cruelty to the elderly and infirm—118 criminal counts all told.

"Many of the jurors were wiping away tears as the indictments were read," the reporter said, choking back tears of his own. "Three female grand jurors were sobbing openly as they entered the room," he reported.

The twenty-four counts of cruelty to the elderly and infirm made my eyes open wider and my jaw drop. I knew this number. The number twenty-four corresponded exactly to the number of residents who were *rescued* by the Manganos in the rush of the unexpected floodwaters. Now they were being charged with cruelty to those whose lives they saved. We would later learn that the government's theory was that these survivors should have been evacuated in advance of the storm. To subject them to the horrors of a swim out of the nursing home, culminating in their being pelted by rain and wind as they clung to life on the roof, was cruelty under the statute. I shook my head in disbelief. "They charged them with criminal cruelty towards twenty-four people whose lives they saved, while risking their own lives to do so," I thought. "Incredible!" The power of a prosecutor's office was fearsome to behold.

I did some math quickly. The penalty for negligent homicide, if one were convicted, was a maximum of five years in prison for each count. Cruelty to the elderly and infirm carried a more serious sentence than did negligent homicide. One could receive ten years in prison for each and every count. If convicted, Sal and Mabel were exposed to 175 years in prison on the thirty-five counts of negligent homicide. On the cruelty counts they were exposed to 240 years each. Thus, their individual total exposure to prison was 415 years on the combined criminal counts. It was mind-boggling, unexpected, and unimaginable. As a practical matter, a conviction on any one count meant a conviction on all counts, as all the counts sprang from the same set of operative facts. Based on the 118-count indictment, if we lost the case, Sal and Mabel would likely go to jail for the rest of their lives.

This reality came crashing down on me like a ton of bricks teetering on a ten-story platform. I was paralyzed with fear, unable to move out of the way. I was gripped by a crisis of confidence that no trial lawyer worth his salt should have to endure: I was in way over my head and Sal and Mabel were about to pay the price for my mistakes and bad judgment. Like Icarus, I was guilty of the sin of hubris for thinking, somehow, that I was capable of flying the Manganos to safety. I wasn't a criminal lawyer—what in hell was I doing trying to defend these people who seemed so clearly guilty? I thought for the better part of an hour about calling Bob and telling him I was withdrawing as counsel and could he please find a *real* criminal lawyer so Sal and Mabel would at least have a fighting chance of avoiding prison for the rest of their lives. I owed it to them, I thought, rationalizing my fear, my cowardice, and my demonstrated incompetence at preventing their indictment. As I sank deeper and deeper into this slough of despondency, my cell phone rang. I answered it without checking caller ID. It was Mabel.

She told me news of the indictment was on all the television stations in Baton Rouge where she was living in the shadows, keeping the lowest profile possible, hopeful that anonymity would somehow provide rescue from her plight. "What does it mean?" she asked, tremulously. Her emotional need snapped me out of my self-pitying funk.

"It means, Mabel, that we're in it for the long haul," I responded. "We're not going to be able to make this go away anytime soon," I said quietly. There was a long pause and the silence was uncomfortable.

"What do we do next?" she asked. Good question. I muttered something about getting together with Bob, discussing options, and formulating a new game plan. Mabel was as disappointed with my answer as I was, but she was resigned to her new fate as the only person, along with her husband, to be charged with criminal culpability for deaths associated with Hurricane

Katrina. "Just let me know what is next, okay, Jim?" Her voice was edged with disappointment in me, and our conversation ended awkwardly.

A week or so later I met with Bob, and at some point I slipped in the question that was haunting me: "Do you think it would be better if I withdrew and you brought in a real criminal lawyer to work with you?" I was half hoping his answer would be "yes."

Bob considered the question and responded, "Jim, you have great instincts and judgment. You are completely devoted to these people and, despite events, have done a great job for them so far. I really wouldn't consider handling the case with anyone else but you. We're in this together."

My self-doubt and fear gave way to emotions with which I was infinitely more comfortable and familiar: anger, fury, and outrage at what this prosecutor's office had done to these two innocent and elderly people. You want to fight? Bring it on you heartless, misguided, rotten bastards! You want Sal and Mabel? You've got to come through me and Bob first, and we're not easily moved. You picked the fight. We intend to finish it. Bravado is an excellent antidote to fear. My hope was that it was not false bravado, the consequences of which are often humiliation and self-destruction.

Chapter 23: Unlit Charcoal Briquette

With the return of the grand jury indictment, a whole new protocol was set in motion. Sal and Mabel would have to appear at an arraignment, where they would be entitled to have the charges against them read aloud in open court. They would then have to respond to those charges by entering a plea—guilty or not guilty. The issue of bail was likely to come up again. They were still free, released from the Baton Rouge jail on their own recognizance. Given the volume and severity of the charges, the court would likely inquire as to whether the defendants should be made to hand over property or post a cash bond to secure their appearance at trial. Judge Winsberg, who was sitting by designation of the Louisiana Supreme Court in New Orleans, called for the lawyers from both sides to attend a conference with him to discuss arrangements, scheduling, and other administrative matters.

We met in his chambers at the old criminal district court building for Orleans Parish, a stately Works Progress Administration (WPA) building of dark gray concrete behind a row of huge columns that swept across the length of the Tulane Avenue façade. The main lobby of the building was ornate and beautiful with enormous art deco chandeliers dangling from vaulted ceilings. The courtrooms were wood paneled, with a creaky swinging gate separating the audience from the area reserved for the judge, lawyers, and defendants. The building's former glory was fading as a result of budget cuts, neglect, and the weight of all the sadness seen here on a daily basis for decades. This courthouse was the last stopping point for tens of thousands of defendants as they made the transition from the presumption of innocence to conviction and, as often as not, incarceration.

In chambers there were no pleasantries exchanged among us lawyers. Usually I tried very hard to avoid making things personal with my opponents. They had a job to do, and so did I; personal rancor had no place in effective representation of one's client. This case was different. We had been misled, lied to, and taken advantage of. Sal and Mabel were victims of the state's chicanery. Every day, every encounter was to be all out war—no quarter asked, none given.

No doubt I ratcheted hostilities up several notches when responding to a magazine reporter from *Esquire*. The article appeared the same month as the grand jury indictment. He seemed to think—correctly, perhaps—that Foti and his prosecutors were on extremely firm legal ground. "Aren't you afraid that the entire weight of the state's prosecution apparatus is lined up against you and the Manganos?" he asked.

My answer became the article's take-away quote: "Charlie Foti has the legal acumen of an unlit charcoal briquette," I said. "And that's being unkind to charcoal briquettes."

When we met with Judge Winsberg, he mentioned that he had seen the *Esquire* piece. "Nice article," he said, with a wink in my direction. The judge had a certain impishness about him, and as a former star high school athlete he enjoyed a good brawl, whether he was in it or just refereeing it. The government lawyers hated the article, of course. They termed it crass and inappropriate. Their marching orders from the head briquette were, obviously, to destroy me.

The judge began the conference noting that with the grand jury indictment in hand, the law required that the defendants be arraigned within a certain number of days. "When do you all want to do it?" he asked. Calendars were checked and coordinated and we all picked an acceptable day.

"The more important question, Judge," I said, "is where do we do it?" I explained that Sal and Mabel had received threats expressed by the deceased's family members in a blog they were coordinating. I was deeply concerned for Sal and Mabel's safety (and mine) if we went down to St. Bernard for arraignment. I noted that the judge was already presiding in a courthouse with better security. "Why don't we do it here in New Orleans?" I suggested.

St. Bernard was a tough, blue-collar kind of a place. Its working-class families labored in oil refineries and sugar mills. Others were hunters, fishermen, shrimpers, and oystermen, and they were all armed to the teeth. There were as many guns in St. Bernard as there were people, probably more, I argued. Family of the dead were desperately hurt and psychologically damaged, and they had been stirred to a frenzy by the attorney general's rhetoric. Many of them had been quoted in the press as saying that the Manganos had let their parents "drown like rats."

"In this atmosphere," I argued, "it wouldn't take much for somebody to snap, step out of the crowd, and start blasting. I don't want to be in the line of fire if that happens, Judge."

Winsberg took my concerns seriously. But he noted that the law required a defendant to be arraigned in the parish where the alleged crime had been committed. "We'll handle the arraignment in the St. Bernard courthouse, and I'll contact the sheriff and have sufficient security in place," Winsberg said. Thus the matter was concluded. The judge was adamant and in control. We would have to run the public gauntlet of shame and condemnation, "down in da parish," as the locals called St. Bernard.

The appointed day came on October 4, 2006. Sal and Mabel drove down from Baton Rouge, as did Bob. We met at my office on Poydras Street in downtown New Orleans, a nineteenth-floor aerie overlooking the Superdome. We would all travel together in one car with me at the wheel. I drove through the still destroyed and uninhabited neighborhoods of a once vibrant city, through the infamous 9th Ward, and into St. Bernard Parish. We passed homes still bearing the markings that rescue teams had painted on them to indicate whether someone had died there in the flood. The irony was wrenching. We were passing through ghost town neighborhoods to answer the charge that Sal and Mabel, through their gross negligence, had caused thirty-five residents to give up the ghost as Katrina's tidal surge raged through St. Rita's. We scarcely said a word for the duration of the half-hour drive.

I had coordinated our arrival with the sheriff's office. We were to drive past the courthouse and present ourselves at the sheriff's substation. Sal and Mabel had to be booked again with mugshots and fingerprints. This time there would be no handcuffs. As I passed the flood-faded sign ("Welcome to St. Bernard Parish"), a sheriff's deputy in a parked police vehicle looked at me, picked up a hand-held microphone, and started talking into it. I imagined what he might be saying: "Suspects and their lawyers have just entered the parish." He pulled in behind us, following at a discreet distance. We continued our journey south and east, past the Chalmette Battlefield where Gen. Andrew Jackson and a ragtag army of irregulars repelled the British, not knowing, neither he nor the enemy, that the peace treaty ending the War of 1812 had already been signed. I couldn't help wondering if, in the courtroom bloodbath ahead, our fate would be that of the British or of Jackson's scruffy gang. As we continued south, the two-story courthouse came into view on our left. There was a grassy area in front of the building lined by live oaks dripping with Spanish moss. Several dozen protesters carried signs which we couldn't yet make out. Mabel said she recognized some of them as relatives of the lost thirty-five. We would have to walk through this welcoming committee in order to gain entrance to the building. Also present and clearly visible were multiple television trucks with their satellite dishes extended towards the sky. For the TV folks this was the next best thing to the "perp walk" they had been denied in Baton Rouge when Sal and Mabel were first arrested. The Manganos, though still presumed innocent in the eyes of the law, would have to navigate a seething throng that firmly believed them guilty. It was never good television for the defendant. At least we weren't in handcuffs.

Several blocks past the courthouse I made a right turn and a squat, one-story building came into view. "That's the police station," Sal said reluctantly. It had a flat roof and as I surveyed the area for a parking space, I saw what appeared to be two SWAT team officers armed and dressed for the part, standing on the roof looking down on our arrival. One of them pulled his hand-held radio from his belt and began speaking into it. Both had automatic weapons draped over their shoulders, and both wore dark sunglasses. As we entered the small substation, I remembered Mabel telling me her father had been a deputy sheriff in the parish for years. How hugely embarrassing this ordeal must be for her, I thought to myself—to be booked in your hometown as public enemy number one. For twenty years, she had been the owner/operator of St. Bernard's best nursing home, a thriving business with hundreds of employees over the years, recognized and respected by most in the community. Now she was an uncommon criminal. Her expression was sad and distant as we walked inside.

We fared much better in this jail than we had in Baton Rouge. Sal and Mabel disappeared in the back, without cuffs, for a few minutes, not hours. Bob and I waited in the non-secure area. After the indignity of fresh mugshots and fingerprinting, Sal and Mabel emerged ashen-faced, and we retraced our steps to the car for the short drive to the courthouse. I glanced up at the roof to see one of the SWAT-like guys grab his radio and announce our departure. At the courthouse, a cluster of uniformed deputies signaled where we were to park. I instructed Sal and Mabel to avoid eye contact with anyone, to look straight ahead, and to say nothing. As I got out of the car, Little Sal emerged from the shadows of one of the large oak trees. "I'll be right behind you, Mr. Jim," he said. "I won't let anyone sneak up on you from behind. I got your back." Complementing Little Sal's brawn, a phalanx of sheriff's deputies formed a protective barrier around us as we walked fifty yards or so to the building's front door. The first words I heard from the crowd were, "There they are!" And protestors rushed in our direction. As they got closer, a chorus of "boos" erupted and grew louder.

"Shame! Shame on you, Sal and Mabel," someone shouted.

"You killed my mother!" sobbed another.

"Bastards!" a deep-voiced man cursed.

We were closing in on the courthouse steps and the relative safety that lay within the building when I heard a shout that scared me. "Murderer!"

I grabbed Mabel's hand. "Come on, sweetie, we're almost there." If it hadn't been for the deputies, this crowd of forty could have become a lynch mob in an instant. Finally, we made it to the front door and passed through metal detectors and more security personnel. There was a large police presence in the lobby and I felt a whole lot safer inside than out.

The arraignment would take place upstairs in the smallest courtroom I had ever seen. Media were seated in the jury box and four rows of spectator seating filled up instantly. We were "inside the rail," but the spectators sat right behind us, no more than four feet away. If stares could kill, Sal and Mabel and Bob and I would have drawn our last breaths in that courtroom. As the four of us sat at the counsel table awaiting the judge's entrance, Bob was on the far left next to Mabel, then Sal, then me on the far right. I noticed that Sal was breathing heavily and sweating profusely. The fifty-yard walk in the heat couldn't have caused this, I thought. I put my arm around him whispering, "Are you going to be okay?" Sal had high blood pressure and other ailments. "I'll be okay," he said. With my hand on his back, I could literally feel his heart pounding and my concern about the mob out in front of the courthouse gave way to worries about his health.

There was a knock on the door and the bailiff commanded loudly, "All rise." The judge took the bench and Bob handled the mumbo jumbo of waiving a reading of the grand jury's indictment. It would have been gasoline on an already scorching fire for courtroom spectators to hear their relatives' names called out one by one. Bob was representing Mabel for purposes of the arraignment and I represented Sal. When asked how his client wished to plead, Bob stood and with his deepest, most intimidating base voice said, "Your Honor, Mrs. Mabel Mangano pleads *not guilty* as to all charges." Those assembled knew he meant business. I followed Bob's lead and entered the same plea for Sal, albeit less impressively. The entire matter was over in less than ten minutes and we prepared to run the media and protestor gauntlet in an attempt to get out of town in one piece.

Outside we beat a hasty retreat with the help of the deputy sheriffs clearing a path through television cameras, reporters, and victims' family members. It was surreal, like a scene from a movie—except we weren't watching the screen, we were on it as the object of the mob's hatred. I drove as quickly as I could out of St. Bernard. "We made it!" I cracked as we crossed the parish line and relished the relative safety of New Orleans—a city notorious for its high murder rate. "Now that wasn't so bad, was it?" It was the wrong time for sarcasm and nobody appreciated my attempt at humor. Thirty years defending corporations and insurance companies had not accustomed me to being well liked. As the one standing between an injured plaintiff and his dreams of a pot full of money, I was often detested, even despised. But the hostility we had experienced this time was jarringly different; the potential for outright violence much greater than anything I had known. I knew one thing for sure: we had to figure out a way to get this case out of St. Bernard Parish. The raw feelings would certainly lead to an unfair trial and an almost certain conviction.

I was parched from my barely one-minute speech on Sal's behalf, so I stopped by the Mexican joint on the way home to lubricate my vocal cords. Later that evening I wound up on the couch at the apartment with Christopher. The girls were out running around, who knows where. The local news came on and the Manganos' walk of shame was, of course, the lead story. Chris watched in rapt silence as he saw his dad navigate the angry mob. I could hear the gears turning inside his little head as he considered the danger we faced. I had seen enough. It was time for bed. I clicked off the set, but before I could get to my feet, Christopher asked, "Dad, what made you decide to want to become a lawyer?" Good question, I thought, well asked. I knew the answer, but I was unprepared to share it.

My mind reeled back over the years to when I was a twelve-year-old boy in love with a book, Harper Lee's *To Kill a Mockingbird*. I had been mesmerized by Atticus Finch and his display of courage and integrity in defending a black man in the Deep South accused of raping a white woman. He became my lodestar. I wanted to be Atticus when I grew up. The law was a noble and honorable profession, I thought. I would defend the little guy. I would help those who couldn't help themselves. Somehow it hadn't turned out quite that way. I was part of a profession whose members—trial lawyers in particular—are considered to be greedy, evil, and dishonest practitioners who will take any client for a fee.

My vision of honor and heroism had been further defined by a television show, broadcast in the 1960s in black and white. *The Defenders* were a father-and-son team of defense attorneys. Dad was a sharp, veteran litigator who mentored his green and idealistic son. They took on wildly unpopular clients and causes. They opposed capital punishment, "no knock" search laws, McCarthyism, and blacklists, while upholding custody rights of adoptive parents and the insanity defense. The show was brutally realistic. Father and son lost as many cases as they won, maybe more. But they always fought the good fight and respected one another. That sort of relationship was sorely lacking amid the boozing and anger of the home in which I was raised. Legal career aside, I had longed for that sort of father-son relationship during my own childhood but never got it.

My reflection on these formative experiences was the reminiscence of a split second, none of it spoken aloud. Instead I answered Christopher's question with a cop-out: "Sometimes I really don't know why I became a lawyer, Chris." What I didn't add was "... especially at a time like this." I didn't want to make him any more afraid for me than he already was. Exhaustion and anxiety cost me a teaching moment with my young, very bright and impressionable son. Perhaps I've corrected that mistake here. I hope so.

Chapter 24: A Secret Deal

Bob and I met again the week after the arraignment. It was now time to get down to the real business of preparing a defense, allocating responsibilities, and figuring out what in hell we were going to do to stop the railroad express. We were puzzled by the fact that the state chose to indict both Sal and Mabel. St. Rita's was owned by a company called Buffman, Inc. Mabel had told us she held 80 percent of the shares and Sal 10 percent. Mabel's brother Tony owned the residual 10 percent. Because Mabel was the majority shareholder, the state license to operate the home was in her name and she was the person ultimately responsible for patient care and safety. With no license and only minority ownership, Sal was not legally responsible, or so we thought. I surmised that the state indicted him to avoid seeming to gang up on a white-haired grandmother. Much later we would learn that Sal was actually the president of Buffman, Inc. That meant defenses could be asserted on his behalf inconsistent with Mabel's interests. Ergo, we had an ethical conflict. Sal was entitled to conflict-free representation. We needed to hire another lawyer for him. We needed the help and another agile mind to prepare and execute a defense not yet fully formed. But who should we get?

I had received more than a half-dozen phone calls from lawyer colleagues wanting to get in on this high-profile, if seemingly impossible, case. Some calls came from as far away as Chicago and Fort Lauderdale. As Bob and I hashed out our options, we looked at each other and both said the same name at the exact same time: John Reed. John was an accomplished criminal lawyer and, along with his partner Robert Glass, was part of the *crème de la crème* of the criminal defense bar in New Orleans. I had known him since I was in law school. He was born in England, came to the United States as a boy, and distinguished himself academically. He was an elegant lawyer, erudite and educated—Harvard College and Yale Law. He had come south after law school as a wild-eyed liberal working for peanuts to represent the poor and disenfranchised. His practice had ultimately evolved into a strictly criminal one. His reputation was impeccable and he was known for his ability to win cases based on his deep knowledge of legal precedent. He could become the legal brains of our operation. Bob and I were instantly agreed and I was commissioned to call him.

"Hi, John," I said. "It's Jim Cobb."

"Well, well, well," he said. "What's an old, broken-down admiralty insurance defense lawyer like you doing in the biggest criminal case in America?" he asked. It would have been impossible for him to have missed my many television appearances.

"Funny you should ask," I responded. "That's why I'm calling." I explained our situation with Sal and Mabel and our belief that Sal needed separate, unconflicted counsel. He agreed.

"Assuming we can work out the financial details," I said, "want to play?"

Without hesitation he answered, "Love to!"

Finally our team was fully formed, and I couldn't have been happier. We were three totally different people who would have to find a way to work together for Sal and Mabel's benefit. Egos would have to be left at the door, a daunting prospect when dealing with veteran trial lawyers. I brought John up to speed on where we stood and what was contemplated going forward. In viewing the case from afar, he had already concluded that the whole prosecution was a grandstanding attempt by Foti to scapegoat the Manganos—an abusive maneuver by a politically motivated windbag. Of course, John felt that way about *most* prosecutions. I teased him: "Are you prepared to give up your membership in the Communist Party for the duration of the case *and* cut off your ponytail?" "Neither," came the immediate and emphatic reply. We were off and running.

"So what do they have on Sal?" he asked.

"Nothing," I answered. "I have no idea why he was even charged. You've got a slam dunk winner, a cakewalk," or so I thought at the time.

Months later as John studiously pored over mountains of documents, he discovered a letter written by Sal that was potentially devastating for both Sal and Mabel. John presented himself at my office, entering the conference room and closing the door behind him. He put his worn, hippie briefcase on the table, opened it, and pulled out the worrisome document: a letter certifying, as part of St. Rita's emergency plan, that a transportation company would evacuate all patients. The transportation company was proudly in possession of one van—one van to evacuate fifty-nine elderly patients and their life-sustaining medical equipment. Who was the owner of the van and, thus, of the "transportation company"? Sal Mangano.

John flipped the document across the conference room table, asking sarcastically, "Is this your idea of a cakewalk?"

"Oops," I said. "I didn't know about this."

"Obviously," he answered. "But it's your job to know about this, and it's a huge problem."

"Indeed it is," I said, smiling brightly. "But now it's *your* problem, John Boy. Great to have you on board!"

I wasn't giving up on getting rid of Foti. The state's initial defense to my motion to disqualify Foti—that "the grand jury might not indict"—was now certified hogwash, as we knew all along. I sent the papers to John asking his view of the motion and whether we should continue to pursue it. He termed the content of what I had written, "incendiary, inflammatory, and deservedly pejorative."

"Foti will hate it, so we should probably re-file it," he said. "The bigger question and issue is how do we get a change of venue, for without it I don't believe we stand a chance." I began to assemble the data supporting a motion for change of venue. We chronicled all of Foti's impermissible press comments. In addition, we compiled an exhaustive record of all the pre-trial publicity, 99-percent of it negative. Finally, the icing on the cake was Foti's solicitation of me and the Manganos for donations. Which was it: an incredibly dumb mistake or a *bona fide* shakedown and extortion? The real answer didn't matter. Having to answer the charges could prove a major political embarrassment to the attorney general. Just as importantly, we charged him with violations of the lawyer's code of conduct, and we had him dead to rights on several rule violations. The Louisiana State Bar Association might have to get involved, which could result in a public reprimand.

I filed both motions and scheduled them to be heard in open court, with both sides making their arguments. To rub salt in the A.G.'s wound, we served him with a subpoena to appear as a witness to be cross-examined by me on the motion to disqualify. Since we alleged bias, prejudice, and improper comments and conduct, we believed we were entitled to his testimony, on the record, in open court. Somehow, all our filings made it into the hands of the major television stations, print reporters, and other interested media. Someone had highlighted the most inflammatory language and charges in the motions, making the job much easier for anyone who wanted to report on the filings. We were in a two-front war. The first front was obvious—the defense of the Manganos in the 118-count criminal indictment. The second front was the media and the impact they could have on public opinion and, ultimately, the jury pool. So far, we were losing both wars rather badly. The two motions were our first opportunity to turn the tide, stop the bleeding, and try to take the high ground.

The attorney general's office acted predictably and angrily. They filed a Motion to Quash the subpoena of Foti, saying our side could not call as a witness the other side's lawyer. As a general rule of law, they were correct. However, given the serious nature of our charges and the now infamous solicitation letter to a criminal defendant *and* her lawyer, Judge Winsberg denied the state's Motion to Quash and ordered the A.G. to show up for the hearing to be cross-examined by me. I salivated at the prospect. After dousing him with starter fluid, I intended to light up the briquette-in-chief. My dream was to disqualify Foti and his office and get a new prosecutor who would then dismiss all the charges. I met with Bob and John, and revealed my strategy. As I outlined my plan of attack, these experienced criminal lawyers were looking at each other, not at me. The look on their faces revealed their thoughts: "Do you want to tell him or should I?"

Because John was the newest team member, he deferred to Bob. "Uh, Jim, I don't know exactly how to say this, but you've got virtually no chance of winning this motion."

"What do you mean?" I shot back. "Foti has violated the rules, committed ethical breaches and basically attempted to extort the Manganos *and* me. How can we not win?"

"Jerry Winsberg is not going to find that Foti has done anything unethical requiring his disqualification. When Foti was sheriff in Orleans Parish for thirty-two years, Winsberg was a judge in the same building. They were on the same team, locking up the bad guys. They probably supported each other politically through bunches of elections. Winsberg may be a stand-up guy. I don't know. But he won't do this," said Bob.

"I agree with Bob," chimed in the pony-tailed communist, "but let it play out. Who knows what might happen. Plus, I know you have your heart set on gutting him, so why not? It'll be fun to watch." It was a reality check I guess I needed.

The state filed its opposition to our motion for change of venue and it was impressive and depressing. The law was totally on their side. Louisiana courts frowned upon changes of venue. The moving party had to prove that it was virtually impossible to get a fair trial in the jurisdiction in which the case was pending. Some judges would even start picking a jury before deciding whether to change venue, in order to see if they couldn't find fair-minded jurors. If that process were to begin, we were toast. John was our resident state law expert and he confirmed that the A.G.'s argument was essentially correct.

"Terrific," I thought. I'm going to further enrage the bullish A.G. in attempting to disqualify him—a motion I'm sure to lose. Plus, the law is against me on changing venue. What else could possibly go wrong? I shouldn't have asked. I came into possession of some terrible information. St. Bernard Parish, a place of hard-headed, self-reliant residents who rarely evacuated for hurricanes, had undergone a change of heart ahead of Katrina. Ninety-two percent of the residents of the parish had, in fact, evacuated. So had the other three nursing homes in the parish, making St. Rita's the *only* home in the parish that had not. Accordingly, if the case remained in St. Bernard, 92 percent of our potential jurors, looking at the same information Sal and Mabel were looking at, made the exact opposite decision about evacuation. Trying a case with this kind of audience in the jury box would ensure only one verdict: guilty.

But something else was happening in Baton Rouge. The assistants handling the case were experiencing extreme gastrointestinal distress at the prospect of their boss having to testify as a witness. I suspect the attorney general was feeling it, too. They filed a writ to the Court of Appeal seeking to have Judge Winsberg's denial of their Motion to Quash the subpoena requiring Foti to testify reversed. They lost. Foti was going to have to testify and they all were clearly disturbed at the prospect. Foti was pretty good on script and on message but was not very nimble intellectually in a cross-examination situation, and his handlers and assistants knew this. They had also read the *Esquire* article and believed that my furious vendetta with their boss had pushed me to the edge of insanity. There was some truth in both their assumptions. Crazy or not, I was a skilled cross-examiner who might well make their boss look foolish. I often told my law students that cross-examination was the anvil upon which truth was forged, a quote from Justice Oliver Wendell Holmes. My intention, as Foti's assistants well knew, was to place the A.G. on the anvil and pound him flat.

The day drew near, and media started buzzing around, drawn by the nectar of our allegations against the state's chief law enforcement officer. Regardless of the outcome, it was going to be one hell of a show. On the Friday before the Monday hearing, I received a call from the lead assistant handling the case. He started by saying that he thought the judge was wrong in forcing his boss to testify. I reminded him that the Court of Appeal had backed Winsberg's decision. "Well, we're thinking about going to the Supreme Court, seeking reversal," he said.

"Go ahead," I said. "You waste your time doing that while I prepare to turn your boss into shish kebab on a hot grill. Frankly, I don't give a shit what you guys do." There was a long pause.

"Would you consider dropping your motion to disqualify our office, eliminating the necessity of General Foti testifying, if we dropped our opposition to your motion for change of venue?" he asked quietly. Uncharacteristically, I met quiet with quiet. I flashed back to Bob and John's strong belief that we were likely to lose the disqualification motion anyway. I thought of the mob scene outside the courthouse as we made our way into arraignment. The only instruments the crowd lacked were torches, pitchforks, and a noose or two. The fact that the state proposed to have no opposition to a change of venue did not mean that the judge would automatically grant our motion and order a change of venue—he was not necessarily bound by their lack of opposition. But no opposition was a huge first step in the right direction.

I responded, "Okay, let me think about it. . . . We'll do the deal!" I said after pausing for about five seconds. Neither one of us trusted the other.

"Who's going to get up first?" I asked. "You drop your opposition to the change of venue and then I'll say we dismiss our motion to disqualify your office."

"No," the assistant said. "You go first since you filed the disqualification motion first and it is scheduled to be heard first."

I feared a double-cross. These were the same folks who had agreed to meet with Sal and Mabel and hear their side of the story, only to cancel the meeting and haul them off to jail.

"Let's take it up with the judge on Monday and ask him how he wants to proceed," I suggested.

"Okay," came the reply.

"But we are agreed, right?" I asked.

"We are," came the government's answer.

It was the right move, even though it denied me a delectable moment in the sun, cross-examining Foti on some deeply embarrassing issues. Plus, we had discovered the government's Achilles' heel—they would agree to anything to avoid my putting their boss on the witness stand. We would threaten this again and again at trial, each time obtaining the desired result. They'd drop objections and agree to the admission of questionable evidence—anything to keep Foti off the stand. It was a powerful hammer to wield and wield it we did.

Monday's hearing was packed. Foti and I had gone at each other tooth and nail through the media. Now reporters salivated over the prospect of watching us duke it out in court. Both sides met with the judge in chambers, beyond the media's prying ears. I began to explain the agreement to the judge, we'd do this if they do that, and he interrupted saying, "I don't want to know about any of your side deals. We're going to do this on the record, not back here." His comments caught me off guard as most judges love it when the parties settle their differences and spare the judge the burden of making the decision for them. The gravity of the case evidently meant that the judge was going to play it by the book. One hundred and eighteen counts of homicide and cruelty trumped our usual way of doing business.

On the way back into the courtroom, I told the assistant, "Look, you guys hosed us once; you're not going to do it again. You've got to trust me on this one. I don't have a boss second guessing and making me break my word. You go first."

"Okay," he said. He announced that the state had no opposition to a change of venue and I stood, saying, we dismiss our motion to disqualify.

"There will be no need for testimony on the motion, Your Honor," I added.

The judge then said, "I was inclined to grant a change of venue, with or without the state's opposition."

An audible groan went up from the press gallery. I made no comment about what we did and why, and, not surprisingly, the press never figured it out. The details of how we got out of St. Bernard Parish are revealed here for the first time. We were triumphant, but we did not pop champagne corks. We still had to deal with a case involving 118 counts and the deaths of thirty-five innocent elderly. We did not know yet to which parish the case would be transferred. But getting out of St. Bernard Parish filled our sails with hope—at least we stood a chance.

The judge asked both sides to submit memoranda on where the case should be transferred. We studied population and demographic data, trying to find a parish similar to St. Bernard in size, racial mix, educational and income levels, and so forth. It was a race to the bottom. There was no other parish in Louisiana quite like St. Bernard. Of course, we would have loved to suggest a parish that was "friendly" or "fair" to criminal defendants. There was no such place in Louisiana and probably no such place in America. We were part of the Deep South and the prevailing assumption was that if you got charged with a crime, you were probably guilty. Conviction rates were and are astonishingly high in America. Most criminal defendants "bargain"—pleading guilty to something or other in exchange for a reduced sentence. If the defendants decided that they wanted to go to trial, forcing the state to prove them guilty beyond a reasonable doubt, those state court defendants were convicted more than 90 percent of the time. The federal system was even worse. Federal criminal defendants, who chose trial over a plea, were convicted 95 to 96 percent of the time. Thus, there was no "friendly" place we could find.

We settled instead on suggesting venues where the residents, the potential jurors, did not have to make an evacuation decision themselves for Katrina. Of those who made an evacuation decision, more than 90 percent chose to flee in advance of the monster. I know I did. Of those who stayed, more than 1,600 had died and the vast majority of the rest deeply regretted their decision to shelter in place. We presented our detailed models and data to the judge weeks later. He called a conference with both sides present to announce his decision.

"We're going to move the case to West Feliciana Parish, in the town of St. Francisville," he announced. West Feliciana was a tiny parish with a population one-sixth that of St. Bernard. There was little racial diversity. More troubling was the fact that the parish was home to the Louisiana State Penitentiary at Angola, America's largest maximum security jail and one of its most dangerous. I worried that we'd wind up with a jury pool packed with prison guards and employees of the big state hospital. After all, our opponent in the case *was* the State of Louisiana, the largest employer in the parish. "Isn't that sort of stacking the deck against us?" I asked the judge.

"I wouldn't worry about that," he answered. "I know the area well. It's a very eclectic place. There are a bunch of artists, writers, and interesting people who live there. We'll get a fair jury," he maintained. What I didn't learn until later was that after Katrina the judge had bought himself a condominium in a development just outside of St. Francisville, known as "the Bluffs." This wasn't a vacation home; it was an "evacuation" home, a safe, high and dry place to which he and his family could flee during the craziness of hurricane season. It was only about ninety minutes north of New Orleans yet far removed from the dangers of hurricane-force winds and flooding. It was a smart move. It also meant that in choosing St. Francisville, the judge, unlike us, wouldn't be living in a hotel room. It also meant that he would be bringing the economic benefits of a five-week trial to his newly adopted home away from home. Hotels and restaurants would be full and the back bar at the Magnolia Café would do a bang-up business.

As we left the conference, Bob turned to me and said in his usual dead-pan voice, "Well, at least we're out of St. Bernard." He was right, of course, but we were both uncomfortable with the insular, lost-in-time town of St. Francisville. Months later, on the first day of jury selection, we were handed the list of 150 or so unlucky residents of West Feliciana Parish who had been called to service. I did a quick count and almost 35 percent of the potential jurors were law-enforcement officers, prison guards, or had a member of their immediate family in law enforcement. Several of the potential jurors were in full police uniform as they sat in the courtroom—not exactly the kind of message a defendant wants sent to other jurors.

At a private conference at the judge's bench, I flipped through the pages of names and occupations. "Where are all the artists, writers, and eclectic people? All I see are cops and prison guards," I said sarcastically.

"Quit whining," the judge snapped back, "and start picking."

It would take us five full days to pick the six jurors and three alternates who would decide Sal and Mabel's fate, but at least we were out of St. Bernard Parish.

Chapter 25: Fighting for the Advantage

The big match was all set. The 118-count indictment wasn't going away. And as per our change-of-venue deal, Foti's office would remain on the case as prosecutor. The judge set the case to begin in early August 2007. We would be in trial for four to six weeks and thus would be in session on the second anniversary of Katrina, the day when the thirty-five were lost. It would be an emotional moment for all.

Trials, especially in big cases, are like pitched battles. More often than not, it is the skirmishes that take place in advance of the battle that determine its outcome. The Union soldiers at Gettysburg didn't win on the last day simply by repelling Pickett's desperate, gallant final charge. The Yankees won it on the first day, when preliminary skirmishes gained them the high ground, forcing the Rebs to attack entrenched, fortified positions. It was a fatal error by Robert E. Lee, one that sealed the South's ultimate fate. Our skirmishes with the state began immediately, with both sides maneuvering to obtain and hold the high ground. We believed we had won the first battle in obtaining a change of venue. The state, confident in the overwhelming strength of its evidence, believed it didn't matter where the case was tried. One of us was about to be proved terribly wrong.

Every American citizen should know that it is the state which bears the burden of proof in a criminal prosecution, for it is the state which has brought the charges. Every American should know that the state's burden is a high one; it must prove the defendants' guilt "beyond a reasonable doubt." Whether all jurors give defendants that benefit is an open question. Theoretically, all we had to do was play "good defense;" we weren't required to prove our innocence, nor were Sal and Mabel required to testify. They were cloaked in and protected by the presumption of innocence and could stand on that presumption without saying a word. Although these principles are the very foundation of our republic, in the context of the

St. Rita's case, they were pure, unadulterated bullshit, and we knew it. We would have to mount an offensive, for the entire world already believed the Manganos were guilty. They had been stripped of a defendant's most sacred presumption.

But while we bore no burden of proof, we did carry what I call the "burden of explanation and persuasion." We had to explain to the jury that the decisions Sal and Mabel made in the teeth of disaster were reasonable under the circumstances, not criminal. And therein lay our biggest challenge: fulfilling our self-imposed "burden of explanation and persuasion" without subjecting Sal and Mabel—or us lawyers—to the uncertainties that would come with putting them on the stand.

The state struck first. They filed a notice of their intent to offer evidence of what the other nursing homes in St. Bernard Parish did in advance of Katrina—*they evacuated!* Only one resident in one of these three homes had died during the evacuation process, a result dramatically better than the thirty-five we lost by drowning. Of course we opposed the state's attempt to use this evidence. We argued that what some other nursing home did with a different patient population in a different location was irrelevant to the central issue in the case: had the Manganos acted reasonably given *their* circumstances, *their* location, *their* patient population, and *their* experience? The "reasonable man" standard hinged on a mythical creature, not what some real person did in real life, someplace else. The fact that the other three nursing homes guessed right did not make our decision wrong, much less a crime. The prejudicial effect of the extraneous evidence would far outweigh its probative value. It was an esoteric legal point, but an important one, and it was not lost on the cagey Judge Winsberg.

At the argument on the motion, the judge put his practical stamp on the issue. "Look," he said, "it's bad enough that I've got to try one nursing home case with thirty-five deaths. I don't want to try the particulars of three other homes and what they did and didn't do." I pointed out that there were fifty-seven nursing homes in the New Orleans area and surrounding parishes in the Katrina impact zone. I told the court that my information indicated that thirty-six of the fifty-seven homes had acted as we had—they didn't evacuate and chose, as we did, to shelter in place. "The state can't just cherry pick three, Your Honor," I said. "If they're allowed to put that in, I'm going to put in the how, why, and when of the other thirty-six homes who did the same as we did! That way the trial can last six months, not six weeks," I added sarcastically.

To be sure, our team loved the evidence that thirty-six out of fifty-seven did as we did, and we would have liked to get that information into evidence. But the stark contrast of the three other St. Bernard nursing homes evacuating was highly prejudicial. As to the state's request, the judge cut to the chase: "Mr. Cobb, do you want it in or out?"

We took a break so Bob, John, and I could confer in private. We were conflicted. We sure liked the data that sixty-three percent of all area nursing homes made the same decision we did, but we hated to admit that had we done what the other three St. Bernard homes did, there would have been no deaths by drowning at St. Rita's. The judge waited impatiently for our answer. Bob finally crystalized our choice, "If they want it in, I'm opposed to it," he said reflexively in his own inimitable way. We were agreed. We returned to the courtroom and I served as spokesman.

"So what is it, Mr. Cobb? In or out?" the judge asked.

"We want it out!" I said emphatically.

"Then out it is!" ruled the judge without giving the state lawyers a chance to speak further.

They went crazy with protest. "If I let you put in what those three homes did, I've got to let the defense put in what thirty-six out of fifty-seven did. You're better off without it," he reasoned.

The state's lawyers, furious at the ruling, asked the judge to set the time for them to appeal, which they announced they intended to do immediately. The judge set the return date and the state filed an aggressive appeal. We opposed it. Their "story," their vision of how they wished to present their case, obviously hinged on getting this evidence in. They also had the advantage of limitless resources as Foti threw more lawyers at the case.

They won. The Court of Appeal reversed Judge Winsberg's ruling, writing that he could not summarily exclude all evidence of what other nursing homes did or didn't do. He would have to allow the state to lay a foundation, as to the similarity of the circumstances of each nursing home. If those circumstances turned out to be "highly similar" to St. Rita's, he would have to allow the evidence. The burden of explanation suddenly weighed heavier; it had expanded. "If all the other homes in the parish left, why didn't St. Rita's?" would be the question burning in the jury's mind. We thought our answer would be that thirty-six of fifty-seven homes in the affected area sheltered in place just as we did, and that answer would be sufficient. We were to be abandoned by a politically tricked-up Louisiana Supreme Court, which disingenuously cited a hearsay rule in decreeing that we couldn't allude to the thirty-six of fifty-seven homes that had *not* evacuated. By a four-to-three vote, the Supreme Court tried to gut our case; the effect was devastating.

As the multiple pre-trial skirmishes continued, we labored to give voice and witness to our own narrative. What was our story to be that would explain the tragedy to the jury and persuade them that Sal and Mabel were not criminals? The linchpin of our defense was Mabel's belief that had she chosen evacuation, many of her beloved residents would have died in the process. That was her clear belief; she had eight to ten special-needs patients—people on oxygen, feeder tubes, or unable to even sit up for any extended period of time. Had she chosen evacuation, she asked me repeatedly, "Whose plug do I pull first, Jim? Your mom's? Sal's mom's? I just couldn't bring myself to do that." But how would we prove that Mabel's concern was rooted in medical fact?

As with all things medical, I turned to my partner Susan Henning. She was my newest partner and the only one in the firm fully supportive of my defense of the Manganos. She had been director of medical records at one of New Orleans' premier hospitals. She knew her way around a patient's chart. She chose to go to law school after being exposed to some of the horrors of nursing homes in that industry's dark days, decades ago. She was a reformer and an advocate for nursing-home residents. The irony of her now joining in the defense of the most notorious nursing home owners in America was not lost on either of us.

The state had seized all the computers, patient charts, and records as part of their crime scene investigation after the bodies were removed from St. Rita's. They stored the data in an upstairs room in the St. Bernard Parish courthouse. They had no idea what to do with the information. Susan did. We filed motions and got the property returned. The written records, soaked and splattered with mud and mold, were a mess. Some needed to be professionally restored to be readable. There was hysteria and widespread fear that even handling items that had marinated in Katrina's toxic floodwaters could have lasting health repercussions. Susan termed the hysteria and fear "foolishness" and dove right in. She suffered no ill health consequences. Susan sat in a closed conference room for weeks on end, meticulously poring over the stained medical records and charts of the fifty-nine residents of St. Rita's. At the end of this exhaustive process, she emerged to state emphatically, "At least seven residents would not have survived an evacuation." Armed with this conclusion, all we needed was an expert witness, a board-certified medical doctor to testify to the grave condition of the residents and the belief that many would have died in an evacuation. Who would it be? We looked at each other and sang in unison and on key, "Brobson!"

Dr. Brobson Lutz was not only a graduate of Tulane's med school and board-certified in both internal medicine and infectious disease, he was also a former health director for the City of New Orleans and the best testifying expert I had ever seen. He loved the stage; he loved the spotlight; and his testimony in this case was to take place in a national and international arena, the biggest on which he had ever performed. His native Alabama accent was right out of central casting and would play perfectly in rural St. Francisville. He would rise to the occasion, and between the two of us, we would design some surprises for the prosecution during their cross-examination. We had worked together a dozen times before and always got great results. When Lutz got done popping one of our surprises on the stand, prosecutors sometimes resembled Wile E. Coyote (*Carnivorous vulgaris*), of *Road Runner* cartoons fame, after opening a door in search of his nemesis and instead getting a face full of dynamite. In my dreams, Lutz leans over the prosecution's table as he leaves the stand and whispers, "Beep! Beep!" I held off on sharing that fantasy with him for only one reason: I was afraid Lutz just might do it!

The next part of our narrative was by now well rehearsed: the loss of life at St. Rita's—and everywhere else—was the fault of the U.S. Army Corps of Engineers, the United States government, the State of Louisiana and St. Bernard Parish, a collective and colossal failure in disaster planning and emergency management. I had the Corps' own report in which they admitted fault, and it would be nicely complemented by Ivor van Heerden's testimony, based on his book.

Several other scientific panels also found fault with the government. A team of scientists from the University of California at Berkley was commissioned and funded by the National Science Foundation (NSF). The American Society of Civil Engineers (ASCE) began its own separate, independent investigation. Even the Corps of Engineers appointed an Independent Performance Evaluation Team (IPET) to look at its operation. Finally, no longer trusting the national government or anyone associated with it, the State of Louisiana had appointed and funded Team Louisiana—which examined the failures from a Louisiana perspective. At various points in time, I plugged into all these investigations, anxiously awaiting their findings—and every one of them delivered. The government had been culpable in countless ways for the catastrophe that only began with a big storm in the Gulf of Mexico. If we were able to get this information into evidence, our chances would improve enormously. The state knew this as well as we did, so they swiftly filed a motion to block any effort on our part to demonstrate third-party fault.

Their argument was simple. This was a case about the Manganos and their failure to evacuate, they said. It wasn't a case about the U.S. Army

Corps, or FEMA, or state and local officials. We couldn't blame others for our failures and any attempt to do so was an irrelevant distraction designed to divert the jury's attention from the only real issue in the case—did the Manganos commit negligent homicide and cruelty to the elderly and infirm? The government was, of course, correct. It was our job to divert the jury's attention. Their job was to narrow the scope of events with a laser-like focus on just what Sal and Mabel did or didn't do. Our job was to expand the focus. There is an old saying among lawyers who do criminal defense work: find someone else to blame other than your client and do a better job of prosecuting them than the government does of prosecuting the defendant. This was our mission, but would the judge allow it? Particularly when the "someone else" that we had found to blame was the government itself?

In the run-up to the hearing on whether evidence of third-party fault would be allowed, I found myself doing something to which I was unaccustomed— legal research. I knew where the library was in our office; I had to walk through it on my way to Susan's office in order to beg for her assistance on the latest medical issue. I didn't know where all the books were kept, but I thought I knew how to find some of them. On one such excursion into the library, I found myself in a back corner reviewing materials in preparation for the class I was teaching at Tulane. In the row next to my materials, a stack of U.S. Supreme Court advance opinions, all loose, unorganized, and not yet placed in binders had been shoved off to the side, hidden by whoever had library duty and was too lazy to do the job correctly. "Look at this shit," I thought to myself, picking up the opinion on top of the stack. The case—*Bobby Lee Holmes v. South Carolina*—was very recent, and was also quite unusual in a divided and increasingly politicized court for yielding a unanimous decision. More typically in a criminal case, the vote would have been five to four, with Justice Anthony Kennedy swinging back and forth between the court's conservative and liberal blocks. Intrigued, I glanced down to the bottom of the first page and read the one sentence summary of the court's holding. I almost fell over. "Holding: . . . that the exclusion of defense evidence of third-party guilt denied defendant a fair trial." I raced back to my office, found a highlighter, and devoured the opinion whole.

On New Year's Eve, 1989, eighty-six-year old Mary Stewart had been beaten, raped, and robbed in her home. She later died of complications stemming from her injuries. Bobby Lee Holmes was convicted by a South Carolina jury of murder, first-degree sexual conduct, first-degree burglary and robbery, and was sentenced to death. The prosecution relied heavily on overwhelming forensic evidence: (1) Holmes' palm print was found just above the doorknob on the interior side of the front door of the victim's house; (2) fibers consistent with a black sweatshirt owned by Bobby Lee were found on Mary's bedsheets; (3) matching blue fibers were found on the victim's pink nightgown and on the defendant's blue jeans; (4) microscopically consistent fibers were found on the pink nightgown and on Holmes' underwear; (5) Holmes' underwear contained a mixture of DNA from two individuals, and 99.99-percent of the population of the planet other than Holmes and Mary Stewart were excluded as contributors to that mixture; and (6) the defendant's tank top was found to contain a mixture of his blood and Mary's. In addition, the prosecution introduced evidence that Holmes had been seen near Stewart's home within an hour of the time the state alleged the attack took place. Talk about a slam dunk! The jury convicted Holmes swiftly and he was sentenced to death.

Holmes appealed, alleging he was prevented from offering crucial evidence in his defense, evidence that another man, Jimmy White, had attacked Stewart. He rustled up some witnesses who placed White in the victim's neighborhood on the day in question. Yet more witnesses were prepared to testify that White acknowledged he, not Holmes, had raped and killed the eighty-six-year-old. The "word on the street" was that White had explained himself by saying, "Well, you know, I like older women." A tough South Carolina trial judge had excluded all this testimony, citing the overwhelming amount of the incontrovertible forensic evidence and that White, predictably, had denied saying the things attributed to him.

In reversing Holmes' conviction, the ultra-conservative U.S. Supreme Court asserted that the trial judge's exclusion of the "word on the street" evidence and the hearsay testimony of others implicating White denied Holmes "a meaningful opportunity to present a complete defense." They sent the case back to South Carolina to be re-tried. A criminal defendant was entitled to present his version of events, even when overwhelming forensic evidence supported a guilty verdict. For our purposes, the ruling was an unexpected gift from on high. Surely, if the murderous Mr. Holmes had a right to put on highly questionable "word on the street" hearsay, then we had a right to put on evidence of the Army Corps' fault and the fault of federal, state, and local officials underlying the deaths at St. Rita's.

At the oral argument on the state's motion, I stumbled upon some unscripted wording that we would use again and again at the trial. It would have an explosive impact on our opponents. "Judge," I said, "this is a homicide case. Under the Supreme Court's decision in *Holmes*, we get to point the finger of blame, no matter how tenuous, at someone we believe responsible for the deaths. Sal and Mabel didn't kill the residents at St. Rita's, *they did*," I said, pointing right at the prosecutors representing the

State of Louisiana. It wasn't a planned argument; it just came out that way. The prosecutors were furious, with smoke pouring out of their ears and steam rising from their collars. "Beep! Beep!" I thought to myself.

The judge denied their motion to exclude evidence of third-party fault, which meant we could draw on the thousands of pages of reports exhaustively detailing the failures of government that had led to a wall of water washing over St. Bernard Parish and the nursing home owned by our clients. A nine to zero decision by the U.S. Supreme Court was unassailable and, for our case, heaven-sent. We would ride it as far as it would take us. No longer were we defending a hapless couple against long odds. We were prosecutors as much as the state was. In the crosshairs at the center of our case was government incompetence and its role in the thirty-five murders for which Sal and Mabel had been indicted.

Chapter 26: What Would Jesus Do?

Our offensive game plan was set, and we were confident that most of our story would be heard by the jury. The question that remained was how to tell that story without using Sal or Mabel in the telling of it. Here's why: Defendants who testify in their own behalf are often their own worst enemy. Sometimes inarticulate and always scared at the possibility of conviction and incarceration, these testifying defendants often come off as shifty, nervous, and possibly untruthful. A jury can read body language well and a testifying defendant always gave away an inescapable emotion—fear.

But if we were reluctant to put Sal and Mabel on the stand, we were downright eager to exercise our rights under another provision of the law, the one that requires prosecutors to turn over everything they might have against a defendant and to do so before the trial begins. Decades ago the U.S. Supreme Court ruled that if prosecutors had knowledge or evidence in their files that tended to "exonerate or exculpate" a defendant they had charged with a crime, they were legally obligated to turn that evidence over to the other side. The exculpatory material became known as "Brady" material, so named because the case which first established the proposition was *Brady v. Maryland*. The case and the principle became enshrined in American law.

Louisiana prosecutors, particularly in Orleans Parish, became infamous for their violations of the "Brady" rule, sending people to prison for decades for crimes they knew they did not commit. The prosecutors and the convictions they obtained were reversed again and again. John filed our "Brady" motion, demanding any and all information in the possession of the state that might tend to exonerate Sal and Mabel. Given our defense—that federal, state, and local officials through their negligence/incompetence had caused or contributed to the deaths at St. Rita's—they were likely to have a boatload of information responsive to our request. It put the state on the defensive and was designed to burden *them* with going through all things

Katrina, to produce information that would help us. Prosecutors hated wasting their time reviewing evidence and information and determining whether it was "Brady" material. If they failed to turn over exculpatory information to us in their possession, it would be excellent grounds for an appeal and reversal of any conviction. Sadly, we were already thinking about an appeal. Although the "Brady" motion was standard operating procedure, its potential negative impact in distracting our opponents and consuming their resources was genius. We had taken the high ground.

The prosecutors counter-attacked and totally outflanked us. In response to our "Brady" motion, they offered to provide us with access to all the material the state was required to produce to the United States House and Senate as part of the congressional investigations following the Katrina debacle. Every piece of paper, every email, every transcript of every meeting, and every document was available. Initially, I thought we had them. We would get to see their entire file which, I believed, would be overflowing with usable information. I asked the assistant A.G. how voluminous the material was and when we could pick it up. There was no picking it up, he responded. Everything had been provided to Congress electronically. They would give us a password and user code so we could see it all ourselves. Terrific, I thought, "How big is the file?" I asked. "A little more than 300,000 pages," he replied with a hint of "Gotcha!" in his tone of voice. I was flabbergasted. This mountain of information looked basically insurmountable.

In opening up everything to us, the government accomplished two important goals. First, they put the onus of finding Brady material on us. It would be unacceptably expensive and a waste of lawyer time to go through 300,000 pages of material when we didn't even know what we were looking for. Second, in giving us everything they had, the government immunized themselves against the charge that they had not shared any exculpatory evidence in their possession. Were Sal and Mabel to be convicted, any appeal based on a violation of the Brady rule would mean a sure loss. Instead of saying good-bye at the end of our conversation, the prosecutor should have said checkmate.

It was a Thursday afternoon and I was in a foul mood as I headed off to teach my class at Tulane Law School. Perhaps I could take it out on some ill-prepared student, I thought. As I stood at the lectern in front of one hundred or so would-be legal eagles, I had an epiphany. Wait a second, I thought, I've got one hundred sets of trained eyes right here in front of me! If I could somehow get all of them to volunteer to review portions of the material, that would be only 3,000 pages per person—a huge amount of information but a whole lot better than 300,000! We couldn't afford to pay a hundred law clerks. Sal and Mabel were strapped financially, had lost their means of income, and were ripping through their savings paying us to fight for their lives. In America, in spite of slogans like "Equal justice under law" and other platitudes, if defendants don't have money, there is nothing equal about the justice they receive. Finances were clearly a huge issue for the defense. The state knew no such limitations as their money pit was bottomless—your tax dollars at work.

I had to find a hook. At the end of class I made an announcement that I was looking for some help in the Mangano case. My students were well aware of it, as we frequently discussed issues in the case and strategies I was considering. It was much more interesting for the students to be discussing a real-life case in real-time than some old case gathering dust in a law book. In making the request for help, I found my hook: "Who knows," I said, "one of you might be the next Darby Shaw."

Darby Shaw was the lead character in John Grisham's suspense thriller, *The Pelican Brief*. She was also a fictional Tulane law student. In the novel, two U.S. Supreme Court Justices are murdered and Darby writes a brief, "The Pelican Brief," suggesting who the murderers might be working for. She presents it to her Tulane law professor, her mentor, with whom she is also having an affair. Her professor/lover and others are promptly murdered and Darby goes on the run, certain that she is the next target. It's a great read that made a decent movie, starring Julia Roberts and Denzel Washington. Julia had hung around Tulane for weeks researching her part, hanging out with students, and attending classes. She never sat in on one of mine. I would have remembered that.

"This is your chance!" I said enthusiastically to my students. "You might find the key to this case and might wind up in a book or movie or both!" When class was over, a half-dozen students approached me saying they were interested in getting into the fight. They helped devise a methodology to research the 300,000 computer pages by scanning them for key words and phrases. The students would review the information and print anything they thought remotely interesting or helpful and bring it to me. I would then determine whether they should dig deeper or go on to another subject. The experience was exhilarating for the students and for me. They mined all kinds of gems from the state's own files, which would prove invaluable. Some of it was quite embarrassing for Gov. Kathleen Blanco. If one wants to even the sides in a fight against the government, sic a half-dozen motivated Tulane law students on your opponent. The scales of justice tip back into even balance, and in a court of law, even-steven means reasonable doubt and the defense wins. The kids were terrific, and while none of them had Julia Roberts' looks, their legal research skills were infinitely better, providing the Mangano defense with a much-needed shot in the arm.

The state started another firefight when it gave notice of its intention to present the jury with photographs of the thirty-five dead bodies. The photographs were delivered to my office in a sealed brown envelope stamped with the following inscription: *"Caution, Graphic Photos. Attorney Eyes Only."* Even without the warning, I dreaded opening that envelope. Somebody had to do it, but I stalled for time. To prevent anyone working in the case file from stumbling upon them, I decided to view the photographs at home and maintain possession of them there. My dread was rooted in an insight I had gained while defending the civil cases for wrongful death filed against the Manganos by angry family members. What really infuriated the survivors of the deceased was the way they believed their relatives' bodies had been handled—or mishandled—after the storm. Admittedly, it took authorities and first-responders a while to recover the bodies at St. Rita's for the simple reason that all resources were deployed toward rescuing the living. Then, as the water receded and swift recovery of the bodies became possible, the state got into a fight over money with the contractor it had hired for the job. And so another five or six days passed before the men in the hazmat suits came to the home to extract the bodies and ferry them away in ambulances. In the incredible summer heat that followed Katrina, the decomposition of the bodies accelerated and their appearance was, quite simply, hideous by the time the state documented these deaths photographically, more than two weeks after the storm.

The anger and sadness of the victims' families was only augmented by additional idiotic decisions made by the State of Louisiana. The bodies were moved to a large, temporary morgue set up outside Baton Rouge. As family members began to inquire how they could retrieve their loved ones' remains in order to bury them, they were stonewalled by more bureaucratic indecision and incompetence. Because the state believed the thirty-five were victims of a crime, each corpse had to undergo a complete autopsy to determine cause of death. This was ludicrous and insensitive in my view as the thirty-five were found floating in water in a building that had been hit by a ten-foot tidal wave. How else did the state think they might have died? Were they struck by lightning? Had they been shot by some crazed mass murderer stalking the halls of St. Rita's before the storm hit? Of course not. The sad reality was that there were 1,600 dead bodies ahead of the thirty-five, which the state had decided were also in need of autopsy. Accordingly, the state retained possession of the bodies for months, preventing family members from arranging funerals and beginning the process of closure. Ironically, at the end of these inexcusable delays, decomposition was so far advanced that coroners were unable to determine cause of death, and all the death certificates were stamped "Hurricane Related." The bureaucratic logjam had been entirely for naught—and grieving families laid all their dismay at the feet of Sal and Mabel Mangano.

I went home and promptly mixed and consumed two dry Bombay Sapphire martinis. How dry? I quietly whispered the word "vermouth" over the glasses filled with gin and ice before consuming them. Armed with liquid courage, I attempted to gain entry to the almost hermetically sealed envelope. The guys who had taped this up had done quite a job—I soon wished they had done even better. The sizable stack of color photographs began with exterior shots of the nursing home, a foot or so of water still lapping against brick. There were multiple photos of a blue van, tossed and turned by the flood, doors ajar, and covered in mud. Only later, and much to our chagrin, would we find out why the photographer was fixated on the van.

The series then moved inside the home and down the darkened, flood- and mud-stained hallways. Some walls were intact; others had been blown out. I flipped to the next photograph and was confronted by the portrait of an elderly woman in a blue nightgown, face down in about two feet of putrid water. I gasped. Many other images were at least as horrible. One depicted a man in a red robe, draped over a wheelchair with his face toward the floor. Yet another showed a man nicely tucked into his bed, but dead. His eyes and face were bloated beyond recognition. I thought I had gotten a pretty good idea of the hell that was St. Rita's final hours from the Manganos' account of their struggle against the storm. But these 8"x 11" color photographs were nauseatingly worse than anything I had imagined. For weeks to come, they were still burnt into my mind as I shut my eyes and attempted to sleep. No amount of sleeping pills could overcome them. I thought for a moment how I would feel if the persons in the photographs had been my mother or grandfather. The anger of the families who lost those thirty-five elderly relatives became suddenly very real for me.

We had to keep these photographs from the jury. Jurors are human beings and it is hard for them not to be swayed by raw emotion. That was obviously the state's plan in attempting to introduce this evidence. I dispatched my law students to research a Motion to Exclude the photographs. The argument was simple. The photos had nothing to do with whether Sal and Mabel had committed negligent homicide and were clearly designed to inflame a jury and engender sympathy for the dead and hostility toward our defendants.

Juries aren't supposed to decide cases based on sympathy or rage. There was a rule of evidence right on point. Evidence that would emotionally sway the jury more than prove any fact important to the case should be excluded, at the discretion of the trial judge. We filed the motion and set it for hearing before Judge Winsberg. We *had* to win this one.

At the argument on the motion, I went first. "Your Honor," I began, "what fact do these photos tend to prove? That people died? We know that and will stipulate to that. This is not a crime of passion where the condition of the body of a victim might be relevant. This is a *negligent* homicide case. How do photos of these poor people, left in water for two weeks by a state too cheap to get them out sooner, prove anything? The only thing this evidence proves is that the state will stop at nothing to unfairly convict the Manganos. The evidence is not relevant, it is not probative of any fact in issue, and it is disgustingly, highly prejudicial. We object."

I was astonished at the prosecutor's brief, confident response. "Judge," he said, "the state is entitled to the moral weight of its proof," and he sat down.

I jumped up in rebuttal, "What does that mean?" I almost yelled. "The government hasn't addressed any of the issues covered in our brief nor answered the question of why these photos are even remotely relevant to the crime charged."

The judge had heard and read enough. "Mr. Cobb," he said firmly, "your motion to exclude the photographic evidence is *denied*. They will be admitted and the jury will see them."

I was blown away. Evidently, this "the state is entitled to the moral weight of its proof" was some magical, talismanic phrase that must work every time. The deck continued to be stacked against us. As a concession, I was able to get the state to agree not to show any photographs where the faces of the victims were visible. Big deal. The jury would only see multiple photos of bloated, dead old people face down in water and mud, draped over wheelchairs and hanging off the edges of their beds. I was crushed at the loss. We would have to figure out a way to deal with the ruling, but at that point, I had no idea how we could possibly combat this kind of prejudice.

Yet another major pre-trial fight was brewing. Its successful resolution in our favor could, I firmly believed, lead directly to an acquittal. This time my opponent was not the attorney general's office nor would the contest be determined by a ruling from Judge Winsberg. This fight took place in private, far from the prying eyes of the law. This time my fight was with the Catholic Church of America.

In our research about which nursing homes had evacuated and which had not, we came across the Lafon Nursing Facility. Their story had received virtually no media coverage locally, owing no doubt to the church's power to control certain elements of the local media. The *Washington Post* had written a major piece on Lafon and I was stunned by the details of their tragedy. The Sisters of the Holy Family, a Catholic order of mostly African American nuns, owned, operated, and ran Lafon. The order was founded in 1842 by a free woman of part-African descent. Her sisters and those who followed in their path had cared for the elderly and infirm for more than a century. As Katrina loomed, Sister Augustine McDaniel was in charge of the nursing home and was licensed by the state as its administrator. Sister Augustine was known as a tough, no-nonsense administrator.

The patient population at Lafon was unique. The home had many private patients as well as those whose bills were covered by Medicare and Medicaid. It also had a large population of elderly nuns who came to Lafon from all over the United States. Across the street from the home was the Mother House where other nuns lived who did not require care. Many worked in the nursing home; some had other missions in the community. As the hurricane approached, Sister Augustine made the decision to shelter in place—the same decision Mabel made. But Sister Augustine's boss evidently disagreed. Mother Superior Sylvia Thibodeaux oversaw the entire congregation of nuns from her headquarters in St. Louis, Missouri. When she found out that Sister Augustine was going to shelter in place, she overruled her, sending air-conditioned buses to Lafon with orders to evacuate all the nuns in the nursing home, as well as the nuns in the Mother House. Sister Augustine, five or six members of her order, and about twenty staff stayed behind to care for Lafon's more than 100 residents. Evidently, Mother Superior's criterion for evacuation was this: if your first name was "Sister," you got out; if your first name wasn't "Sister," you stayed.

Lafon was in flood-prone eastern New Orleans, perhaps ten miles from St. Rita's as the crow flies. As the levees failed all around, the water began to rise into the nursing home to a level of three to five feet. Fearing more water would come, the staff used bed sheets to carry frail residents to the second floor. Much of the food, potable water, and medicines were left behind on the first floor and destroyed. With the loss of electricity and generator power, there was no air conditioning or fans. Temperatures soared to unbearable levels.

Staff members attempted to flag down help, but emergency vehicles swept past the home to rescue people trapped on rooftops and in attics. Finally, on the fourth day without electricity, medicine, or water, a staff member's relative found a bus. Approximately three-dozen of the one hundred residents were taken to a nursing home in Houma, ninety minutes away. The bus driver was supposed to return but was scared off by random gunfire in and around

New Orleans. Two days later FEMA workers arranged for a squadron of Black Hawk helicopters to transport the remaining residents to a triage area at Louis Armstrong New Orleans International Airport, from which they were evacuated to homes outside the flood zone. In the half-dozen days it took before help arrived, Lafon residents died horrible deaths—heat stroke, dehydration, and lack of required medicines. Twenty-two elderly angels lost their lives. The nursing home's chapel was turned into a morgue to store bodies wrapped in sheets. Some of the nuns visited the chapel, falling to their knees in prayer for their dearly departed.

Boy, did I want to meet Sister Augustine! Not for the purpose of questioning her decision-making and judgment, but for the purpose of embracing it—if what she did was reasonable under the circumstances, then so was Mabel's conduct, under Judge Winsberg's ruling as to what other nursing homes did. Equally interesting to us, Sister had been neither arrested nor charged! I imagined my line of inquiry were I to put her on the stand:

> "So, Sister, you chose to shelter in place?"
> Answer: "Yes."
> "And you used your best judgment and experience to come to this decision?"
> Answer: "That's correct."
> "And twenty-two of your residents died in the nursing home after the storm?"
> Answer: "That's right."
> "When is your trial for negligent homicide scheduled, Sister?"
> Answer: "It isn't."
> "You mean you did the same thing Sal and Mabel did, you lost twenty-two lives, and you haven't been arrested or charged with anything?"
> Answer: "That's correct!"

That testimony, I believed, could win the case, hands down. The unfair, disparate treatment of Sal and Mabel as compared with that of this Catholic nun could turn the day. More than anything, it would demonstrate the arbitrariness of the prosecution. I was not unmindful of the fact that St. Francisville was a majority white venue. In eliciting this evidence, I would, in effect, be playing the race card, but for two *white* people. Foti, a Democrat who garnered 98 percent of the black vote, would never charge or arrest a black Catholic nun.

So I began the process of going through the byzantine layers of Catholic bureaucracy to get to Sister Augustine. I was first referred to the civil lawyers for the Archdiocese of New Orleans. I knew these guys, had gone to high school with one of them, and felt like they would understand I was not out to get Sister, but to save my clients' lives. Sister's story was our story. All we wanted her to do was acknowledge that she sheltered in place, that people died, and that she had not been arrested or charged with a crime. Simple. These few facts were indisputable and would not compromise her position. After multiple efforts to reach the woman, I was finally informed that she had retained a criminal lawyer and I would have to deal with him. They told me to call Ralph Capitelli.

Ralph was one of New Orleans' premier criminal defense lawyers. He got his start in the Orleans Parish District Attorney's Office, rising through the ranks to first assistant. When he was the powerful head of the Screening Division of that office, the person who decides whether to accept or reject charges against someone arrested, I worked for him in the Economic Crime Unit as an investigator. I held this position for a year and a half after college as I attempted to cobble together enough money to attend law school. More recently, I had become a student of Ralph's lovely wife Linda, a Pilates instructor at the health club both Ralph and I used. I had been expelled from her Pilates class for conduct unbecoming a Pilates student. At least that's the story I told everyone in explaining why I was no longer attending. The truth was the exercise class was much too hard and caused me to be perpetually sore in places where I didn't even know I had muscles. Embarrassingly, I was a Pilates class dropout, but I had known Ralph for thirty years and felt confident my request to speak with his client, Sister Augustine, would get a fair hearing.

The church's selection of Ralph to defend Sister Augustine was brilliant. He had tried plenty of cases in his day, but his specialty now was in preventing people from being indicted or arrested. He flew below radar, which is partly why the local press had not picked up on the Lafon story, in marked contrast with Sal and Mabel's very public ordeal. Ralph had been briefed by the archdiocese about my inquiry and was expecting my call. Knowing Ralph to be an early riser, I called him first thing the next morning. His assistant put me right through. Ralph picked up the phone on the first ring.

"Hey, man," he said, "you got a tough one on your hands."

"I know," I said. "That's why I'm calling you. I need your client to testify."

I told him a little about Sal and Mabel. They were devout Catholics of Italian heritage; so was Ralph. They had attended Mass multiple times per week for years; so did Ralph. They were upstanding members of their community with never a hint of trouble or scandal; so was Ralph. I told him I only needed three pieces of information from Sister: first, using her best judgment, she had decided, for the safety of her residents, to shelter in place. Second, because the levees had failed, her home flooded, and because the emergency response was late and woefully inadequate, twenty-two of her residents died. Third, she had been neither arrested nor indicted.

"Those are all facts, none of which hurt your client," I said, "and they are all the truth."

Ralph immediately recognized the tremendous positive impact such testimony would have in our defense. "Look, Jim," he said, "I understand . . . but I can't help you."

He explained that Lafon had been sued for damages by the family members of the twenty-two who lost their lives and the plaintiffs' lawyers had taken Sister Augustine's deposition. When asked questions, she had invoked her rights under the Fifth Amendment and refused to testify.

"Plus, the A.G.'s office has an open criminal investigation pending against her and Lafon, and so long as that is the case, I can't allow her to testify—anywhere."

"Aw, come on, Ralph," I pleaded. "What are the chances of Charlie Foti arresting, handcuffing, and indicting an African American Catholic nun who has devoted her life to caring for the elderly? That will happen the day after we have two feet of new snow on Canal Street in the middle of August! It ain't gonna happen, and you know it."

"I don't know it until it doesn't happen, and I can't expose my client to the risk of your questions *and* the A.G.'s questions," he shot back.

"Well then, I'll just subpoena Sister for the trial, put her on the witness stand and see how it plays out," I replied.

"She'll take the Fifth," Ralph said calmly.

"I guess I'll have to live with that," I said. "I'd kind of enjoy seeing the headline: 'Nun Takes Fifth' in the newspaper."

"Uh, Jim, you don't get to do that. The jury will never see or know that she took the Fifth. Winsberg will send the jury out, you will ask your questions, she'll take the Fifth, and she'll be done."

I was, once again, trapped by my naïveté regarding criminal law. The conversation got real quiet.

"Look," he said, "I wish I could help, but I can't. My duty is to *my* client. I'm sorry."

"It's still Sister's decision, isn't it?" I asked desperately.

"It is," he said.

"Could you present all this information to her, especially Sal and Mabel's devotion to the Catholic Church?"

"I will," he answered.

I knew he would recommend against her testifying, and I knew she was likely to follow his advice. I wasn't sure how many more losses, disappointments, and blind alleys I could endure. I wasn't angry with Ralph, just crushed that another promising avenue of defense was closed to us.

"When you present this to Sister, could you do me a favor and ask her a question from me as she considers her decision?"

"If I can," he said.

"Ask her for me, what would Jesus do? Would Jesus take the Fifth, while these two good Catholics are ground up by a politically corrupt system? What would Jesus do?"

He never responded directly to the request, and instead, ended the conversation by saying truthfully and with emotion, "Good luck to you guys. I hope you can save the Manganos."

We never spoke about it again. Sister never testified, she never took the Fifth Amendment, and the jury never heard the strikingly similar Lafon story. Once again prosecutors had blocked our attempt to expose their hypocrisy and patent unfairness. We had lost another one.

Chapter 27: Stacked Deck

The loss of the Motion to Exclude the photographs of the thirty-five deceased residents raised another question. Given that the jury was going to see this gruesome, highly prejudicial evidence, what kind of person could view it and *not* be swayed by sympathy and emotion? More importantly, and more generally, what kind of person could sit in judgment on this highly emotional and publicized case and be fair and impartial? In other words, who did we want on our jury and why, and who did we *not* want on the jury, and why not? I had no clue and neither did Bob or John. We needed to figure out whether there was some group of people who would be more susceptible to our line of reasoning than to the government's blatant appeal to sympathy and prejudice.

Bob took the lead and commissioned a grizzled political veteran to do a poll of West Feliciana Parish, the parish from which our jurors would come. His choice of pollster was a name I knew well: Joe Walker. "I've worked with him before on big cases and Joe has forgotten more about people and their attitudes across the state than most people ever know," Bob said. Joe Walker was a character and a pro. He smoked cigarettes and drank whiskey, both in extremely large quantities. He was our kind of guy. He was a veteran of political wars in the New Orleans area and throughout the state. He wasn't just a pollster—he managed campaigns, hired and deployed canvassers, and knew the intricate details of how to identify *his* voters and get them to turn out on Election Day. He won more than he lost and his knowledge of people in general and what motivated their decision-making was encyclopedic. When I was a college student, I had worked for Joe going door to door in a number of campaigns he was managing. Together, Bob and I provided him with some insight into what we wanted to know about the attitudes of the residents of West Feliciana Parish. Joe did the rest, constructing an intricate poll that his workers would conduct by telephone. The results were most disturbing.

The poll's basic sample was 45-percent male, 55-percent female, 77-percent white, and 23-percent black. This closely approximated the demographics of West Feliciana Parish. Thirty percent of respondents had a high school education or less; twenty-five percent had some college. It was a surprise to me to learn that 29 percent had a college degree and 15 percent had some sort of post-graduate degree. It was a fairly well-educated sample. Occupations ranged from professional to white and blue collar, "other," and homemaker. Twenty-eight percent of those surveyed worked for the State of Louisiana—our opponent in the case. Many of them were police and prison guards, who were not our best possible jurors. Do prison guards and police officers presume the guilt of someone charged with a crime? You bet they do. This would prove to be a large, troublesome group for us if those called for jury service on the case turned up in this percentage or higher. They did.

We first wanted to gauge the residents of the parish and their knowledge of and attitude about the events involving nursing home deaths after Katrina. Eighty-seven percent had some familiarity with the events at St. Rita's. This was an astonishingly high recognition number, we were told by Joe Walker. Thirty-eight percent of those surveyed felt they were "very familiar" with the events at the home. Again, this was a very high "very familiar" number. The problem with these recognition numbers was that anything these people knew about the case came from media reports, virtually all of which were extremely negative about the Manganos. Thus, they were likely predisposed against us. The data got worse. Thirty-six percent of the entire sample felt they had an opinion about the case. Of that 36 percent who had an opinion, 17 percent thought the owners were innocent, 72 percent felt the owners were guilty, and 11 percent had some kind of opinion which did not neatly fit into guilt or innocence. Thirty-five percent of all respondents felt the owners' actions constituted recklessness or gross negligence. This was, unfortunately, the very definition of negligent homicide.

We also wanted information on general attitudes towards nursing homes and Joe obtained it. Twenty-eight percent felt they had a lot of knowledge about nursing homes, 56 percent had a little knowledge, and 10 percent felt that they knew nothing at all about nursing homes. The next number blew me away. Sixty-five percent of all respondents had had a family member in a nursing home. This meant that almost two-thirds of those polled had formed opinions about nursing homes based on their own personal experience. Only 8 percent felt their relatives had received "extremely good" care. Twenty-six percent felt their relatives had received "good" care. Twenty-nine percent felt the care was "only fair" and 15 percent felt the care was "poor." What impact would these opinions have on a prospective juror's ability to be fair?

While Joe was collecting his data, I was preparing to deliver a speech before the American Health Lawyers Association's annual meeting in New Orleans. Health lawyers, nursing home associations and administrators, and hospital administrators and associations nationwide were all following the Mangano case very closely. There, but for the grace of God, could go any healthcare worker in America, so the lawyers were keen to know about the case. When I finished the speech, I was surrounded by lawyers wanting more information. One of them asked did I have a jury consultant on the case. I did not. He told me he had worked with a guy out of New York in a number of nursing home cases and that he had great insight.

"He might be interested in helping out. Want me to see if he is?" he asked.

"Sure," I said, handing him my business card. "Have him give me a call."

It was one of those encounters which I expected would never bear fruit. I was wrong. About a week later the consultant called: "Mr. Cobb, my name is Phil James. I'm with Trial Solutions, Inc. You spoke with an attorney I've worked with before, sometime last week."

"I did," I said sounding somewhat surprised. "What can I do for you?"

"Actually, it's what can I do for you?" he responded.

He told me he had been keeping close tabs on the case from afar and how disgusted he was at the way Attorney General Foti had bludgeoned Sal and Mabel in the media, destroying their presumption of innocence. Phil was a trained lawyer *and* a psychologist, an interesting and unique combination. Given all the negative publicity and the horror surrounding the deaths of thirty-five nursing home residents, "I can't conjure a more challenging jury-selection scenario than trying to get a jury that would fairly try the Manganos," he said.

"Nursing home cases start off behind the eight ball anyway," he said. "The bias and prejudice out there against these institutions is palpable. I know. I've done a number of nursing home cases. They're tough. The one you've got might be impossible. I love that kind of challenge. If I can, I'd like to help."

This was an odd offer, I thought: someone with knowledge and experience of the challenges we faced wanting to jump aboard a sinking ship. "I don't know that we can afford you, Phil," I said. "Sal and Mabel are paying for this out of pocket, and finances are a big issue, as you can imagine."

"I've thought about that," he responded, "the case is so important and I believe they have been so unfairly treated that I'm willing to waive my fees and work for expenses only." This was an incredibly generous offer. "I want to be in this fight on Sal and Mabel's side," he concluded.

"Let me check with them and I'll get back to you," I said.

Phil's credentials were impeccable and Sal and Mabel agreed to pay his expenses, which would be considerable but a fraction of what they would have paid if he billed them for the hundreds of hours he would come to spend on the case. He sat through most of the trial even though his work was essentially done after the jury was picked. Phil massaged and organized JoeWalker's polling data, combing it for detail that proved stunningly revealing. He did a statistical summary of the survey slicing it into frequency tables, data sub-sets, and all sorts of additional categories I didn't understand. Fortunately, he authored an explanatory executive summary, which I did understand. There was good news and bad news in the data. Even though 72 percent of those surveyed thought the defendants were guilty, when presented with factual information which we knew we could prove, the disturbingly high number began to come down.

When told that Sal and Mabel had actually stayed with their residents, as opposed to the widely held public perception that they had abandoned them, the 72 percent who believed them guilty dropped into the mid-60 percent range. When told that no mandatory order to evacuate St. Bernard Parish had ever been issued, the needle moved down into the mid-fifties. When told that the nursing home had been constructed to withstand hurricane-force winds *and* had never flooded in twenty years of operation, the needle of presumed guilt dropped into the mid-forties. The takeaway? *We could change people's minds, even those who first believed Sal and Mabel guilty.*

As I surveyed the data, laid out in long spreadsheets, I noticed that one column of people did not change their opinions, no matter what fact they were presented with. "Who are these guys?" I asked. "And what is it about their shared demographic that makes them so unmovable?"

The answer was simple. The people who couldn't be budged were those who had had personal experience with nursing homes. Those who had a negative opinion of nursing homes in general believed the owners guilty. Those who felt their relatives received "extremely good" care were far less likely to find guilt. Virtually all those who felt their own family members' care was "only fair" or "poor" felt the owners were guilty. These attitudes did not correlate with other demographics or even with whether a prospective juror did or didn't know a lot about the case. The quality of care received by a relative in a nursing home seemed to be the determining factor. This insight suggested two strategic responses: First, it would be absolutely essential to eliminate anyone who felt that a relative didn't get at least "good" care at a nursing home. Second, and contrary to my strong assumption, negative media coverage was not the only factor driving the high rate of presumed guilt among those who had heard about the event. The problem was, however, that those with "only fair" and "poor" impressions of the nursing homes they dealt with comprised almost 50 percent of the sample. We were going to have to eliminate every other juror if we were to winnow people all but incapable of finding the Manganos not guilty out of the pool.

Each side only has a limited number of "strikes" or "challenges" to knock people off the jury they don't want. Through questioning, a juror can be stricken "for cause" *if* that juror demonstrates an inability to be fair and impartial *and if* the judge grants that motion to strike. These were two huge "ifs." We all believed Judge Winsberg would be disinclined to strike 50 percent of all potential jurors upon our request. Everything would depend on how we questioned the prospective jurors and on what we could get them to say. The case could not be won in jury selection but it could be lost there, especially if we wound up with jurors who had negative views about nursing homes based on their own personal experience. Our challenge was immense, but at least we had a game plan and a road map, thanks to Joe's and Phil's excellent work.

Phil suggested that we do something I had never done before—engage in a mock trial before the real one began. Bob and John, as high-profile criminal defense lawyers, had gone down this road before and both believed it could be helpful in trying out themes, theories, and arguments and getting feedback from regular folks on how they played out. Phil recruited two sets of jurors from the area in and around St. Francisville, paying them a day's wages to sit through a mock trial and answer our questions. The mock jury was carefully selected, in an attempt to mirror the demographics of West Feliciana Parish as closely as possible. Phil would steep the jurors in the case by giving them a summary of all the facts that were largely uncontested by both sides. Thereafter, they would listen to the closing arguments of both sides—the government and the defendants. Someone would have to play the prosecutor, arguing forcefully what we assumed to be the state's case. I drew the short straw and was instantly transformed into an avenging assistant attorney general. Bob would argue for Mabel and John for Sal. After our presentations we would leave the room and the jurors would deliberate and try to reach a verdict. We would watch and listen to those deliberations through closed-circuit television, as we had hidden cameras and microphones set up in the room. It would prove to be a fascinating and illuminating exercise. After jurors announced their verdict, Phil would lead us in de-briefing them on what they made of our evidence, our arguments, and our style of presentation.

As the venue for the exercise, we picked a cheap motel in Port Allen, with emphasis on the cheap. Port Allen was a small, poor, industrial town directly across the Mississippi River from Baton Rouge. The motel was circa 1955, with a flat roof and parking spaces aligned with each door. The interior was dark and dingy, but we were able to rent the required spaces inexpensively. It was still going to be a pricey exercise as we needed video equipment and several conference rooms. The location's saving grace was a locally owned donut shop right next door, with a blinking sign that said "Hot," whenever a fresh batch went up for sale. I kept one eye on my notes and the other on the "Hot" sign, waiting for it to come alive. Phil and his assistant spent the night before the big day in the motel setting up the equipment so we would be ready to go first thing in the morning. I was the first lawyer to arrive. John arrived next. "Somehow, I always knew I'd wind up in a cheap motel with you," I said by way of greeting, as I met him in the faded lobby with its dark carpeting and even darker furniture. "You can't afford me," he shot back. "Where are the hot donuts?"

As the prosecutor, I presented to the jury first and became instantly immersed in the part. I gave a stinging, angry, and vengeful argument against the people I had been defending now for almost two years. It was over the top and emotional, appealing to the mock jury's sympathy, as I expected our opponents would do in the real trial.

"Every nursing home in St. Bernard Parish got out . . . except Sal and Mabel's," I started. "Thirty-five frail, elderly citizens lost their lives in the most horrible way imaginable. They sat in their wheelchairs and lay in their beds, helpless to escape the rising flood waters and died tortured deaths. All because they were there . . . and shouldn't have been."

I pressed the attack saying Sal and Mabel, like the ostriches they had penned up on their property, stuck their heads in the sand and ignored the days and days of warnings that this was going to be the big one. One of Sal's and Mabel's hobbies was the keeping of exotic birds on the property next to the nursing home. One of the birds they kept was an ostrich. I suspected the prosecution would use this against them, so I tried the line on the mock jury.

"Ninety-two percent of the residents of St. Bernard left in advance of the storm. Sal and Mabel should have left with the people they were legally charged with caring for. They didn't because they didn't want to spend the money on buses and lose the revenue of patients moved to another facility. They gambled with their residents' lives and lost; it is now time for them to pay the house for their losing bet."

I displayed the ghastly photos of the dead residents that we knew were coming into evidence. Several of the mock jurors wiped away tears. Even though it was a mock argument to a mock jury who wouldn't actually decide anything, I was overcome with emotion. I finished and returned to the private room where Bob and John had been watching the TV monitor. I choked back tears as I confronted in a very real way, for the first time, the power of the state's case and the distinct possibility that Sal and Mabel would be convicted. John put his arm around my shoulder in an attempt at comfort saying, "I know that was hard to do. It was also very, very good. Unfortunately."

In turn, John and Bob gave their closing arguments and I watched from the private room. Phil did not want any of us to be in the room when the others made their arguments, and we would have minimal contact with the mock jurors during the exercise, save for our presentations. Bob went first. He met my fire with brimstone. He was aggressive in his defense of Mabel and outraged that the government would even bring these charges, given the multiple governmental failures at every level that were the real cause of the deaths at St. Rita's. Bob's presence in the mock courtroom was huge, and if I were a juror, I would fear doing anything other than what he was telling me to do. His command of the facts and the jurors' attention was impressive. John went next. His voice and approach were different from Bob's but equally effective. In softer, gentler tones, he cast Sal and Mabel as victims. It was heartening to see these skilled practitioners do their stuff, and I was glad they were on my side.

They returned to the private room and we all watched in rapt attention as the mock jurors began their deliberations. They forgot very quickly that there were cameras in the room and went at each other tooth and nail. Initially, they were evenly split, but as the process played out, leaders emerged—the same thing that happens with real juries. Eventually, the two separate juries coalesced around the same verdict—*not guilty*. For the first time in my career, I was glad I lost a case. The de-briefing session that Phil conducted was invaluable in helping to identify those themes and arguments that had been most persuasive. It was also a confidence booster to have gotten not-guilty verdicts from both mock juries—in spite of the brilliant (if I say so myself) closing argument I gave on behalf of the prosecution. We were uplifted by the results but had a lot of work to do as a result of the information we obtained.

We would learn later that as we held our mock trial, the state was off doing the same thing. They did theirs under the supervision of a Texas research company owned by Dr. Phil, the television talk-show host. Their mock trials took place in a swank hotel on the outskirts of Dallas. And based on what intelligence we could gather, they had mock tried the case five times—clearly they had a lot more time and money than we did—and they got guilty verdicts every time. The immovable force was about to meet the irresistible object. Mock juries in Dallas and Port Allen had reached diametrically opposite conclusions. What verdict would a jury seated in St. Francisville bring? We were all about to find out.

Chapter 28: "At Each Other's Throats"

In the run-up to the trial in the early summer of 2007, I was a basket case. I was juggling trial preparation for a projected four-to-six week trial with myriad other responsibilities. My singular focus on defending Sal and Mabel cut me off from my regular insurance defense business—clients who paid their bills, usually on time. As a family, we were back in our rebuilt home but at the cost of crippling debt and greatly reduced cash flow. I had law partners with whom I was barely speaking, one of whom had pronounced that I shouldn't have taken the case because the Manganos were guilty. My new *de facto* law partners were Bob and John. Both of them were solo practitioners and I was the only one with secretaries, paralegals, and access to law students and clerks; I shouldered the responsibility of organizing and coordinating all of these moving parts.

The cumulative effect of the past two years had certainly taken a toll on my psyche. Jimmy "Roach" Roussel, a trusted fellow admiralty lawyer, mentor, and friend, called one day and suggested that I needed counseling. He thought I was losing it. His was a voice I trusted completely and his observation stunned me. My golf buddies were trying to coax me back out on the course to relax, decompress, and have some fun. Golf sounded better to me than counseling, so I joined my old group early one Saturday morning. Even starting at 7 A.M., playing golf in New Orleans in the summertime can be an exposure to oppressive heat. By the time we reached hole number six, I was drenched in sweat. The sixth hole at TPC Louisiana was par four, the hardest of the course, with a pond on the left side occasionally inhabited by a three legged-alligator. I hit a decent drive in the middle of the fairway, leaving about a two hundred yard second shot over water. My mind wandered, thinking about the case and things that needed to be done. I took a short, too fast swing at my ball, promptly cold-topping it into the water right in front of me; the ball never even left the ground. Determined not to let this pathetic shot faze me, I dropped another ball in the exact spot and took another furiously fast swing. The second shot was identical to the first and sank into a watery grave. Undeterred, I dropped a third ball and opened up the club's face in an attempt to get it airborne. This resulted in a dead right shank that put the ball in a waste bunker. I blew a gasket. I hurled my club at the water hazard, fully intending for it to join the white orbs it had already placed on the bottom. With sweat dripping down my arms onto my hands, the club slipped out of my grip and wound up on the bank. I couldn't even throw a club in the water! Talk about pathetic.

Golf is a game of rhythm, timing, and tempo. I had none in my life and, therefore, could not bring any of these qualities to the golf course. Ball-less, club-less, and clueless, I stormed back to my golf cart, grabbed the struts that held up the canopy, and began shaking them violently. Dennis "Sideswipe" Sabrio, ordinarily the most volatile member of our group, walked over to me slowly and carefully. Dennis had a hair-trigger temper and was as explosive as a vial of nitroglycerin on a trampoline. He placed his right hand on my left shoulder and dropped his head slightly, his eyeglasses sliding down to the end of his nose. He looked me dead in the eye through the small space between the top of his glasses and his hat brim. Quietly, he said, "Son, you've got to calm down. You're going to have a heart attack out here and there ain't nobody gonna go mouth to mouth with you! Relax. Try and have some fun."

That's when it hit me. I was on a terrible trajectory; a descent into madness awaited me at the end of this road. Miraculously, the drink cart appeared. I had a cold beer and calmed down, rode a couple of holes without playing, and finished the round in one piece. The warnings from trusted friends sent a strong message and I tried to be more circumspect going forward. I never got the counseling but probably should have.

Back on the battlefield, the bullets continued to fly. Two weeks before the trial we filed yet another Motion to Disqualify Foti. This time we cited his civil lawsuit against the United States in which he swore that all the damages sustained by the State of Louisiana were the sole fault of the U.S. Army Corps. The lawsuit asked for $200 billion. Just as in other cases, the federal government could claim sovereign immunity and a judge would have to rule on the case. This was inconsistent with his prosecution of the Manganos and constituted a breach of legal ethics, we argued. In a fourteen-page memorandum rife with boldface type, exclamation points, and capital letters, Foti responded by claiming that he and his staff were the victims of "character assassination as part of an ill-conceived and desperate attempt to thwart the jury process."

Foti also accused us of "carrying out a conspiracy of public relations activity" with attorneys for Dr. Anna Pou, one of three people charged with murder for allegedly euthanizing elderly and terminal patients at Memorial Medical Center during the Katrina crisis. Foti accused John Reed and me of working with Pou's attorneys to sway public opinion against the attorney general's office. He was mistaken. I engaged in those activities with Bob, not John. In strong language the A.G.'s team wrote: "They have assisted, conspired and consulted with counsel for other defendants to create a nefarious conspiracy of public relations activity designed only to affect the public sentiment and potential jury pool in the present matter and that of other high profile cases in the office of the attorney general."

Were I to have made such a stunningly obvious pronouncement to my daughter, Collette, on any topic, she would have had a succinct reply: "Uh, duh, Dad! You think?" *Of course* we were trying to influence public opinion, just as the state had tried to do in maligning Sal and Mabel at the time of their arrest. John Reed rejected my suggestion that Collette's "Uh, duh!" be our response to the state's motion. Instead, he authored a one-page response citing the old Native American expression that he who points a finger of blame at another has three pointed back at himself. The relief Foti sought from the judge—a forced public apology from me for impugning his ethics and integrity—was rejected by the judge. And so was our Motion to Disqualify Foti—again.

At another particularly contentious hearing, the prosecutors had gotten wind of our polling activity in West Feliciana Parish. Joe Walker's troops had evidently made a random phone call or two to an assistant D.A. in the parish, as well as to an employee of the A.G.'s office who resided in St. Francisville. They had falsely ratted us out, saying that the poll was trying to *shape* public opinion, not *gauge* it. Knowing it would grab a headline, the assistant A.G. accused us of "jury tampering," a ridiculous charge as we didn't even have a jury seated yet, but it made the papers. I slammed my palm down on the table in front of me, jumping to my feet in objection to the prosecutor's scurrilous charge. Unfortunately, there was a microphone on the table, which made my hand slap sound like a bomb exploding. The judge told me that if I ever did that again, he was going to "put me in the back"—that meant jail. The mild-mannered judge was clearly displeased by the level of vitriol displayed by both sides. After this particularly heated exchange, Winsberg picked up his gavel, showing it to the participants, and said, "I've never used a gavel before in my life. I might have to have it removed from the courtroom because I really feel like hitting it!" He got my attention. The page-wide headline in the next day's *Times-Picayune* read: "Foti, defense team at each other's throats." With knives drawn, indeed we were.

In the last, desperate days before the trial commenced, the state filed another motion to prevent Governor Blanco from being forced to testify. They argued that this would be the first time in Louisiana history that the state's chief executive would be compelled to testify involuntarily in a criminal case.

"There is no legal precedent to force the executive to testify in a criminal case," the governor's lawyer argued.

"Really?" I shot back, "Perhaps my learned opponent is forgetful. There was a little case he may have heard of titled *United States v. Nixon*, in which a unanimous United States Supreme Court ordered the President of the United States to comply with a subpoena and testify in a criminal case—his own."

I had waited my entire career to cite *United States v. Nixon*. Finally, Tricky Dick was of use to me.

The assistant A.G. responded, "We urge the court to proceed with extreme caution because this could serve as a precedent. It could be inflammatory to put the government on trial and put the governor on the witness stand."

"Uh, Duh?" This was, of course, our most fervent hope and objective. Keeping that thought to myself, I responded instead, "Your honor, the governor is the captain of our ship of state. That ship foundered during Katrina and we want to know what course she set and what she did. The Louisiana ship of state was run hard aground and she was at the wheel."

Winsberg's decision was swift, "The governor will have to testify, the state's Motion to Quash her subpoena is *denied*."

The pre-trial skirmishes invariably turned into bloodlettings, but there were victories on both sides. Sleepless night followed sleepless night as the clock ran down. Three days before the opening gavel, I received a phone call from the lead prosecutor. We were barely speaking outside the courtroom. We did all our talking *at* each other, on the record, in open court. His tone was different this time, less combative.

"Jim, I've just spoken with General Foti, and I am specifically authorized to have this conversation with you." That's good, I thought, what bomb are they going to throw at me this time? Much to my shock and surprise, it wasn't a bomb; it was an olive branch.

He started with a rhetorical question: "You know there are 118 counts pending against the Manganos, 59 counts against each one of them individually?"

"That's correct," I answered.

"The A.G. is prepared to offer your clients the following," he continued.

"If they will plead guilty to only one count of negligent homicide and one count of cruelty to the infirm, we are prepared to recommend to the court that any sentence be suspended and that neither Sal nor Mabel will ever spend a day in jail. We have every reason to suspect that the judge will follow our recommendation on no jail time."

You could have knocked me over with a feather or a small gust of wind. As plea bargain offers go, it was hard to imagine a more generous one. We had fought and fought and fought, and perhaps the A.G. now realized that *he* could lose the case just as easily as we could. He also had his re-election to consider. If the trial lasted four weeks, the first primary would follow in just a month and a half. A guilty plea would be a notch in his gun belt, virtually assuring his re-election for another four years. But if he lost the case, how would he explain to voters that he had blown the biggest, most publicized case of his entire time in office? I did not want to comment on the offer. "Of course, I'll need to talk to my co-counsel," I said, "and ultimately it's Sal and Mabel's decision. So let me get back to you." It was Friday morning. The trial was set to begin Monday.

I immediately got Bob and John on a conference call and told them about the offer. "That's about as good as it gets," Bob said. "Eliminating any possibility of jail time is always attractive," chimed in John. As veteran criminal defense lawyers, anytime Bob or John could resolve a case with no jail time through a plea, when the possible incarceration time exceeded four hundred years, such a deal had to be considered a major victory. Our objective, after all, was keeping this elderly couple out of jail. The case could break either way, and the certainty that neither Sal nor Mabel would spend the rest of their lives in jail was enormously attractive. This was not a decision the lawyers could make. It was up to Sal and Mabel. They would be the ones pleading guilty and accepting responsibility before the whole world.

"What do you think they'll do?" Bob asked.

"I have no earthly idea," I replied, "but I'll call them and find out."

I called Sal on his cell phone and he answered almost immediately. I relayed the attorney general's offer to him: a one-count guilty plea and no jail time.

"What do you think?" he asked.

"Well, Sal," I said, "as plea offers go, they don't get any better. It's only one count, each, and you'll never spend a night in jail. That takes all the uncertainty out of the case."

"Do you think we can win the case?" he asked.

This was the dreaded moment of truth for me; the one all lawyers who hold other people's lives in their hands fear. I needed to be careful. I did not wish to paint the picture too darkly, nor did I wish to paint a rosy view of how things would turn out.

"Mr. Sal," I said, getting formal with him, "I've won cases I should have lost, and I've lost cases I should have won. I believe we have a compelling story to tell. But make no mistake about it; jury cases are a crapshoot. I can't tell you what to do. I can't even recommend what you should do. The decision is so personal and so important, only you can make it."

There was a long silence as my words sank in. The silence lengthened. To break it, I was about to ask if he had any questions for me. Before I could get the words out, Sal spoke. "Mr. Jim," he said, "I ain't pleading guilty to something I didn't do. I didn't kill those people and I sure wasn't cruel to the people whose lives we saved. What about my name and my family's reputation? I could never look my children or grandchildren in the eye again if I plead guilty to something I didn't do. I trust *you* to make this come out right."

"What do you want me to tell the A.G.?" I asked quietly.

"Tell him to go f— himself. We're not pleading guilty to something we didn't do."

I was awed by the man's courage but could not resist a quip: "May I tell him that in exactly those words, Sal?"

"If you want to, go ahead, Mr. Jim. I'll see you on Monday in St. Francisville."

The conversation gave me goose bumps. I hoped that Sal's bravado had not overpowered his intellect, but his rejection of the plea offer was the measure of a proud, defiant man. I had to save him from prison and the pressure to do so now mounted toweringly.

I called Bob and John and told them Sal's decision. They, too, were speechless for a few moments. Finally, Bob broke the silence. "Well, I guess I'll see you guys up here on Monday morning." There was not much else to say.

It fell to me to call the A.G.'s office and relay our response. I got the prosecutor on the line right away and there was much anticipation in his voice. If the truth be told, the lawyers on both sides would not have been disappointed with the deal. The state would have gotten its admission of minimal culpability, and we would have prevented our clients from spending a single day in jail. For the lawyers on either side, this was not a bad outcome. Plus, a plea would have spared us all the life-shortening stress of a four-week trial carried out in the glare of national and international publicity. With the trial now inevitable, the upshot would leave one team of lawyers crushed and broken, with lives and careers possibly damaged irreparably. The other team would be exultant— hailed as conquering heroes. Which team would wear the laurel crown?

"I've got an answer," I started.

"Okay," came the tense reply.

"As I understand it, this offer came directly from Charles Foti, himself, right?"

"That's correct," my opponent replied.

"Well, our answer comes directly from Mr. Mangano, and I'm going to ask that you communicate his exact words to the Attorney General. Will you do that?" I asked.

"I will," he said.

"Tell the Attorney General to go f— himself. The Manganos are not pleading guilty to something they didn't do. We'll see you sons-of-b—es on Monday morning." I hung up.

Chapter 29: Picking a Jury

The weekend before the trial was a mind-numbing flurry of activity. We had to pack up boxes and boxes of information and evidence, making sure not to leave anything behind. We were hampered in our preparation by the state's refusal to tell us which witnesses they were calling first. Accordingly, we had to be prepared for *all* of them. I was also studying and reviewing the jury selection materials. Jury selection, the first phase of the trial, would be followed by opening statements, and the prosecution would then call its first witness. John and I would take the lead in questioning prospective jurors, and Bob would give the opening statement for Mabel, followed by John's opening statement for Sal. The court had ordered about 150 prospective jurors to fill out a comprehensive questionnaire, the answers to which we had all analyzed in excruciating detail. Phil, John, and I had engaged in a jury-ranking exercise. Separately, and without consulting each other, we reviewed every juror's questionnaire, assigning each one a ranking of one to ten. One was a juror leaning strongly toward the prosecution; a rating of ten meant the prospective juror leaned strongly in our direction. We then collected our separate rankings for each juror and averaged them to come up with a final ranking. We needed to have these at the ready, so Phil color-coded them on computer spreadsheets. Names highlighted in red were strongly pro-prosecution; those in yellow meant caution; those in green were pro-defense jurors. The final tally was a downer. The jurors highlighted in red outnumbered those in green more than two to one. Our work was cut out for us.

On the home front, I had to prepare the troops because Dad was going off to war and would be totally absent from their lives for at least a month, maybe more. No help with homework; no friendly ear to help solve a problem. From their questions, I was keenly aware that they were following the case closely with their classmates. Everyone was. Like it or not, they were fully invested in the case and would bask in the glow of a victory or hide in shame at a defeat. They could also see close up the toll that this was taking on me. Debbie and I thought it was a good idea to let them ride up with me on Sunday, see the place I would be staying for the foreseeable future, and give them some comfort that I would be all right. Packing up a month's worth of coats, ties, suits, shirts, and trousers was no easy task. It was as if a child were being bundled off to summer camp, except the child was me. It was a role reversal and it felt kind of odd.

We formed a two-car caravan for the ninety-minute drive to St. Francisville. One vehicle was packed with boxes of file material and evidence. The other was packed with my clothes. Although the trip was a relatively short one, the sparsely populated St. Francisville was a world away. The flat, below sea-level New Orleans was an ethnic and racial gumbo spiced with its own music, food, and all kinds of excesses. St. Francisville was high ground in rolling hills with bluffs overlooking golf courses and the Mississippi River. St. Francisville's population was a mere 1,700 souls. The Orleans Parish Prison held more than 2,000 inmates at any given time. These were dramatically different locales and the inhabitants clearly had different outlooks on life. Tiny stores dotted the town's main street, selling glass items, antique lace, and Civil War bullets. Compared to New Orleans, it was rural and lily white—a tiny country town compared to the Big Easy. What would these people make of Sal and Mabel and the horror that had befallen them? The residents of this small, southern town were about to decide the biggest criminal case in America.

We unloaded our files at the wood-framed office we had latched onto directly across from the courthouse. Mike Hughes, a gentleman country lawyer, had graciously granted us the use of his historic building as our command center. Mike was a lawyer who drafted contracts, read title abstracts, and helped people write their wills, but he was just as comfortable riding on his tractor, cutting grass, or plowing up a field for spring planting. He was a gem and a godsend. Even with all our jury data, polling information, and mock trial experience, we longed for some local information about prospective jurors. I asked Mike Hughes if he could provide insight. In addition to his private practice, Mike was an assistant district attorney for West Feliciana Parish. He did not think it was appropriate that he consult with us about prospective jurors, given his position.

He was, of course, correct. He did, however, refer us to another local lawyer and another Mike. Michael Hesse was a practicing lawyer with a beautiful office in "downtown" St. Francisville and he agreed to help. John and I spent a great deal of time with him, drawing on his encyclopedic knowledge of local residents whose names were on the jury list. He helped us pick a jury and rendered service to the Manganos far beyond his meager charges. He stayed fully engaged throughout the trial and handled inquiries from the *New York Times* and other national news outlets at a time when we could not. He was always available for observation, consultation, and advice. He was quiet and reflective, another educated and nimble mind brought to bear on Sal and Mabel's behalf. His contribution was invaluable.

As we unloaded box after box of our evidentiary "ammunition" the day we arrived, I noticed four or five vehicles parked in front of the courthouse. All of them had that government look about them: Crown Victorias with black tires and no frills. I wanted to show Christopher the courtroom, so we strolled on over. We climbed the stairs to the second-floor courtroom, and I opened one of the tall wooden doors. There, much to my surprise, was the entire prosecution team setting up their bells and whistles so they could be sharp and ready first thing in the morning. They were four in number, an A-team of trial lawyers who had replaced the assistant attorneys general in the state Medicare/Medicaid Fraud and Abuse section who had been handling the case earlier.

I recognized the lead dog immediately and I was none too happy to see her. Julie Cullen was the director of the Criminal Division, having worked

St. Francisville attorney Michael Hesse in the courtroom where the case was tried.

Country lawyer Mike Hughes on his office front porch.

there long before Foti came to office in 2003. She was a career prosecutor with more than thirty years experience and had spent the last sixteen of them in the attorney general's office. She had a reputation for being extremely aggressive—a woman who went for the jugular and seldom lost a case. We had known each other thirty years earlier, working together in the Orleans Parish District Attorney's Office. She was a law clerk and I was an investigator in the office's Economic Crimes Unit. I was a twenty-two-year-old punk who drove an unmarked police car with a police radio, had a badge, and carried a gun. I must have been insufferable. I have no specific recollection of any atrocities I may have committed against her, but that's not to say that she didn't remember some slight. She would soon make no secret of her contempt for me because of what I had said in the *Esquire* piece. She would maintain that attitude unwaveringly, right through to the verdict.

Second fiddle, though he would actually handle more witnesses than Cullen, was Paul Knight, the deputy director of the A.G.'s Criminal Division. If Cullen was pushy and abrasive, Knight was smooth as cane syrup. Both his undergrad and law degrees were from LSU, and he had been in the public defender's office for seventeen years before switching sides and becoming a prosecutor, a role he had performed with distinction for more than a decade. Working both sides of the fence like that always sharpens a lawyer, and Knight, however courtly, was also sharp.

Burton Guidry was sort of the self-proclaimed "executive director" of the A.G.'s Criminal Division and was in charge of politics, spin, buttering up the sheriff, and who knows what else. He liked to say he had an undergrad degree from LSU, a law degree from Loyola University, and a master's from the School of Hard Knocks. He was a French-speaking Cajun, and to say he brought color to the prosecution team would be a huge understatement. His motto was: "Have Law—Will Travel; Have Injustice—Will Travel Swiftly." Guidry was a farmer, a professional musician, and a writer. He also appeared as "Crawdaddy, Cajun-at-Law," a comedy act which I regret never having seen. He performed with a touring band, "Crawdaddy and the Crustaceans," playing Cajun, Zydeco, and "swamp pop." The word was that he was a decent bass player and also stroked a mean washboard. He signed his correspondence "Crawdaddy," somewhat undercutting the dignity of the attorney general's letterhead.

The final team member was a fellow named Steven Cooper, a baby-lawyer fresh out of LSU, who probably provided research and writing to the other members of the state team. He was a nice kid, but I warned him not to drink too heavily from the prosecution's pitcher of Kool-Aid. There

Prosecutors Paul Knight and Julie Cullen. Courtesy of CBS News, from *48 Hours: No Way Out* (02/02/08).

are truly three sides to every case, I used to tell him: your side, my side, and the truth, somewhere in between.

As Chris and I strode in on them, they turned in our direction with looks on their faces like we had caught them with their hands in the cookie jar.

"You guys having a party and forgot to invite me?" I asked.

"We got the sheriff to let us in so we could set up," one of them said. "We were going to call you and let you know you all could do the same."

"It's 4:00 on Sunday afternoon," I shot back, "exactly how much longer were you going to wait before calling me and letting me know that you'd been given the keys to the courthouse?"

They had no answer. I learned through Mike Hughes and others that Guidry, the prosecutor in charge of political connections and spin, had been working the town for weeks, with special attention to the sheriff. In rural Louisiana, the sheriff isn't just the law; he is the tax-collector and, thus, the most powerful political figure in the parish. The A.G.'s men had been seen buttering him up, treating him to lunches and dinners at the Magnolia Café. Simply being seen with the sheriff was a sign to residents that the government was on the right side of the case. Had I known that the sheriff was subject to buttering up, I would have bought a couple of pounds of

The battlefield on which the war was fought. The old courtroom in the old courthouse.

the yellow stuff myself. It wouldn't hurt to be seen as one of the good ol' boys, but we had definitely missed that boat. Just hours from the opening gavel, I didn't even know what the sheriff looked like, yet he had given my opponents the keys to the courthouse on a Sunday afternoon. We had been out-politicked, and the realization was deflating.

Christopher and I beat a hasty retreat. We drove the short two blocks to the Shadetree Inn, the sort of bed and breakfast (without the breakfast) where I would be living for the foreseeable future. The place was quaint and close, on a beautiful piece of property overlooking rolling hills and tall southern pines. The inn was owned and operated by the son of a former Louisiana governor, who had gone the hippie-commune route in the 1960s. He was pleasant and helpful and, more importantly, was cheering for us. He knew the excesses of government first-hand and identified as a staunch libertarian. Everyone helped me unload my clothes and set up my small room. There was a bathtub but no shower. I hated that, but it was all that was available. We sat out on the back deck overlooking the beautiful lawn and tall trees for a spell. Chris, who had grown very close to Sal and Mabel, spoke first.

"You're not going to lose, are you, Dad?" Precisely what I needed—a little more pressure from my only son.

"Chris," I said, "I'm going to do my very best," and left it there.

It was time for them to head back home, get some sleep, and be ready for school the next day. There were long hugs all around. I watched Debbie's white SUV pull out of the gravel driveway and turn down the street that led to the courthouse. I watched until they disappeared from view. I was all alone and instantly sad. I wallowed in my sorrow for about thirty seconds, then picked up my briefcase, went inside, and got to work. One thing on my to-do list was immersing myself in the ghastly photographs of the victims. Having lost the fight to keep them out of evidence, I now planned to show them to prospective jurors in the morning. It was a risky strategy for jury selection, but I was committed to doing it, if the judge allowed.

Sleeping during trials was always difficult for me. In this case, it would prove almost impossible. My brain just would not turn off no matter how tired I got. I closed my eyes around midnight, tossed and turned until about 4 A.M., got up, and started reviewing notes for jury selection. I vowed to get into some sort of daily exercise regime. It would release energy. Maybe it would also tire me out enough to sleep the next evening. I slipped on some running shoes and went out the door for a run of one to two miles. I would do this every day for the next month. The courthouse was shrouded in the pre-dawn darkness on my way out, and gently bathed in a hot summer sunrise on my way back. This first time, as I returned, sheriff's deputies were stringing tape, putting out traffic cones, and preparing for the crush of people about to descend on this iconic building at the center of town. The first television trucks had arrived in the dark and were setting up in hopes of ambushing the judge, the lawyers, the Manganos, jurors, and anybody who looked like they might be somebody.

Even though the Shadetree Inn was only two blocks from the courthouse, I drove that first morning as I would every day for a month to our office across the street from the court. To walk in the stifling August heat would have been to arrive in court looking like I'd been for a swim. As it was, the police needed convincing that I was a lawyer working the case before they'd let me pass their barricades. I parked in back of Mike Hughes' office and arrived about the same time as Sal and Mabel. After hugs all around, I quickly herded them inside before media could document their ashen faces, frozen in fear.

The walk to the courthouse would be more of a challenge. Peeking out the front window, I could see about a dozen still photographers and a dozen TV crews lined up like a firing squad. Although the jurors would be told not to look at television, invariably they would. I wanted the defense team, including Sal and Mabel, to project a positive, confident aura. All too often, defendants walking in and out of court, *look* guilty—sending a message I definitely wanted to avoid. I called our group to order.

"Look everybody," I said, "let's get together and go to and from the court the same way every day. Sal and Mabel, I want you in the middle; John, you're next to Sal on the outside of him, and I'm next to Mabel, on the outside of her. Bob, you walk right behind Sal and Mabel."

I knew he would tower over their barely five-foot-tall frames. "Everybody smile and try not to look nervous. Sal, you hold Mabel's right hand and I'll hold her left. We ready?" There were silent nods. "Let's go," I said.

Media engulfed us the moment we stepped off Mike's front porch. Smiling broadly, I tried for affability: "Good morning, how you guys doing?" As we pressed forward toward the courthouse, the phalanx of still and video photographers walked backwards, not wanting to miss a thing. Some of the reporters shouted substantive questions, but the judge had imposed a gag order and I kept my mouth shut. Another week would pass before I got myself in trouble that way. As we got to the front door, a line which no photographer could cross, I let Sal, Mabel, Bob, and John enter first, holding the door open for all of them to pass. A TV reporter from New Orleans who knew me well shouted a last question: "How you feelin', Jim?" I turned, stared into the assembled multitude of TV cameras and uttered two words with all the confidence I could muster: "We're ready!" With that, I ducked inside and climbed the wooden staircase to the room in which Sal and Mabel's fate would be decided.

It was packed—standing room only. Court personnel were bringing in folding chairs and lining the aisles with them. These chairs filled quickly. With so many people, and all these moving parts, it was going to be a long day. The judge started jury selection with some general questions for the pool. "This case may last four to six weeks. Would jury service for this length of time work a hardship on any of you?" Virtually every hand in the room went up. The judge summoned those with hands raised to the bench and ordered them to form a line. It went down the center aisle, snaked out of the room, and spilled down the stairs. Each in turn was invited to explain why each couldn't serve. Some had jobs they were afraid of losing if they were absent for six weeks; others spoke of kids who needed rides to school; elderly parents needed care and feeding; and some prospective jurors cited illnesses of their own. The judge listened patiently, but briefly, to every story, excusing very few. The disappointment of those retained was evident. *Nobody* wanted to be here, least of all when judging this heartbreakingly sad case was going to eat up six weeks of their lives.

One prospective juror in particular had a compelling story. He was a middle school teacher who had not yet signed a contract for the coming school year. He was in the middle of job interviews, desperately seeking work for the next nine months. It was mid-August and if he didn't find something soon, he would be unemployed for the entire school year and unable to provide for his family. When asked by the judge what impact on his life jury service in this case would have, he gave an ominous answer, "I would be doomed!" In another moment he commented that he had seen a ton of publicity about the case and had already reached a verdict: "I think they're as guilty as sin," he said. He sure sounded like the kind of juror we wanted to get rid of, but was he *really?* Bob and John voiced legitimate concerns. I had a different view, in spite of his comments. I had given him a high rating as a prospective juror. Once he resigned himself to serving, I had a hunch he would favor our side. Ultimately, I made the decision to keep him. He would play a pivotal role in the case's outcome.

I wanted to accomplish two objectives in selecting those who would decide Sal and Mabel's fate. First, I wanted to eliminate the squeamish, the faint of heart, people who would be overwhelmed by raw emotion. I didn't want people screaming or fainting at the first sight of those lurid color photographs we had failed to exclude. Second, I wanted to identify and eliminate those who had a relative in a nursing home who had received only fair or poor care. Our task during jury selection was to establish that these two types could not be fair and impartial. Further, we had to convince the judge to strike them "for cause." Successful for-cause challenges did not count against the twelve peremptory challenges possessed by each side, the ones that allowed us to strike any juror we chose for any reason whatsoever—or no reason at all.

As we began working through the groups of jurors brought forward in groups of twelve and seated in the jury box, I decided to tackle the photographs issue head on. "Ladies and gentlemen," I began, "you will see photographs in this case that you might find deeply disturbing. The government intends to introduce pictures of some of the victims in this case, drowned in the nursing home. We objected to this, but the judge in his wisdom (yeah, right!) overruled our objection. It is the state which will introduce these photographs, not us." I was glancing over my shoulder, half-expecting an objection from prosecutors and a chewing out by the judge, but one never came and I kept rolling.

"But what I need to know now is whether you will be so affected by these pictures, that it will compromise your ability to be fair and impartial. So I am going to show them to you *right now* during jury selection." My goal was twofold—to eliminate the squeamish and the overly emotional and

The defense team with their clients. From left to right, *John Reed, Sal, Mabel and, the author; rear, Bob Habans.* Courtesy of CBS News, from *48 Hours: No Way Out* (02/02/08).

to take the sting and surprise out of the pictures by bringing them to the prospective jurors' attention even before they were selected. In this way, I hoped, they would be desensitized to the emotional impact the photographs carried and would credit me with being up front and honest with them. Jury cases aren't just about the evidence. More often than not, cases turn on which lawyer the jury trusts and believes. Honesty and candor with the jury is always the best policy, even if you have to fake it.

I approached the jury box and handed the set of five color photographs of the dead, bloated old people to the man sitting in the front row on the far left. I sat down and watched quietly and intently as each prospective juror flipped through the photos then passed them on to the next person. Most of them were expressionless. A couple of women winced and recoiled as they looked at the evidence. After each prospective juror had seen the batch, I went right after the wincers. "Ms. X," I said, "I couldn't help but notice your reaction as you looked at these pictures. How did they make you feel?" This was the big question in *voir dire*—getting at the jurors' feelings. Too many lawyers waste this moment by turning it into an opportunity to do the talking. I wanted to get the jurors talking, and I wanted to do the listening. *Voir dire* is French; literally translated it means "to see, to speak." This is the only time in a trial when lawyers are allowed to have a conversation with prospective jurors in order to gauge their ability to be fair and impartial. It is a critically important time, and one mostly wasted by most lawyers.

"It made me feel terrible," one woman answered. "I just don't think I can do this. It's too sad and I would be affected by sympathy for these poor people. I'm a sympathetic person; I'm just not sure I could put that sympathy aside."

I asked to approach the bench with all the other lawyers and we had a conversation in hushed tones, outside the panel's hearing. "I move to strike her for cause, your honor," I said forcefully.

"Granted," said the judge before the state could object.

This became a pattern with each succeeding group of prospective jurors. In total, we struck "for cause" ten prospective jurors so overcome emotionally by the grisly events of St. Rita's that they conceded they might be incapable of a fair and impartial verdict. Several prospective jurors refused to even look at the photographs, and they were excused. It was a time-consuming process whose outcome would not be known until those selected returned with their verdict on a stormy Friday night, four weeks away.

My second area of inquiry was even more emotional than the photographs because it required prospective jurors to talk about their own loved ones— not photos of strangers—and the kind of care they had received in nursing homes. I had to be extremely careful for this was opening old wounds and bringing back potentially sad memories. Rub somebody the wrong way and he might carry a silent grudge against the defense all the way through the trial and into the final deliberations. But it was a road that our pre-trial jury analysis told us we had to go down, so I forged ahead. In the first group of twelve that we questioned was a man who said on his questionnaire that the nursing home care received by a relative was "poor."

I engaged him in a conversation: "Who was your relative who was in a nursing home?" I asked quietly.

"It was my mother," he almost whispered back.

"I note from your questionnaire that the care she received you thought was poor. Could you tell me a little bit about that, please?"

He related a number of problems he encountered: lack of attention, lack of cleanliness, and a generally bad attitude among the home's employees.

"What impact do you think that had on your mom?" I asked.

"Well, she was unhappy and her health deteriorated. We couldn't care for her and I felt helpless."

"How did it make you feel to see your mother the recipient of poor care?" Once again, I asked the "feel" question, hopeful for a window into his soul and attitude.

"It made me angry," he said. "Here we were paying all this money for her to get poor care. I was angry, hurt, and felt like the home didn't really care about us."

"How did it make you feel about the owners or operators of the home?" I asked.

"I couldn't stand them. I thought they were greedy and just didn't give a damn about my mother."

I let his answer sink in and placed a long pause between his answer and my next question, the one I hoped would be my last of this juror.

"Knowing how you feel and knowing that the defendants in this case are nursing home owners and operators, don't you think that your anger and negative feelings about nursing homes, based on your own legitimate experience, would somehow spill over into this case and you would be ever so slightly pre-disposed against Mr. and Mrs. Mangano?"

He thought long and hard and the courtroom got real quiet. "I'd like to think it wouldn't, but I can't be sure; I might be biased against them based on my own personal experiences."

Bingo! "May we approach the bench?"

"Yes," the judge said dryly, his head lowered in disappointment as I approached.

"Move to strike the juror for cause, your honor," I said.

The state opposed it, asking for the opportunity to "rehabilitate" the prospective juror through their questioning. "You ain't gonna get there with this one," the judge deadpanned. "Motion to strike for cause, *granted*."

My questioning of this juror and his answers took place in front of the entire jury pool. Accordingly, those who also had issues with nursing homes involving their own relatives were instructed on how to evade four weeks of jury service, if that's what they wanted to do. Time and again, as prospective jurors entered the box and were asked questions about their attitudes towards nursing homes, I bore down on those whose relatives had received only fair or poor care. The vast majority of them fessed up to their potential bias and were successfully challenged for cause. A handful resisted, stating that in spite of their own personal experiences, they could be fair and impartial sitting in judgment of the Manganos. I knew this was either wishful thinking on their part or pure bullshit. For these individuals, we used our peremptory challenges to eliminate them from the jury.

We were rapidly approaching the moment of truth. The judge had excused a number of prospective jurors for personal reasons—their health, child-rearing responsibilities, job conflicts, etc. We had eliminated for cause a number of others who admitted they had formed opinions about the case, and/or had bad experiences with nursing homes which could cause them to be biased against Sal and Mabel. The state had challenged for cause a number of jurors who expressed an anti-Foti sentiment calling into question their ability to be fair and impartial to the State of Louisiana. What were left were those jurors who were deemed by the judge to be "qualified" for service in this case. The identification numbers of the remaining jurors were mixed together, shaken up, and then randomly selected by the clerk as she pulled numbers out of a large box one at a time. It was a game of chance, with Sal and Mabel's freedom hanging in the balance. As the jurors' numbers were called, they were placed in the jury box in the order they were called. It was now time for both sides to exercise their "peremptory" challenges, if either side had any. This process was nerve wracking, with the judge tendering to each side the prospective juror. The state and the defense would alternate voicing their acceptance or rejection of a prospective juror until we had six jurors and three alternates. Ultimately, we would both use all twelve of our peremptory challenges, but that's not the way things started out.

Judge Winsberg spoke first, "Mr. Knight, does the state accept juror #29?"

The prosecution team engaged in a private, whispered conference. After several minutes, Knight responded, "Juror #29 is acceptable to the state, your honor."

"Mr. Cobb, I tender juror #29 to the defense. Do you accept or reject?"

Bob and John and I engaged in a mini-conference, checked our juror rating sheet, looked over at the juror again without being too obvious, and decided to accept her.

"Juror #29 is acceptable, your honor," I said.

"Okay, Mr. Cobb, it's your turn to go first, I tender to you juror #113. Accept or reject?"

We had high marks on this juror and quickly decided. "We accept juror #113," I announced.

The prosecution team conferred and Knight announced, "Juror #113 is acceptable to the state, judge."

"All right, sir," the judge said. "Right back to you, Mr. Knight, Juror #75, accept or reject?"

The state's lawyers had a lengthy conference on this one, finally emerging and announcing, "#75 is acceptable to the state."

We had been having our own conference on #75 while they were having theirs. We liked him and I announced quickly, "#75 is okay with us, judge."

In this way, we selected the first three jurors very quickly, in shockingly agreeable fashion, neither side objecting to any of the tendered jurors.

As we were contemplating the next juror tendered, and recognizing that both sides were accepting and picking the *same jurors,* I whispered to Knight, "One of us is f—ing up!"

"Yeah," he whispered, "I guess one of us is. But which one?" We would both wait another three weeks before finding out the answer to his whispered question.

At the end of four long, emotional, and torturous days, six jurors and three alternates took the oath to judge the case fairly and impartially and were seated in the box: four women and two men. Two of the women were Sunday school teachers; a third had studied to be a Catholic nun. It was a deeply religious jury in a Bible Belt area, north and slightly west of the state capital of Baton Rouge. Would the God these folks worshipped be a kind and forgiving God, or one who required penance for the sins the government alleged Sal and Mabel had committed? Judgment day was more than three weeks away. I was certain of one thing—these jurors would pray for help and guidance in the momentous decision they faced.

Chapter 30: My Cousin Vinny

Opening statements are a key piece of any trial, particularly in a case that is expected to last weeks and weeks. Jurors need a road map that will guide them through their long journey to deliberation and a verdict. Both sides want to present an overview of their case and the evidence they will present, a sort of preview of coming attractions. It is a conversation designed to persuade without being argumentative, because argument is not permitted in an opening statement. The best opening statements are like the best movie trailers: they compel the listener/viewer not to miss what's being previewed. "Man, let's go see that one!" is the reaction the lawyer seeks to create in his audience of jurors. More than just a preview, we try to create a story that, if we prove everything we say we're going to prove, has the juror leaning in our direction, sort of prejudging the case based on the opening statement— which isn't even evidence! In my teaching, I had reviewed many studies which revealed that jurors who leaned in a particular direction after opening statements wound up rendering a verdict consistent with that first impression about 70 percent of the time!

The state goes first as they have the burden of proof and must first allege something that needs proving: *i.e.* that a crime was committed and that they know who did it.

The honor of initiating the state's case fell to Paul Knight, the second in command. He was short in stature, but his savvy and experience on both sides of the bar cast a long shadow. Now in his sixties, he described himself to the jury as "just an old country lawyer, who's going to help you folks find the truth and do justice in this case." I had learned long ago to watch out for those "old country lawyer" types. His approach was simple and disarming and had great appeal. He was immaculately attired in a deep blue, pin-striped suit, with a crisp white shirt and a red power tie. Every hair on his head was perfectly in place; its mostly salt and diminishing-pepper color attested to his decades of practice. He was charming and annoyingly complete in his approach. Never getting excited and rarely raising his voice, he was a plodder, a lawyer who meticulously crossed every "t" and dotted every "i," but with an ease about him that I feared would inspire trust and confidence in the jury. He was the exact emotional opposite of everyone on our team, and that contrast of calm and competence was unnerving. We were the yellers and the screamers; he was the quiet "old country lawyer" who would play well in these parts, I feared. "Quick," I thought to myself as I listened to his opening statement, "somebody get me a slow drawl and a country accent."

Knight started his opening by conceding that the Manganos ran a "good, clean nursing home," but he pointed out that "they were not saints." In fact, they were "handsomely paid" business people who may have been too focused on financial considerations when they decided against evacuating St. Rita's as the monster named Katrina approached. He told the jury they would see documents that would show the couple's combined salaries exceeded $1 million in 2004, the year before Katrina. He told the jury they would hear testimony from three former employees of St. Rita's who heard Sal and Mabel both say that they would never evacuate because "it cost too much money." Thus did the old country lawyer establish motive—a financial motive—as the inspiration for the heinous crime of negligent homicide by failure to evacuate, all thirty-five counts of it.

Knight told the jury they would also see documents from St. Rita's Emergency Operations Plan, a plan required under state law. As part of this plan, the Manganos had to verify that they had a contract with a transportation company to evacuate residents in advance of a storm. "And this is all they had," he said. He flashed up on the fifty-two-inch high definition plasma screen the same document John Reed had discovered and tossed at me in my office. It was a letter on the stationery of a company called Regional Transportation Services, Inc., promising service in an evacuation. The letter was addressed to Mrs. Mabel Mangano as administrator of St. Rita's and was signed by the President of RTS, Inc. The president was Sal Mangano, Mabel's husband and co-defendant. "He could have just signed it 'Love, Sal,'" said the prosecutor sarcastically.

The fifty-two-inch screen was mounted on the wall to the jury's immediate left. It was clearly visible to the jury, the judge, the lawyers, and the audience. The courtroom was like the town of St. Francisville—quaintly gorgeous and lost in time. The parish had built a new courthouse with computerized electronic courtrooms right next door to the "old" courthouse. Our trial was being held in the old courthouse so as not to disturb the schedule and rhythm of the business of the new courthouse. The courtroom, with its eighteen-foot-high ceiling, wooden rails, and antique wooden floors had character. It reminded me of the courtroom in *To Kill a Mockingbird*, where Atticus Finch had defended Tom Robinson. It was an old-fashioned courtroom, a throwback to another century. And I loved it.

That document was just the beginning of the bad news. Knight proceeded to tell the jury that the *only* vehicle RTS, Inc. owned at the time of the storm was a blue van, and he flashed on the screen a photograph of the trashed, muddy, and flooded blue van that I had seen before in the batch of pictures of dead residents of St. Rita's. I had wondered why the state took so many pictures of it. Now, alas, I knew. There was no way this one van could evacuate fifty-nine nursing-home patients, and the implication was that the Manganos had lied in their Emergency Operations Plan and cut another corner in order to save money. It was devastating. He concluded quietly and methodically.

"Katrina was an act of God," he said, "but God did not send her unannounced. This storm was expected and predicted with as much certainty as we have ever seen." He said the Manganos' decision exhibited a "gross disregard for the safety of others," resulting in thirty-five innocent elderly people drowning. "Why did they die?" Knight asked, almost in a whisper. "Because they were there . . . and shouldn't have been."

John Reed opened for us and immediately went on the attack. "If there's any crime that has been committed here," he said, "it's that a government that so badly served the public during the hurricane would now turn on its own people afterward."

He pressed our central theme: the fault lay with the U.S. Army Corps of Engineers for building a faulty flood defense and with state government for failing to develop an adequate evacuation plan and for the government of St. Bernard Parish for failing to call a mandatory evacuation. They, too, were paralyzed in indecision.

"Had they been told to evacuate by the government, they would have," John intoned. "These are good, law-abiding people. They are a family of first responders. They follow orders. None were given."

Bob jumped into the breach next, giving us a second bite at the apple. The attorney general's office made a mistake in charging both Sal and Mabel, giving us two chances at every witness, two opening statements, and two closing arguments. The magnitude of that mistake became instantly apparent to me. The prosecutor had termed the Manganos' decision to shelter in place "foolish" in his opening statement. Bob pounced on it, destroying the other side's advantage in one, clear sentence.

"The only way you could conclude Sal and Mabel foolish," he said, his booming voice rising to the eighteen-foot ceiling of the stately courtroom, "is to say they were foolish for trusting their government."

He then painted a picture of Mabel that countered the negatives the other side was counting on planting in jurors' minds. Mabel stands barely five feet tall, he told the jurors. "And she can't swim," he said. She stayed at the nursing home, never dreaming it would flood to a depth of ten feet in less than twenty minutes. After the water hit, "she stood outside on a planter to maintain her balance, holding onto the roof gutters with one hand, while holding onto a sixty-two-year-old mentally handicapped resident with her other hand. These folks are heroes and these charges should never have been brought," he concluded, looking directly at the prosecutors with all the contempt he could muster—and that was always quite a lot.

It didn't take long to figure out what the prosecution's focus was going to be. They next called the grizzled police photographer of the St. Bernard Parish Sheriff's Office, the man who took the photographs of the dead. This was a guy who had been to hundreds of crime scenes, murders, shootings, and accidents. But he choked back real tears as he described what he saw that day at St. Rita's. The photographs he took were admitted into evidence, over our preserved objection, and immediately published to the jury. Again I watched the jurors carefully. They looked at the photographs quickly and with little emotion, numbed to them, as I had hoped, from viewing them during the jury selection phase. The photographs' shock value already appeared to be diminished, and I would remind them in my closing argument that the only reason the photos were used was to appeal to emotion, bias, or sympathy, none of which had any place in an American courtroom.

Next the government took a misguided turn into the science of Katrina. They called a storm surge expert formerly employed by the National Hurricane Center in Coral Gables, Florida. He testified that, in his opinion, levee breaches contributed little to the catastrophic flooding that killed the thirty-five residents at St. Rita's. The flooding came from overtopping of the levees by a predicted eighteen- to twenty-foot storm surge, he opined. I could barely sit still waiting for my chance to cross-examine this scientific outlier. On cross, I confronted him with all the studies that concluded the flooding was due to catastrophic levee failure.

"Aren't you familiar with the Army Corps' own report—I.P.E.T.," I asked, "which concluded the exact opposite of what you just told this jury?"

"I am, I just disagree," he said sheepishly.

"Really?" I asked incredulously. "Well, let's talk about all the other studies that conclude the exact opposite of what you just told this jury." Whereupon I picked up binder after binder of reports, stacking them on the witness box right in front of the witness. Each report was almost a foot thick. "I.P.E.T., Team Louisiana, National Science Foundation, the American Society of Civil Engineers," I said, piling these reports in front of him to the point where he almost disappeared from view. "Every one of these studies and reports totally contradicts what you just said, don't they?"

"I guess so," he said.

"No, sir," I said, my voice rising, "I don't want you to guess. Go ahead and review the reports and tell me whether or not *all* these voluminous reports totally and completely contradict your testimony."

He made no attempt to do so, deciding instead on surrender. "They do," he replied.

"I guess you're sort of the Lone Ranger on this one, aren't you?" I said sarcastically.

"Objection!" the prosecutors screamed, jumping to their feet. The judge sustained their objection, but my point had been made.

Next, the state called the executive director of the Lake Borgne Basin Levee District, Borgne being the lake Katrina washed across St. Bernard Parish. Why are they calling this guy, I wondered. He gave the jury a primer on the St. Bernard levee system. He used maps to show how St. Bernard is surrounded by water, and how precarious and vulnerable the parish is, especially in the face of a monster hurricane. It looked like a place anyone in their right mind would want to leave before a hurricane struck. They had orchestrated a conclusion to the witness's testimony that was dramatic. He testified that Katrina's surge was predicted to be eighteen to twenty feet high, a wall of water pushed ahead of this tropical cyclone. It would hit with the force of a nuclear bomb.

"Do you have something that can demonstrate to this jury how high eighteen feet is?" asked Knight.

"I do," he answered. Then he pulled out of his briefcase a telescoping pointer, which he extended upward inside the courtroom. "That's eighteen feet," he said as the pointer touched the ceiling. The jurors' necks tilted backwards looking up at the ceiling. From our seats, it was absolutely horrifying to contemplate a wall of water this high. The prosecutor had made his point vividly: you would have to be nuts not to flee a predicted tsunami like that, especially if you were charged with the care and protection of fifty-nine nursing home patients.

I rocketed out of my chair and went on the attack. I did not attack the witness; he was a nice enough guy. I attacked the prosecution's premise. I had the maps that he used brought back up on the plasma screen.

"Can you locate St. Rita's Nursing Home for us on this map?"

"I can," he said, whereupon he placed a big, red, electronic "X" on the spot.

"Now what is this long, raised structure here?" I asked, pointing to a map that showed in simple terms a structure between St. Rita's and the Mississippi River Gulf Outlet.

"That's the levee protecting the parish from the Mississippi River Gulf Outlet, the MRGO, we call it," he said.

"Who designed, engineered, and constructed the MRGO?" I asked.

"The U.S. Army Corps of Engineers," he replied sharply.

"And what is this other long, winding structure on the map?"

"That is the Caernarvon levee structure," he answered.

"So, St. Rita's sat behind *not one, but two* sets of protection levees, correct?"

"That's right," he said.

"They were surrounded by hurricane-protection levees, right?"

"Yes," he said.

I modulated my voice volume to rise several levels as I asked, "And the levees did *not* protect them, did they?"

"No, sir, not for this particular event," He answered. I took a long pause and let his answer sink in.

"Were you around for Hurricane Betsy?" I asked. Betsy was the seminal flooding event for St. Bernard Parish, having completely inundated the upper parts of the parish in 1965, killing scores of people.

"I was a teenager," he said.

"As part of your duties as executive director for the levee district, have you studied what parts of St. Bernard flooded in Betsy and what parts didn't?"

"I am familiar with that, yes," he answered.

"Did the area where St. Rita's was located flood in Betsy?" I asked.

"It did not!" he snapped back.

"And prior to Katrina, Betsy was the worst flooding event in the history of the parish, wasn't it?"

"That's correct," he said.

"And between Betsy and Katrina the U.S. government built *two* sets of protection levees between St. Rita's and the water, didn't they?"

"Correct," he said, suddenly sounding almost as angry at the Corps as he was with his interrogator—me.

"And those levees failed catastrophically during Katrina, didn't they?"

"They did," he answered.

"Do you still have that telescoping pointer that you used in response to the prosecutor's questions with you?" I asked.

The MRGO meets the Intracoastal Waterway and becomes the "Hurricane Highway." Courtesy of CBS News, from *48 Hours: No Way Out* (02/02/08).

"I do."

"Please go ahead and extend it out towards the ceiling just as you did for them."

The witness complied and I watched the jurors' heads tilt back, following the pointer up to the eighteen-foot-tall ceiling as the pointer touched it. I reminded him that he used it to demonstrate how high Katrina's storm surge was predicted to be. I looked up at the ceiling, pointing, and asked, "And that's how high the levees were supposed to be, weren't they?"

"You're correct," he said.

"In fact, the levees were supposed to be twenty feet high, higher than the storm surge, correct?"

"That's correct," he replied. Had I been Joe Pesci in *My Cousin Vinny* and had Winsberg been the southern judge played by Fred Gwynn, I would have said, "I'm done wid dis guy!" Instead, I said, "No further questions, your honor. I tender the witness."

The fact that the levees failed did not really answer the question of whether the Manganos should have evacuated. But the issue was joined and the jury appeared to be fully engaged. The A.G.'s office was prosecuting the Manganos; and we were prosecuting the United States government and soon would turn to prosecuting the State of Louisiana, the very government that was prosecuting us. The courtroom was already an emotional and legal tinderbox. As we trained our weaponry on our opponents, things were about to explode.

Chapter 31: Evidence Through a Looking Glass

Every witness's testimony has the potential to be both helpful and harmful to the side that calls one. There is no discovery in criminal cases, no deposition testimony during which we could find out what a witness might say in response to a particular question. In civil cases, like the wrongful death suits filed against the Manganos by family members of the victims, we have the opportunity to put every witness under oath in a deposition and "discover" what each is going to say in response to a particular question in advance of the trial. No such discovery mechanism exists in criminal cases and cross-examination of witnesses in criminal cases is thus a high-wire act for the questioning lawyer. In civil cases, a lawyer should never ask a question to a hostile witness to which the lawyer doesn't already know the answer. In criminal cases, we almost *never* know what the witness is going to say in answer to a particular question. Accordingly, criminal trial lawyers are like two gun-slingers meeting in the center of town at high noon ready to shoot it out, not knowing who is faster on the draw.

Often what is important and memorable to the jury is not what the witness says, but *how* he says it. Such was the case with the state's next witness, Larry Ingargiola, the director of the Department of Homeland Security and Emergency Preparedness for St. Bernard Parish. I got him to admit that St. Bernard never issued, formally and legally, a mandatory evacuation order. This admission was a huge part of our case. I had copies of videotapes of the parish council broadcasting on the parish's cable access channel demonstrating the musings and contradictions of elected officials as they tried to encourage people to leave. One council member, a well-known crackpot, was encouraging people who were staying to get closer to the Mississippi River, as this was higher ground than in the rest of the parish. Being a crackpot in St. Bernard was not a disqualification from holding political office. In fact, it was almost a requirement.

As I pressed the witness about the mixed messages the government sent to its people, he gave me one of those memorable answers: "Mr. Cobb, you've got to understand that in St. Bernard we do have people . . . who would tie themselves to a tree rather than evacuate."

He was referring to the crackpot councilman who had used these exact words on more than one occasion. He then gave me a gift answer that I would use in closing argument. I was questioning him about how well what happened to the parish could have been foreseen.

His answer was pure gold: "I don't think anyone in their wildest imagination could have foreseen the mass destruction Katrina caused," he said, "I couldn't."

"Well, if you, as Homeland Security Director, couldn't foresee what happened, then neither could the Manganos, could they?"

"*Objection!*" the government yelled. The objection was sustained, but the point was clearly made.

The state began to call witnesses who were related to the victims. These relatives all spoke of their loved ones in glowing terms as role models and doting grandparents. Every witness wept. Seeing no benefit in prolonging their time on the stand, we rarely asked any of them a single question on cross. But their presence in front of the jury brought another question to everyone's mind. Why didn't you go and pick up your mom or dad and bring your relative with you when you evacuated? It was a huge question and drove the guilt and anger that these family members felt towards the Manganos. It also raised larger societal questions: What duty do family members owe to their own blood in a nursing home during a hurricane? What does the home owe? Whose responsibility is it? More than a dozen residents were, in fact, picked up by family members in advance of the storm and taken out of harm's way.

One family member, a daughter, called inquiring about what St. Rita's was going to do. One of the nurses said they were staying put for now but that if they received a mandatory evacuation order, they were leaving. The nurse told the daughter that her mom was in pretty good shape, and that St. Rita's could pack up her clothes and meds and have her ready to go in a matter of minutes. This daughter had to drive right by the front door of the nursing home on her way out of town, so it would have been convenient for her to stop by and get her mom. "Nah," she was reported to have said. "You know, we're driving to Florida, and I've got those two big yellow Labs that I'm taking with us. We ain't got no more room in the car."

Although she was on the state's witness list, they never called her to the stand, and I never got to ask her how her dogs were doing, a question I was very much looking forward to asking. It was an issue never openly discussed during the trial, but one which we would later find out the jury thought about and talked about. As issues go, it was the 800-pound gorilla in the room—never mentioned and widely feared. And as to the daughter with the two yellow retrievers who drove by the front door of St. Rita's on her way to the Florida panhandle, her mother drowned in St. Rita's on that horrible August day. Not surprisingly, this woman was one of the very first to file a civil suit against St. Rita's seeking money damages for "wrongful death."

Every trial has its own unique rhythm, pattern, and pace. The lawyers' personalities, the judge's rulings, and the daily back and forth define that rhythm. In this case, every time the state called a witness and we rose for the cross-examination, it was like hand-to-hand combat, with each side trying desperately to make a point or diminish one made by the other side. The state's strategy was to object to almost every question I raised, usually before I had fully phrased it. This was intentionally disruptive, making it more difficult for me to develop my argument cogently and persuasively. This is a trial advocacy no-no. One should always allow one's adversary to finish a question before stating an objection. The judge then rules on the objection—overruling it or sustaining it.

Unfortunately, in this trial, the state's obstructionist tactics found an appreciative audience in Judge Winsberg. Not only did he allow the state to interrupt constantly, worse yet, he invented a new ruling on objections. Rather than saying what the rules allow—objection overruled or sustained—the judge would embrace a premature objection by saying to me, "You're starting off bad, Mr. Cobb." I felt like screaming back at him, "You're starting off bad by not ruling correctly on objections." But this would have been a fight with a judge that a lawyer rarely wins in front of a jury. "You're starting off bad," became the most-often-heard comment from the court in the trial's early days. In choosing this language, was the court trying to send a message to the jury that I was a bad lawyer who didn't know how to ask a question? Would that be the jury's impression? I couldn't allow this call and response pattern to continue. I had a choice to make. Do I take on the judge, head on, and risk alienating the jury? Or, do I figure a way to minimize the government's bogus objections and the court's misguided rulings? I chose the latter path.

After two or three days of, "You're starting off bad," I started to respond: "I'm sorry, judge, let me start over." I didn't mean it—he was wrong—but it changed the rhythm of my cross-examination. At one point, after receiving another, "You're starting off bad," I said, "Gosh darn it, judge, I hate it when I start off bad. Can I please start over?" Now I was being as facetious as possible, with my tongue firmly planted in my cheek, but the judge bought it. I noticed some jurors smiling at my disingenuous apologies, and it appeared that they were on my side as I struggled not to "start off bad." This pattern went on for weeks and became the foundation of my closing argument—an argument that I began by turning to the judge and saying, "May it please the court, I don't want to start off bad, your honor, ladies and gentlemen of the jury; I'm going to be *positive*." I didn't mean it and the jury and the judge were about to hear my definition of *positive*. It would be a shock to everyone in the room and it would not have worked without the judge's gratuitous repetition of his "you're starting off bad" mantra.

About two weeks into the trial, as we returned to the courtroom after lunch, there was an ambulance parked in the handicapped space out front. In the stifling August heat, three attendants were struggling to get an elderly gentleman in a wheelchair out of the vehicle. As we passed them, I whispered to Mabel, "Who's that?" "That's Mr. Jack," she answered. "He was one of our residents on the day of the flood." Oh, shit, I thought, more emotional testimony, this time from a *survivor* as opposed to a victim's family member. This witness's testimony had the potential to be more emotional and explosive than any the jury had heard thus far. The luncheon recess at an end, the court asked the state to call its next witness. "The state of Louisiana calls Mr. John Jack Denton," the prosecutor said.

The witness was pushed into a hushed courtroom, an audible squeak of one wheel highlighting Mr. Jack's infirmity. The area where the lawyers, judge, and jury sat was at least a foot higher than the spectators' gallery, requiring attendants to lift his chair. They did so a little roughly, I felt, and Mr. Jack was jostled around. There was no way he could climb the two steps into the witness box, so he testified from his wheelchair, shrinking the distance between himself and the jury he faced and increasing the drama of the moment. Mr. Jack said he was sixty-eight years old. He looked much older. His skin was that bright white color, approaching opaque, that one sees in the elderly; he was clearly in extremely poor health. I wondered why they were making this poor old man come out on this brutally hot day to testify. What could he possibly add except another layer to the already over-baked sympathy cake the state was force-feeding the jury? Maybe he was the icing on that cake. I hoped so.

In a low, raspy voice, Mr. Jack told how he survived a flood that killed thirty-five of his fellow residents and friends. He said the water came up very quickly, rising to the ceiling in less than twenty minutes. He described the chaos as a staff member pulled him onto a boat and took him to the roof.

"How was it on the roof?" the prosecutor asked.

"The wind was still blowing and it was cold," he said. Everyone in the quiet courtroom was leaning forward to hear the whispery words of a frail old man who had endured the unthinkable. "It was raining hard and the raindrops hurt," he said.

"Did you have any friends at St. Rita's?" the prosecutor asked.

"My best friend," he answered softly.

"What happened to him?"

"He didn't make it out." Near the end of his testimony, the bailiff brought him a box of pink tissues, and Mr. Jack took one, using it to dab both his eyes. Of the many things I had seen and heard in the previous two years, this was one of the saddest.

I then did something I rarely did and instruct my students never to do: I asked a question on cross-examination to which I did not know the answer. I only asked one. "Mr. Jack, I represent Sal and Mabel," I said to him.

He turned slightly in his wheelchair to face me. "Yes, sir," he said.

"How would you describe the care you received at St. Rita's?"

He answered, "The care was very good."

"Thank you, Mr. Jack," I said, "I'm sorry for your troubles," and I was done.

My colleagues breathed a sigh of relief. Turns out Mr. Jack would have passed the litmus test to sit on our jury. Sitting next to me, Mabel dabbed her eyes as Mr. Jack was rolled out. I was uncertain how much more of this raw emotion Mabel could take. I didn't know how much more I could take. I wondered how much more the jury could take.

Perhaps the prosecution called Mr. Jack to prove the charge of cruelty to the elderly and infirm. The state had lodged twenty-four counts against the Manganos for exposing these residents to the flood and the elements, which they charged constituted cruelty and abuse. Each count carried a ten-year maximum sentence, so the Manganos were faced with 240 years jail time, each, if convicted. But did they really need to roll this poor old man into court through one-hundred-degree heat to accomplish this goal? And weren't they laying on the pathos just a little too thick for the jury's taste? None of us knew. The state's next two witnesses could have accomplished their goal of buttressing the cruelty charges, but their impact as witnesses was severely diminished by my cross-examination. I was breaking rules. Once again, I asked questions of witnesses without knowing the answer, except this time they were expert witnesses.

The state called Dr. Sandy Finkle, a geriatric psychiatrist from Illinois. That made him a Yankee in my book and, I hoped, the jury's. "You're from up north in Illinois, aren't you?" was my first question. Finkle testified that he had examined many of the survivors of the flood, including Mr. Jack, and had reviewed their medical records. He testified that these survivors all suffered from post-traumatic stress disorder (PTSD). The symptoms were depression, nightmares, flashbacks, and fear of water. Some were fearful of even taking a bath, he said. At a sidebar conference, outside the jury's hearing, I indicated that I wanted to go into how much money the state had paid this northerner for his testimony. The assistant attorney general handling the witness argued that I could ask how much he was being paid by the hour, but could not inquire into how much his total bill was. This was preposterous and I finally prevailed over a prosecutorial objection: the judge would allow me to fully probe the doctor's financial remuneration. The fact that the A.G. didn't want me to get at the information telegraphed to me that there might be gold in them there hills—a lot of gold.

"So, doctor," I asked, "your conclusion and opinion is that this event had negative health consequences on the survivors?"

"That's correct," he snapped back.

"And how many hours did it take you to figure this mystery out?" I asked as sarcastically as possible, somehow without drawing an objection.

"I spent approximately 160 hours on the task," he replied, a little sheepishly.

"One hundred sixty hours?" I almost yelled. "That's eight hours a day, five days a week, for an entire month, isn't it?"

"Well, it was spread out over time. I didn't work straight through a month on it."

"But my math is correct, isn't it, doctor? You worked the equivalent of a full month of time in order to reach your conclusions?"

"Your math is correct," he said, barely hiding how annoyed he was with me.

"And what is the hourly rate you charged the attorney general's office?" I asked slowly.

"$300 per hour," he responded.

"So your bill is $48,000 for this analysis and testimony?" I said, barely able to contain the fact that his answer flabbergasted me.

"That's about right," came his subdued reply.

"Did you really need to spend that much time and taxpayer money to figure out that this was an awful, terrible event for those who experienced it—something no one would disagree with?"

"*Objection*, argumentative," said the prosecutors.

We had a huge dust-up at the bench and I lost, but I caught a glimpse of the unemployed middle school teacher on the jury shaking his head in what I interpreted as disgust. I hoped he was thinking, "Man, the state could have spent that $48,000 on me as a teacher and gotten something for its money." We would not have contested the facts and the opinion that the state spent $48,000 trying to prove. There was, I hoped, some erosion in the prosecutor's credibility in the minds of the jury. That erosion cascaded into an avalanche with the next witness.

The state called Dr. R. Stahl, another Yankee physician, this one from Buffalo, New York. I wondered if either of these Yankee doctors had noticed the memorial statue to the Confederate war dead that graced the front lawn of the courthouse in which they were now testifying. Once again, my first question to him was essentially, "You're from up north in upstate New York, aren't you?"

"Buffalo," was his curt reply.

Sarcasm surging in my veins, I decided to have some fun. "Don't they have any geriatricians in Louisiana?" I asked.

Dr. Stahl specialized in geriatrics, the treatment of the elderly. "I don't know," came his annoyed answer.

"Well, wouldn't you think LSU Medical School or Tulane Medical School would have some geriatricians on their faculty?"

"I would think so, but I don't know," came his answer. He was no longer annoyed; he was visibly pissed off.

Having way too much fun, I pressed the attack. "Well, surely you know that there are geriatricians between here and Washington, D.C.," I inquired, tacitly alluding to the Mason-Dixon Line. "I'm just trying to figure out why the state of Louisiana had to go all the way up to Buffalo, New York, to get you?"

"*Objection!* Approach the bench," Cullen, the hardened prosecutor, demanded. She was furious, her loathing and contempt for me written all over her face. I loved it when the other side hated me. I felt like I must have been doing my job well, but the judge was not nearly as impressed with me as I was. "Cut that shit out, Cobb," he whispered.

"Judge, I think I have a right to show that the state had to go almost all the way to Canada to find a witness to do their bidding and say what they want him to say."

"I said objection *sustained*; move on or I'll put you in the back," the judge said. I moved on quickly.

Dr. Stahl's testimony on direct was, essentially, that he had reviewed medical records of many of the residents at St. Rita's. Their health problems, he opined, were not unusual for a nursing home and "with proper care and preparation they could have easily been transported elsewhere and not suffer adverse consequences."

"Really, Dr. Stahl?" I asked, "And how many times have you been involved in nursing home evacuations as a result of a threatened hurricane up there in Buffalo, New York? Never! Right?"

"That's right, but it still could have been done," he answered testily.

"So where was Katrina located on August 26, 2005, at noon?"

"I don't know," he said.

"Where was it located on August 27, 2005, at 1800 hours?" I pressed on.

"I don't know."

"August 28, 2005, at 0800 hours?"

"I really don't know," he said.

"Moving right along, doctor," I said. "The second part of your testimony deals with a statistical analysis that you made of the residents of St. Rita's, correct?"

"That's right."

"And as I understand your conclusion, the data showed that the residents who died tended to be the oldest and in the poorest health, correct?"

"Yes," he said.

(I could hear my inner Collette succinctly affirming his answer—"Uh, Duh?"—but resisted the temptation to say the words aloud.) Instead, I asked, "So, how many hours did you spend discovering that the older and sicker residents at St. Rita's were more likely to have died in the flooding event on August 29, 2005?"

"I spent a total of ninety hours on the entire project."

"And how much per hour are you charging the attorney general's office?" I asked.

"My rate is $500 per hour," he responded.

"So, if my math is correct, your charges to the State of Louisiana for your work on this case are $45,000, correct?"

"That's right."

I let the answer and the number slowly sink in and thought I detected the unemployed schoolteacher's eyebrows rise up in disbelief, as he glanced at jurors on his left and right. My interpretation of the silent look on his face was, "Can you believe *this?!*" Whatever information and testimony the two doctors attempted to impart was overwhelmed and discredited by the $93,000 the state spent buying it. I looked forward to having a field day at these guys' expense in my closing argument.

I felt we were in control of the case as the trial's second week came to a close. I wasn't the only one who felt that way. The sheriff's deputy in charge of courtroom and jury security approached me with a puzzled look on his face.

"Can I ask you a question, Mr. Cobb?"

"Sure," I said.

"These last few witnesses we've heard, are they your witnesses or the state's witnesses?" the deputy asked.

"They have all been called as witnesses for the prosecution," I answered. "Why do you ask?"

"Because," he said, "it sounds like their testimony is more favorable for your side than the state's side."

"I sure hope you're right, captain," I said

I was starting to feel cocky. Imagine that—a trial lawyer with a big head. I started chatting with some members of the press during breaks in the trial. The first two rows of the gallery had been reserved for the press. Directly behind them was reserve seating for the victims' families, a constant presence in the courtroom. Under the state's "victim assistance program," the attorney general's office had arranged to transport these people to and from the trial every day, often buying them breakfast and lunch. They were an unpaid cheering section for the prosecution and a constant reminder to the jury that these deaths left shattered survivors, several of whom wore black each day.

During one of the breaks, I started talking with a producer from New York, Paul Ryan, who was covering the trial for the CBS show *48 Hours Mystery*. They were producing a one-hour special on the case that would air nationally months after the trial. He had asked for my cooperation in advance, but I had declined. Ryan knew of my early morning runs in the dark through the town of St. Francisville, headphones on, oblivious to the outside world. He wanted to know what I listened to. I told him that the last two songs I listened to every day before trial commenced were the same: Bruce Springsteen's "No Surrender" ("We made a promise, we swore we'd always remember/ No retreat, baby, no surrender") and Tom Petty's "I Won't Back Down" ("Well, I won't back down, no, I won't back down./ You could stand me up at the gates of hell, but I won't back down.") I was joking around with him, oblivious to the family members who were seated right behind him. After the next break, the lead prosecutor asked for a conference in chambers with Judge Winsberg. We all assembled in his tiny office.

"Judge," Cullen said, "Mr. Cobb's been talking to the press in violation of the court's gag order."

I explained that the network guy I was talking to wasn't doing any daily reporting, so there was no violation.

"That's not why I'm bringing it up, judge."

"Then why?" asked the judge.

She related that several of the family members had taken great offense at me in general and, in particular, at my joking around with this producer.

"As an officer of the court, judge, I believe I am obligated to report that there have been several death threats made against Mr. Cobb. I don't want something to happen if I failed to report the death threats against him." There was no more joking around in the suddenly somber chambers.

"Look," the judge said, "I want you to stop talking to this guy and everybody else. These people are hurt and everybody in St. Bernard is living on the edge of crazy, and they've all got guns. Get me the sheriff in here."

The captain came in and the judge ordered that he provide an armed escort for me and the Manganos as we walked to and from court every day. He then told the captain to have someone follow me back to the Shadetree Inn every night. "Sit outside the Inn in a marked police car for a couple of nights and, hopefully, this will die down. Anything else? Okay, let's go to work."

As we filed out of the judge's office, I was the last to leave. He put his hand on my shoulder and I turned my head in his direction. He whispered so no one else could hear, "Now, shut the f— up!" I said I would. Having a death threat made against me, reported by an adversary who loathed my existence, was sobering. Its impact lasted until dinner that same evening when John Reed, his wife Jon, and I finished off two bottles of El Portillo Sauvignon Blanc, a wonderful wine from Argentina which we consumed at the rate of one case per week throughout the trial. Tom Petty's "I Won't Back Down" lyrics danced in my head. And while I resolved not to back down, I also resolved not to talk to reporters anymore, at least not while family members were in the vicinity.

Either the prosecutors agreed with my sense that they were falling behind in the case, or they wanted to close out the week on a high note with the next "evidence" they offered. The state had compiled more than two-and-a-half hours of video clips from New Orleans television stations in the days leading up to Katrina. The selection of the clips and the editing of them had been done by the prosecutors themselves. The clips showed the near hysteria of local newscasters and weathermen as the Category 5 monster named Katrina swept toward Louisiana. It included satellite photos showing that the storm took up the Gulf of Mexico almost in its entirety, with an eye so well defined it was visible from space. TV's talking heads were going nuts with anxiety, and their rants were chock full of factual error.

We had objected to use of the tapes. It was rank hearsay. There was no foundation the state could lay to show that either Sal or Mabel had seen any of these carefully selected excerpts. Further, the people talking on the tapes were *not* under oath and could *not* be cross-examined. How do you cross-examine a videotape? Such "testimony" violated more constitutional amendments than the number of hangovers the stars of the *Jersey Shore* suffer in an entire season, but the judge was going to allow it. Was it now part of the crime of negligent homicide not to watch television? Or, if watched, was it now a crime not to obey the hysterical raving of meteorologists? And what did weather broadcasts have to do with how a nursing home with special-needs patients should react to a hurricane? I objected again. "Overruled," the judge replied testily.

The state played their edited videos for the last forty-five minutes of that Friday afternoon. It was devastatingly bad for us. Anyone paying the slightest attention to what was going on the weekend before Katrina would have run for their lives! I did, with my family and elderly parents. Ninety-two percent of the residents of St. Bernard Parish did the same, and so did the other nursing homes in the parish, all three of them. We had previewed the videos on laptop computers, as had the judge. They were bad enough on a ten-inch screen. When the prosecution played them on a fifty-two-inch, high-definition plasma screen, they were infinitely worse. The jury sat transfixed by the pictures, unaware that they really didn't qualify as "evidence." We were getting killed, and I had to sit by silently and take it. I was fuming inside, trying not to show it. It was, by far, the worst part of the case for us to date.

The judge told the jury to come back on Saturday morning. We were going to work a half day that weekend to move the case along, and the prosecutor had every intention of continuing with the video orgy. As the jury exited the courtroom Friday afternoon, the judge asked, "Do any of the lawyers have anything else?"

"I do," I said popping out of my chair. We waited until the jurors had cleared the building.

"All right, Mr. Cobb, what you got?"

"Judge, I want to re-urge our objection to this evidence, which isn't really evidence. I'd like to cross-examine what they are saying on the video but I can't. I've got no witness to talk to. It's going in one-sided and without cross-examination, a right guaranteed the Manganos under the Constitution." As the last thing jurors saw that day, the video had already had a devastating impact that was well orchestrated by prosecutors—to give credit where credit is due. I was almost shaking I was so angry. I was about to go off the reservation.

"Judge, you just put the state back in the fight. They haven't won a round, and *you* just put them back in the game." The judge had boxed as an amateur so he understood the analogy.

John Reed tugged on my coat, put his hand over his mouth, and whispered, "Careful."

I didn't give a shit and pressed on: "You can't allow the government to play two more hours of this tomorrow. In addition to all the Constitutional violations, it's repetitive and cumulative and may mislead the jury into giving these videos greater weight than they should have."

The judge got pensive and quiet. I think he was as surprised as I was by how much more of an impact the tapes had on the fifty-two-inch plasma screen, compared with the tiny laptops on which we had first viewed them. It was certainly the most graphic evidence in the case thus far, and the prosecution sought to extend that advantage by playing even more of it.

"I'm going to take your motion for reconsideration under advisement and rule on it in the morning. Mr. Knight, make sure you have live witnesses here tomorrow in case I rule in the defense's favor. Court stands adjourned." And he was gone. The next morning the judge allowed about thirty more minutes of video "evidence," frustrating the prosecution's ambition to play another hour's worth from another channel.

"Mr. Cobb, would you stipulate that if this next tape were played, it would essentially be the same as what the jury has already seen and heard?" the judge asked.

"I would," I said instantly.

"Then we're not going to watch any more of the videos. State, call your next witness." Winsberg had fashioned a compromise of sorts, for which I was thankful, but he had single-handedly put the prosecution back in the fight. We wouldn't find out the jury's reaction for another two weeks. But we'd had two really bad days, and our perceived advantage was disappearing quicker than you can say barometric pressure. Everyone in the room could feel the shift of support to the prosecution's side wrought by the illicit "evidence." We were, once again, in trouble.

The prosecution moved swiftly to press the advantage they had gained. They began to make their case for introducing evidence of what the other nursing homes in St. Bernard Parish did ahead of Katrina. With jurors not present, they called the administrators of the three homes. They told the judge of their homes' geographic locations, focusing on their elevations above sea level. They next spoke about their patient populations, presence of special-needs patients, and the level of sickness and disability within the home's residential population at the time of Katrina. The data were all too similar to St. Rita's. Prosecutors then sought permission to present all this evidence to the jury, concluding with the fact that all three homes had evacuated. Of course, we objected. So what if these homes evacuated, we argued. What *they* did is not the legal standard.

"The question for the jury is what did Sal and Mabel do, and was it reasonable under the circumstances," I argued forcefully.

The judge began to sound like a broken record to me: "Objection *overruled!*"

The jury was brought back into the courtroom and soon knew that all the other nursing homes in St. Bernard Parish had evacuated—leaving St. Rita's the "Lone Ranger" who stayed, said the prosecutor, playing on the name I had given their storm-surge expert. Together these three homes had evacuated approximately 188 residents, more than three times the number in residence at St. Rita's. And only one of the 188 residents had died as a result of the evacuation. This was a dramatically better result than losing thirty-five old folks in a flash flood. The testimony significantly undercut one of our central themes, that evacuation would have cost us many lives given our patient population. The one casualty of the evacuations had been a ninety-year-old woman, and she died in the parking lot of the home to which she was transported. Even she almost made it.

On cross-examination I tried to slip in the fact that the nuns at Lafon Nursing Facility, up the road and across the parish line in Orleans, had also chosen to stay, and that twenty-two residents had died there. We believed jurors would view Sal and Mabel's decision to shelter in place more favorably if they knew a group of nuns who dedicated their lives to caring for the sick and the elderly had made the same decision to shelter in place. I was only just beginning to venture down this road when someone jumped up from the prosecution's table and threw up the predictable barrier: "Objection." Before I could respond, the judge had ruled—"Sustained"—cutting me off at the knees before any information was revealed. In an instant, I decided to say something I knew would infuriate the judge but just might make a lot of sense to the jury.

"Your honor," I said, "if they get to put in evidence of homes that left, why shouldn't we be able to put in evidence of those who stayed?"

Prosecutors blew a gasket, "Objection, approach the bench."

They were furious at me and so was the judge. They asked Winsberg to instruct the jury to disregard what I had just said, as it was not evidence and was highly improper. A lawyer never wants to be called down by the judge in front of the jury, but my sense in that instant had been that it was a risk I needed to take. The judge agreed with the state.

"Ladies and gentlemen, I instruct you to disregard what Mr. Cobb just said; the only evidence in this case comes from the mouths of witnesses on the witness stand. What the lawyers say is not evidence. Now move on, Mr. Cobb!"

As I walked back to the defense table, I noticed a surprised look on the face of the unemployed middle school teacher. He appeared to agree that evidence of who stayed and who left should go both ways, and he appeared puzzled as to why I was being cut off. Or was my observation of him wishful thinking? There would be ten more days of hand-to-hand combat before we knew for sure.

The state continued to call former employees of St. Rita's, each of whom attempted to sink a dagger between Sal's shoulder blades. One, a licensed practical nurse, said that a few months before Katrina she overheard Sal say he was reluctant to evacuate because Medicare wouldn't pay unless the residents were under his roof. This testimony sounded like bull to me, but I was going to have to peel the onion to get at the truth. The witness appeared to be high on something, but how to establish that delicate matter? Once again I prepared to break the cardinal rule about not asking questions when you don't already have the answer. Sometimes fortune favors the foolhardy. As good luck would have it, she admitted that she took prescription pain killers, anti-anxiety pills, and two drugs for migraine headaches.

"Are you loaded right now?" I asked.

I heard the usual call and response pattern between prosecutor and judge: "*Objection . . . Sustained.*"

"Let me re-phrase," I said. "Did you take any drugs today before coming to court?"

She admitted taking anti-anxiety medication as well as painkillers.

"Didn't you first make this allegation of hearing Mr. Mangano say the things you just told this jury, in connection with a wrongful death suit filed against the Manganos by a friend of yours?"

"I did," she said.

"And weren't you hunted down, pursued, and badgered by plaintiff lawyers in the wrongful death suits filed against St. Rita's?" I said, my voice rising.

"I object," she snapped. Apparently the witness had been on the stand so long she had forgotten that she was a witness, not a prosecuting attorney.

"No, ma'am," I responded. "You don't get to object, only the lawyers do; now answer my question." I had half expected the judge to sustain the witness's objection to my question, but he restrained himself. I reminded the witness that she had given a deposition in the civil cases against St. Rita's and that she was under oath when she did so.

I handed her a copy of the transcript of her deposition: "Read what you said on page 28, beginning at line 17, please."

Not without evident difficulty, she tried to focus on the page in question and managed to read the following: "I was hunted down, pursued, and badgered by plaintiff lawyers, and I didn't like it."

"Thank you, Miss," I said. "No further questions, your honor."

The prosecution took a hit, I thought, for putting such a shaky witness on the stand. She was just as shaky negotiating the two steps that brought her down from the stand. I hoped the jury would find her as hard to believe as I did.

Chapter 32: Toe to Toe with Governor Blanco

The prosecution's case was winding down. They had called thirty-eight witnesses thus far. Rumors began to circulate that they were planning to call Governor Blanco. This was odd; they had fought tooth and nail to prevent us calling her in *our* case. When the Louisiana Supreme Court finally denied her appeal to avoid testifying, she would make history. She would become the first governor ever compelled to testify in a criminal case involuntarily. Hearing the rumors, I asked Judge Winsberg to prevent the state from calling the governor.

"She's not on their witness list; they can't call her. And having fought against her appearance all the way to the Supreme Court twice," I argued, "it would be disingenuous and misleading to the jury to allow them to call her now." Not surprisingly, in view of his honor's earlier rulings, the judge denied my request.

What the prosecutors didn't know was that my opposition to their calling her was a sucker punch, *designed* to get them to call her. If we called her in *our* case, we could not ask her leading questions on direct examination; we couldn't put words in her mouth, which is the foundation of effective witness examination. The ability to use leading questions on cross-examination is a powerful weapon. The questioner is allowed to suggest the answer, often putting words in the witness's mouth, making it difficult for the witness to disagree with the leading question. By contrast, leading questions are prohibited on direct examination of witnesses. The question must be open-ended and not suggest its answer. Thus, the witness has more freedom to answer any way he or she wants. If they called her as a witness in *their* case, we would automatically be allowed to ask leading questions on cross-examination. They took the bait and announced to us that she would be their first witness the following day. I feigned disappointment, slamming my briefcase shut and storming out of the courtroom and down the stairs. Out of our opponents' sight, I began smirking like the cat that swallowed the canary even before I reached the front door. Newspaper accounts speculated that by calling Blanco, prosecutors hoped to mitigate the impact of what would surely be a less sympathetic line of questioning by defense attorneys. If this was their thinking, they were sadly mistaken. It's not what the witness says first that is most important; most memorable to the jury is what the witness says last and how he/she weathers cross-examination.

First thing the next morning the prosecutor announced, "The state calls Governor Kathleen Babineaux Blanco." The governor entered the courtroom with a phalanx of plainclothes state troopers, her security detail. Judge Winsberg commanded everyone in the courtroom to "please rise," so everyone stood as she entered. This was odd and inappropriate. No one stood up for any other witness; that courtesy was reserved for the judge and jury. I probably should have objected but everyone knew how that would turn out. The governor was clearly nervous and halting in her early testimony, muffing the address where she lived, the governor's mansion. Thereafter, she testified that evacuation was an "individual responsibility," and that she had repeatedly encouraged citizens to leave and head for safer, higher ground. She refused any blame for the thirty-five deaths at St. Rita's. She had hit rock bottom in public-opinion polls partly because of her handling of the hurricane disaster effort. The governor, a Democrat, had announced months earlier that she would not seek re-election later in the fall; defeat was obvious, even to her. She really had very little to add to the state's evidence and burden of proof and was tendered to us for cross-examination.

The governor, an otherwise likeable grandmother, had to be approached carefully on cross-examination. If we were too strident or mean-spirited with her, we risked engendering sympathy for her and alienating women on the jury, which included four of six members. Blanco admitted that the only two people under state law who could have declared a mandatory evacuation for St. Bernard Parish were the parish president, "and me." She explained that she did not issue such an order, "because all of the local governments were deeply engaged in getting people out and helping people evacuate." She was clearly passing the buck to local government and her answer was unimpressive. The government was objecting to virtually every question I asked and had a receptive umpire in the judge. The constant interruptions made it a difficult examination. I focused in on how the state's response to Katrina was totally changed a mere three weeks later for Hurricane Rita. She described the state's decision to order nursing home evacuations for Hurricane Rita and the provision of National Guard troops to aid that effort as a "lesson learned."

"You didn't do that for Katrina, did you?" I asked.

Her answer was offered meekly: "We were relying on individual responsibility for Katrina."

"And that didn't work, did it?" I shot back.

"No, it didn't," she said.

"And you corrected it three weeks later, right?" I asked.

"That's right," the governor said.

"With some foresight and planning, you could have implemented the plan you had for Rita before Katrina and the thirty-five lives that were lost at St. Rita's could have been saved?"

"*Objection*," and, of course, it was sustained, but I believed the point had been well made.

I next tried to question Blanco about the state's $200 billion lawsuit blaming Katrina-related death and destruction on the U.S. Army Corps of Engineers, the agency responsible for the failed flood-control system. The governor said she was not familiar with the suit, an answer that caused mouths to drop. How could a state's chief executive not know that such a suit had been filed? Winsberg blocked any questions about the suit because the governor denied, incredibly, any knowledge of it. At a bench conference I vowed to call as the defense's first witness Atty. Gen. Charles Foti himself, as the state official who had filed the suit and signed it under oath. Prosecutors, petrified at the prospect of their boss being called to the stand, made a deal and agreed to allow the suit to be entered into evidence. This was a major victory for us, for now we could argue to the jury that the same attorney general who was prosecuting us had, in *another* sworn pleading, blamed the United States Government for everything that he had blamed Sal and Mabel for. I would have a field day with this evidence in my closing argument.

Consistent with her effort at self-exoneration, the governor had already testified on direct that the levee failures played a major role in Katrina's catastrophic flooding.

"If the federal levees had not failed," she said, "the people in the Superdome would have been able to walk home. It would not have been such a huge national and international spectacle."

I reminded her of her testimony before the U.S. Senate, when she was called on the carpet to explain the failures of her administration. "Do you remember saying, under oath, governor, 'We in Louisiana know hurricanes and hurricanes know us. We would not be here today if the levees had not failed.'? Remember that?"

"I do," she answered.

"And that testimony was true on that day, wasn't it?"

"It was," she said.

"And it remains true to this day, doesn't it?"

"Yes."

I walked over to Sal and Mabel, placing a hand on each of their shoulders: "And Mr. and Mrs. Mangano wouldn't be *here* today if the levees had not failed, would they?"

"*Objection!*" (of course). We had a huge blow up outside the jury's hearing.

"Judge," I said, "that's a perfectly good question. If it works for the governor in explaining her predicament before the U.S. Senate, why shouldn't it work for the little guy?"

"*Sustained,*" said the judge. "You should know better."

"Know better than *what*?" I responded, "I believe the court is giving undue deference to this witness. That's all she is here, a witness, and I have a right to fully cross-examine her on behalf of my client."

"I said sustained, now move on before I impose sanctions against you." Winsberg's eyes narrowed; he wasn't playing around.

I moved on, but my question, I thought, made abundantly clear that a double standard was being imposed against the Manganos. As I walked back to the podium, a couple of jurors appeared uncomfortable with the court's ruling. Jurors want to hear *all* the evidence and often hold it against lawyers who try to hide the ball. In this instance, that was the A.G.'s office.

I concluded my examination of the governor with an area of inquiry from which she had no escape. A few months before Katrina, the state's Emergency Operation Plan (EOP) was amended to require the Louisiana Department of Transportation and Development (DOTD) to "direct the evacuation and sheltering of persons with mobility limitations," including those at nursing homes.

"And you signed the EOP, making it an executive order and the law of the state of Louisiana, did you not?"

"I did."

"Did you know that your secretary of the DOTD, Mr. Bradberry, testified before the Congress of the United States, under oath, that he had done *nothing* to fulfill that responsibility?"

"I did," she said.

"And he told the truth, didn't he? He didn't direct any evacuation nor did he shelter anyone at St. Rita's or anyplace else, did he?"

"That's correct," she said softly.

I pressed the attack, "Why would Secretary Bradberry, having been assigned the task of being in charge of evacuating nursing homes pursuant to the state EOP, fail to do so?"

Her answer blew me and several jurors away: "He was very annoyed with himself that this new duty hadn't fully focused," the governor responded.

"He was *annoyed?!*" I exclaimed. "You think he was more annoyed than the relatives of the thirty-five people who lost their lives because he didn't do his job?" I said, almost yelling.

The state's *"objection!"* was followed by the most quickly uttered *"sustained"* in the trial's three-plus weeks. Annoyed indeed, I thought.

"Thank you for your time, governor. I tender the witness."

It was my feeling that the governor acquitted herself as a witness just as she acquitted herself as governor—poorly.

Later in the day, several relatives of drowning victims took the stand. These witnesses were there to reveal the depths of their emotional loss and to continue icing the sympathy cake the prosecution had been baking for weeks.

Wesley Kramer, who was seventy years old, said his mother Mildred could have survived an evacuation. "I think I could have gotten my mother out by myself in my own car, if you don't mind me saying so," Kramer said, his voice rising in anger. We asked him no questions on cross, saying simply, "We're sorry for your loss, Mr. Kramer. No questions." But his answer raised again the question of the 800-pound gorilla in the courtroom. If you could have gotten your mother out on your own, then why didn't you? We hoped the unasked question resonated in the jury's mind.

The day ended with what was for me the most gripping, emotional, and genuinely heartfelt testimony of the week. The state called Louisiana State Trooper Karla Billiot, the first law enforcement officer to have arrived at St. Rita's the day after Katrina's landfall. She was a petite woman, in full uniform: dark blue trimmed in gold with sharp creases in her trousers which continued vertically and perfectly to the creases in her dark blue matching shirt. Her flat, black firearm was clearly visible in its holster on her belt. She carried her trooper's hat to the stand, a carbon copy of those iconic hats worn by the Royal Canadian Mounted Police. I loved the hat, the same dark blue as her uniform. It reminded me of Dudley Do-Right, a childhood cartoon hero of mine. Billiot was a very impressive woman who spoke with just a trace of a Cajun accent. To have become a Louisiana State Trooper was a tribute to the woman's tenacity and toughness. In the witness box she snapped to attention as she raised her right hand, shoulders square, eyes fixed on the clerk as she took the oath. Whatever she said, everyone in the room knew it was going to be the truth, the whole truth, and nothing but the truth.

Trooper Billiot described to jurors her efforts to get surviving nursing home patients out of St. Bernard Parish after finding them at the old parish courthouse with a box of crackers and two or three bottles of water. She began to weep as she described the conditions in which she found the twenty-four survivors.

"They weren't sweating any more, even though it was incredibly hot. They appeared very dehydrated," she said. "One or two were moaning. The rest weren't even moaning any more."

Choking back tears, the trooper testified that upon her arrival at the helm of an airboat, a nurse stepped forward. When Billiot asked where the Manganos were, someone offered to get them from a nearby house. Five minutes later, she testified, Sal Mangano showed up, as "disheveled and battered as everyone else." Their confrontation was an angry one.

"I asked him, 'What the f— were you thinking?' Sorry about that word, judge, but it's exactly what I said."

"That's okay, trooper," the judge said.

Billiot continued: "Mr. Mangano kind of shrugged his shoulders and said the home had never flooded before and he didn't think it would be this bad."

Billiot said she made six or eight trips by airboat taking nursing home patients out of the parish. She was a first responder and a heroine who saved lives on that day; her testimony was, perhaps, the most emotional and impactful of the entire week. One of the female jurors dabbed at her eyes. If I hadn't been on the job, I would have probably dabbed at my eyes, too.

The state had now called thirty-nine witnesses. Their fortieth and last told a harrowing story that capped their case against Sal and Mabel. Steve Galladoro, the St. Bernard Parish firefighter who had been heard from with me on Dan Abrams's MSNBC show two years earlier, gave a gut-wrenching account of his effort to recover his father's body from St. Rita's. The witness was overcome by emotion several times during his ninety minutes on the stand. When he first arrived at the flooded nursing home, he was unaware of his father's fate. Initially, it appeared that everyone had been evacuated. But when he waded inside and attempted to walk through the muddy water, he bumped into an object. It was a dead body floating in the hallway. He pushed on and bumped into another. All of a sudden, he was overcome with fear and trepidation—I don't want to run into my father like this, he thought. He immediately exited the home, heading towards the river and the old courthouse. There he found employees and some residents on the second floor in squalid conditions. No one would look him in the eye. Finally, he testified that one of the nurses came up to him and broke into tears: "Mr. Steve," she said, "your dad didn't make it out."

Galladoro, who had logged more than thirty-five years as a fireman, described his father as "a wonderful man." He said he went to St. Rita's two days before Katrina's landfall to check on the home's evacuation plan. He said he asked about sending his partially paralyzed father off with his sister who was evacuating that day, but Sal Mangano assured him the home had two buses lined up to evacuate the fifty-nine residents if necessary.

"Sal said 'Leave him with us; we're the professionals,'" Galladoro said, wiping away tears. "He assured us that my father was in better hands with them than with us."

Galladoro had returned the next day. St. Rita's still was not preparing to evacuate. He became alarmed. "I told Sal, 'One phone call and I'll get thirty-five firemen to help load these people onto buses and get them out of here,'" he said. "But he said, 'No, no. We're not evacuating. We're going to stay.'"

There had been previous testimony to the effect that parish officials offered two evacuation buses to Mabel less than twenty-four hours before Katrina's landfall. She refused them.

Galladoro was thin, weak, and without hair due to chemotherapy for cancer that had been diagnosed just three weeks earlier. He was unsteady on his feet and used a cane, shuffling instead of walking. Getting into the witness box was a struggle, but he was determined to make it. His testimony came on the two-year anniversary of Katrina's landfall. Numerous relatives of the dead wept openly as the gallant Galladoro struggled and failed to maintain his composure. The sight of this once powerful firefighter breaking down repeatedly, his eyes and nose running freely, made the courtroom uneasy. It was a hard thing to watch, and I noticed several jurors avert their gaze.

His crying stopped almost immediately—odd, I thought to myself—as John Reed started to cross-examine him. As to the sharp encounter that Galladoro had with Sal, he agreed that took place when Sal was being questioned by sheriff's deputies. Sal "had lived with death all around him for two days" and was probably in shock, Galladoro surmised. Our cross-examination was mercifully brief, and when it was over, Knight rose from his chair, faced the judge and jury and said, "The State of Louisiana rests its case."

Chapter 33: "Nice, Very Nice"

For us, it was show time! As we turned to the presentation of our evidence, we still had not made a decision about whether Sal and/or Mabel would testify. We had not even broached the subject. Thankfully, Sal and Mabel had been exercising their right to remain silent for two years. The couple had refrained from making public statements since their arrest. It had gotten to the point that reporters no longer yelled out questions to the couple as they walked to court each morning, holding hands and surrounded by TV cameras. I had done all the talking to the media for two years, before the court imposed a gag order, and now both sides were barred from public comment. Even in off-the-record conversations with reporters, we had declined to say whether the couple would testify. We declined to say so because we hadn't yet reached the decision ourselves.

Some legal analysts and experts said that we had little choice. The *New Orleans Times-Picayune* ran a huge case analysis in the Sunday paper on the last weekend before the jury would decide the case. "I think they have to testify in order to be acquitted," said Dane Ciolino, a professor at Loyola Law School in New Orleans. "There are not a lot of facts in dispute in this case. It's all about why they didn't evacuate, and the Manganos need to explain that to the jury."

One of my colleagues on the Tulane Law faculty, David Katner, agreed that an explanation by the Manganos was necessary for a verdict of acquittal. Most criminal defendants are not called to testify in their own defense, because most of them have prior convictions and juries are entitled to hear about prior convictions. Professor Katner said that wasn't a factor in this case as the Manganos had spotless records and no criminal convictions. Under those circumstances, conventional legal wisdom (if there is such a thing) dictates that you put your clients on the stand and let them explain their actions. Jurors hear about the presumption of innocence and the right to remain silent, but at the end of the day, they all want to hear the defendants' explanations. We would have some time before confronting the Manganos with yet another of the most important decisions in their lives. We would call other witnesses first and assess where we stood at the end of that process before asking Sal and Mabel, "Do you want to testify?"

With that difficult issue still pending, our overall strategy was to strike back hard and quickly at the prosecution's case. We believed the state had dragged the case out with redundantly emotional witnesses. They had gone on and on and on for almost three weeks. If we could be done with our case in short order, establishing just those evidentiary points we needed for a closing argument, the jury might appreciate our brevity and straightforwardness. The state's presentation had also been anything but straightforward. It was my view that after more than a combined three weeks of jury selection, emotional and combative testimony, and constant squabbling among the lawyers for both sides, the jury's mind was probably already made up. I hoped that it was made up in our favor, but that was a pure guess. We should present them with clear, direct evidence and argue the case, empowering the jury in spite of the horror, sadness, and emotion, to set Sal and Mabel free. Easier said than done, perhaps. We knew we still had an uphill climb.

As our first witness, I decided to call someone who could challenge the basic assumption underlying the state's entire case: that evacuating nursing homes in advance of hurricanes saves lives. I called Dr. Brobson Lutz, the sly Southerner with the thick Alabama accent who had already helped us review patient medical records. Lutz had followed college at Vanderbilt with medical school at Tulane and then, just for good measure, picked up a master's in public health, also from Tulane. For a time he had even run the New Orleans Department of Health. But in my book, his most valuable credential was that accent, not unlike what jurors would hear on a Saturday night at St. Francisville's Magnolia Café. In jurors' minds, it would establish him as one of their own, not one of those high-priced Yankee doctors the state had flown in.

Medical studies on nursing home evacuations showed that the number of elderly residents in an evacuated region who die in transit is about the same as the number who would have been killed by the storm if they hadn't left: "The bottom line on all the research is that there is no evidence-based proof that you actually save lives by evacuating patients from nursing home," Lutz said.

He made it clear that he was speaking of nursing homes in general, not suggesting that thirty-five residents of St. Rita's would have died on the road had they been forced to evacuate. I then questioned him about Mabel's fear that some of her residents might not survive the ordeal of a last-minute evacuation. He called that a valid medical concern on her part. He had reviewed medical records of the fifty-nine residents who were present for the flood and concluded that, "One or more residents likely would have died in an evacuation."

That's all I needed from him: corroboration of those two points. And so, in stark contrast to how the state had gone on and on with their witnesses, I said, "That's all I have for you, Doc. Please answer the state's questions."

Cross-examination—and Julie Cullen handled this one herself—is where the good doctor's testimony got interesting. He had testified on direct that early in his career, right out of medical school, he had been the medical director at a nursing home named St. Margaret's.

"Was that a paid job, and how much did you make?" Cullen asked.

"Gosh, you're talking about way back," Lutz answered. "I don't know, maybe $100 a month."

"So it was more of a nominal fee?"

"It wasn't nominal to me at that time," he said. "I had just started practicing and $100 was good money to me back then."

There were some chuckles among the jury members, always a good sign, provided they're laughing with—not at—your witness. Cullen then started arguing with Lutz, never a good idea when the witness is an expert and well experienced in courtroom testimony, as this one was. What Cullen chose to quibble about was the cause of death of the resident at St. Rita's who died right before the storm and was taken out in the last ambulance to leave the parish.

"So you don't know what she died from?"

"No," he said.

"If I suggested to you it was cardiac arrest, does that sound like something that might happen in a nursing home?"

His answer was a stinging rebuke. "Well, everybody eventually dies of cardiac arrest. That's not really a cause of death."

The prosecutor should have left our rattlesnake alone, but she pressed on, arguing with Lutz about evacuation plans and pre-existing contracts with bus companies and ambulance companies to move patients in advance of a storm. He explained that in his review of every article involving evacuations of nursing homes, there were always problems.

"Even with contracts it's very, very seldom that it works out like it's supposed to," he explained. She then asked the one question too many, and got an answer that even I didn't get.

"And isn't that why if you're dealing with a sick, elderly population, you should have a back-up plan?"

I objected to the question and was, of course, overruled, allowing the witness to launch this zinger: "Sure. I guess you need a back-up plan for everything. But if I had been medical director at St. Rita's, and I had gotten a phone call and been told we have food, water, fuel, and medicines to last us a week, and we have never flooded here before—should we try to get everybody out, or should we stay? I'd say it never flooded there before; you sound like you're ready for it; I think there would be more harm done in trying to leave than staying put."

The question had exploded in Cullen's face like an envelope opened by Wile E. Coyote. The doctor's answer was the Road Runner saying, once again: "Beep! Beep!"

Undeterred, she did not stop at one question too many, she asked another. "What about old people who can't get out of bed? Don't you think they could drown if there is flooding from bank to bank in the parish because of a hurricane?"

His answer was a shocker: "Absolutely. And that's why at St. Margaret's, which had flooded before, their plan was absolute evacuation. That had not been their plan before they flooded. That was not the plan at Lafon Nursing Home, the one in Gentilly run by those Creole nuns of color, which flooded and twenty-two people died."

She looked anxiously to the judge for help digging her out of this hole, but he apparently had resigned himself to allowing jurors to hear at last about the nursing homes that *didn't* evacuate. "Just ask your next question," Winsberg said.

The truth of the tragedy at Lafon made it to the courtroom without the head nun's help, although in due course the judge would incorrectly rule against my mentioning it in the closing argument. The "L" word (Lafon) had been uttered and the cat was out of the bag. Lutz's answer was not exactly responsive to the question asked, but that's the risk a lawyer runs when asking the one question too many, especially if it's asked in a non-leading fashion as this one was. He killed her.

Frustrated, Cullen seemed to remember the field day I had had with her two doctor experts, exposing all the money they had been paid, diminishing, if not destroying, the impact of their testimony. So she decided to try the same tactic with Lutz, not knowing where it would lead or what his answer would be. I knew where it was going and how it was going to end, because Lutz and I had prepared for it. First, she attempted to show that Lutz had not reviewed sufficient information.

"Did you talk to any of the surviving residents yourself?"

"No, ma'am," he said in his best Alabama drawl.

"Did you talk to any of the family members of any of the residents who died to get their impressions of their loved ones' physical and mental status before Katrina?"

"No, ma'am."

"How many hours have you spent in preparation since whatever date Mr. Cobb hired you for this case?" she asked with a dismissive wave in my direction.

"About twenty."

"And what are your hourly charges?"

"Two hundred fifty dollars an hour for review of records, which is the same that I charge your office when I review records for you."

(Boom! Beep! Beep!)

"Have we ever met before, doctor?" Cullen asked.

"Your *office,* I said."

"Have *we* ever met before?" she asked again, her voice rising in anger and frustration.

"No, ma'am."

"Have I ever asked you to review any records for me?"

"No, ma'am, but aren't y'all with the office of the Attorney General of the State of Louisiana?"

"Yes," she said, answering a witness's question—a classic symptom that she had lost control.

"Well, then, I've done plenty of work for your office and I am charging Mr. Cobb the same thing I charge your office."

(Beep! Beep!)

In an instant, the state's expert medical testimony was forgotten and Dr. Lutz, who had worked before for both sides, was clearly the more credible and memorable witness. It didn't hurt that he was polite with his Southern drawl, replete with his "Yes, ma'ams" and "no, ma'ams." His use of "y'all" instead of "you" or "your" was the topper. Clearly, he wasn't a Yankee, and we of the defense suddenly felt that we were, indeed, back in the Land of Cotton, High Cotton.

As good as Dr. Lutz turned out to be, he wasn't my first choice to be our first witness. That honor would have gone to Joseph Donchess, executive director of the Louisiana Nursing Home Association (LNHA), a former lawyer for the Louisiana Department of Health and Hospitals. Donchess was physically present in the state's Emergency Operations Center (EOC) as Katrina approached. He and other LNHA staff manned the nursing home desk in the EOC, staying in contact with the homes and relaying information to and from emergency personnel. On Sunday night, just hours before Katrina struck, Donchess had telephoned some fifty-seven nursing homes in the greater New Orleans area. He kept track of which homes were sheltering in place and which homes were evacuating. That tally turned into a document showing that thirty-six of the fifty-seven were staying put, just as Sal and Mabel had chosen to do.

We gave notice that we intended to offer his testimony and the document in evidence and, of course, the state objected. Winsberg overruled their objection, reminding prosecutors that he had previously said if they offered proof that the other three homes in St. Bernard evacuated, he was going to allow this evidence. He reasoned that if the state put in question what other homes did, then, in fairness, we ought to be able to show what thirty-six out of fifty-seven did. "I warned you," he said, overruling their objection. They asked for time to take an emergency writ to the Court of Appeal and Winsberg granted them twenty-four hours, which had the effect of pushing Donchess back in our order of witnesses. The First Circuit Court of Appeal denied the state's writ by a two to one vote. Now in a near panic, the state asked for time to take an emergency writ to the Louisiana Supreme Court—anything to keep the jury from seeing this eye-popping evidence. If we were able to show that thirty-six hurricane-area nursing homes had sheltered in place, how could the state argue that what Sal and Mabel did was "gross negligence?" Was the whole nursing home industry guilty of gross negligence? If so, why were only Sal and Mabel on trial?

Winsberg gave them another twenty-four hours. In the meantime, we were forced to juggle witnesses and re-order the sequence of our proof, which was having a negative impact on our presentation. The state had asked for a "stay" at the state supreme court. A "stay," if granted, would order the trial court to preserve the *status quo* until the full court had a chance to consider the writ.

"Judge," I said, "the supreme court hasn't granted their requested stay; the court of appeal has affirmed your ruling. I want to put Donchess on the stand *now* and elicit this critical testimony for *our* case. Don't we get to call our witnesses when *we* think it best to put them on the stand?"

"You do," said the judge, "just not right now. Court stands in recess," whereupon we took an extended lunch break.

Winsberg was stalling, giving the supreme court the chance to consider and rule on the state's emergency writ. Nobody, including the judge, thought the state's writ stood a snowball's chance in hell. The criteria for writs to the supreme court are extraordinarily narrow in scope, and the issue of a witness's testimony or the admissibility of a document in evidence during a five-week trial did not fit any of the high court's criteria. In addition, the trial judge is given wide latitude to make sure a trial is fair. The trial judge, present in the courtroom, knows what's really going on and how to make things fair; for that reason appellate courts are extremely reluctant to second-guess him. After all, the Louisiana Supreme Court had appointed Winsberg to handle the St. Rita's case in the first place, when all the St. Bernard Parish judges recused themselves. He was probably the most seasoned judge we could have hoped for, said John Reed, himself an experienced practitioner in state court. At various times in the case, both sides were furious with Winsberg for his rulings. I know I was. He managed to piss off both sides with some regularity. In some quarters, pissing off both sides with regularity is mistaken for doing a good job. Surely, I thought, the supreme court is not going to meddle in an ongoing five-week trial, presided over by their hand-picked choice. But it was taking too long. The writ was such bull it merited a swift, two-word decision: "Writ denied."

I got back early from lunch and was walking the back hall which led to Winsberg's office. He was at his desk and he was clearly troubled by the undecided Donchess issue. On the one hand, he wanted to give the supreme court the opportunity to weigh in and decide the issue. On the other hand, he knew I was right. The state in their initial application to the supreme court had asked for a stay and the court had not granted one. The court of appeal had affirmed Winsberg's ruling two to one. The judge would have been on firm legal ground to allow me to put Donchess on the stand right away and elicit this critically important testimony. It could be a game changer. I gave Winsberg a searching look as I passed by his office, and he waved me in and offered an explanation.

"I talked to the clerk at the supreme court and he told me he's trying to round up all seven justices so they can consider the state's writ," he said.

I had a vision of the clerk going from restaurant to restaurant in New Orleans' French Quarter searching for his judges. Were they at the Rib Room of the Omni Royal Orleans across the street from the stately supreme court building? Perhaps Galatoire's or Antoine's? Wherever they were, I feared some of them might be getting liquored up, a judicial phenomenon I had personally witnessed on many occasions. They rarely picked up their own restaurant checks, relying instead on the kindness of lawyers or anyone else who curried their favor. Perplexed, Winsberg mulled over his dilemma. "What do I tell the supreme court clerk?" he mused. I wasn't sure he was looking for an answer from me, but he got one.

"I don't care what you tell him. Tell him to go f— himself. We're in the middle of a trial and their delay is prejudicing defendants on trial for their lives. Let me put Donchess on!"

"Get outta here," he said, trying unsuccessfully to suppress a grin. We went back into court and continued with the witness who was on the stand. About an hour later, the sheriff walked up to the bench and handed the judge a sheet of paper. The judge unfolded the message, his eyebrows rising slightly as he read it.

"Let's take a break, ladies and gentlemen. Stretch your legs and get some coffee. I want to see the lawyers in the back," he said jumping off the bench and heading towards his office. By the time the thundering herd of lawyers reached his cubbyhole, he was seated at his desk, still staring at the message that had been handed up to him.

"The supreme court has ruled," he said somberly. "By a vote of four to three, they granted the state's writ and have excluded the document and the evidence that thirty-six of fifty-seven area nursing homes had sheltered in place. They say the document is hearsay and, therefore, inadmissible because the information was obtained from nursing home administrators and not independently verified by the nursing home association. The evidence is excluded." I was flummoxed, flabbergasted, and apoplectic, all at the same time. The supreme court had *never* intervened in an ongoing trial to rule on a hearsay objection. It was absolutely unprecedented. I felt like I was having an out-of-body experience, a psychic grand mal seizure.

Winsberg appeared as stunned as I was. This incredible turn of events was a huge and undeserved victory for the prosecution. Now, the only evidence the jury would hear was of the other three homes in St. Bernard fleeing ahead of Katrina, successfully evacuating 188 residents with the loss of only one life. In allowing this evidence, Winsberg had assumed the jury would later hear ours—that thirty-six of fifty-seven homes had stayed put. He had promised as much to both sides. That would be a fair and balanced representation of the truth of what happened and the jury could make its own decision as to what was appropriate. The supreme court had now forced Winsberg to break his promise to us, and he was clearly regretful. We elect our supreme court justices in Louisiana and Foti was a powerful politician, whose endorsement in a judicial race would carry great weight. He was the chief law enforcement officer for the state, and we were a law-and-order state. But also a very political state. Indeed, Foti was up for re-election within six weeks of the close of the Mangano trial. We all concluded that four of his "friends" on the supreme court had thrown him a life-preserver in this unwarranted and legally dubious ruling. It was a joke but the jury would never find that out, and the joke was on us.

Unsure what to do next, we retreated to a small ante-chamber in the back of the courtroom where we stored some of our file materials. I was so furious that I punched the wall, damaging the sheetrock and almost breaking my hand. "Calm down," John said, "You're gonna have a heart attack." I had a flashback to "Side-Swipe" Sabrio telling me the same thing on the golf course a while back. "Focus," John said softly. "You'll figure it out." Donchess was to be our next witness, and, as lead lawyer, I would be conducting his examination. I took a long, deep breath, folded my hands on the table in front of me and leaned forward until my folded hands cushioned my forehead. I closed my eyes and tried to go into a trance. It looked like I was an inattentive student in a grade-school class, about to nod off.

A lawyer has two options under these circumstances: to accept a court's ruling and move on—after all, the Supreme Court is the final word on all things legal in Louisiana—or to ignore the court's ruling and press on, trying to slide the information in some other way. John and Bob had exited the small room leaving me alone. They had other business to attend to. I played the hearsay rule over and over in my head, trying to figure out a way around it. Hearsay is an out-of-court statement made by someone who isn't available as a witness, offered to prove the truth of the matter asserted in the out-of-court declaration. *Eureka!* I had an idea. I snapped out of my trance, hopped to my feet, and strode confidently back into the courtroom. John looked at me with a question mark etched on his brow. "I got it," I told him.

Court was gaveled back into session: "Who's your next witness, Mr. Cobb?" Winsberg asked me.

"The defense calls Mr. Joseph Donchess."

Donchess testified that the morning Katrina made landfall, he got a report from Mabel that she and her patients had weathered the storm with no major problems. He also stated that he was in touch with other New Orleans area nursing home administrators while manning the desk at the Emergency Operations Center in Baton Rouge. In addition to maintaining the flow of information between the homes and emergency officials, Donchess was also handling requests from the homes for assistance or supplies. He testified that in his conversation with Mabel on Sunday night just before Katrina made landfall, she had reported to him that everyone was okay and the nursing home didn't need any additional help or supplies.

I attempted to introduce the tally sheet. The state objected. I argued that the document was a business record kept in the EOC. As such, it was admissible in evidence pursuant to the business record exception to the hearsay rule. "Judge," I said, "we got the document from the state; it's *their* document! How can they argue that it's inaccurate hearsay? They provided it to *us*."

I received a kinder, gentler, *"sustained,"* meaning this approach wasn't going to work either, even though legally, it should have. I was down to my last straw.

"Mr. Donchess, you told us you spoke with Mabel at St. Rita's on the night before the hurricane."

"I did."

"Did you call any other homes in the hurricane area that night before Katrina struck?"

"I did."

"How many calls did you make that night to nursing homes?"

"Fifty-seven."

"Without telling us what anybody said or what anybody told you on the phone, as that would be hearsay, you understand that?"

"I do."

"Don't tell me what anybody said. Out of those fifty-seven calls you placed on Sunday night, how many times did someone pick up the phone and answer the call that you made?"

"Thirty-six times," he answered quickly and firmly.

"Bingo!" I thought to myself. It's out there, *in evidence,* and now we can argue to the jury that thirty-six out of fifty-seven did the same thing we did. I hoped this would take the sting out of the fact that the other three nursing homes in St. Bernard Parish had evacuated, leaving St. Rita's as the Lone Ranger that didn't. I had lulled the prosecution to sleep in the preface to the question I finally got the witness to answer. Because I specified "don't tell me what anybody said," my opponents believed I would not be eliciting hearsay testimony. But the mere fact of someone answering a phone call was *itself* hearsay; it was an out-of-court answer, with the person who answered not testifying, and used to prove the truth of the matter asserted. That matter asserted was the fact that thirty-six homes answered the phone because they were sheltering in place just like St. Rita's. I returned to the counsel table and John leaned over and whispered, "Nice, very nice."

Chapter 34: A Courageous South African

Lutz's testimony that hurricane evacuations don't necessarily save elderly lives and that some of St. Rita's residents likely would have died on the bus was one of the three legs on which our case stood. The second leg was Donchess's evidence that thirty-six out of fifty-seven area nursing homes also decided to shelter in place, yet no one else was on trial for a crime from other homes. The third leg was to be provided by the testimony of Ivor van Heerden, the deputy director of the LSU Hurricane Center. He was the intrepid scientist who had challenged the U.S. Army Corps of Engineers' explanations of what happened and why. His book, *The Storm,* had become my Bible when it came to understanding the mechanics of storm surge and levee failure. I had spoken to him much earlier in our preparations for trial and he seemed interested in helping Sal and Mabel. Weeks before the trial was to begin, I tried to reach him. I left a dozen messages for him at his office and home. None were returned. From years of experience, I sensed when a witness was getting cold feet or was trying to duck me. I was convinced that's what was going on, but I didn't know why.

I dispatched a private detective to find van Heerden and, at the appropriate time, to serve him with a subpoena compelling his attendance in court on the trial's opening day. My guy got him at home one night late, waking him up and dropping the subpoena on him. Van Heerden was neither pleased nor amused. The very next night, I received a late night phone call. He was finally returning the dozen or so messages I had left for him, and he was angry. He felt that I had invaded his personal space—his home—causing his wife and children to worry and wonder.

"How could you do this to me?" he asked.

"I've been calling you for weeks, Ivor, and you wouldn't call me back. You left me no choice. I've got a job to do."

His speech was slurred and his tongue was thick. He had clearly been drinking and the conversation was difficult. He didn't want to testify; he didn't want any part of this process. It was not the appropriate time to have a conversation of substance with him and I suggested we speak the next day. He rejected the suggestion.

"What if my opinion and testimony is that your clients should have evacuated and thirty-five lives would have been saved?" he asked.

I paused for a long time before answering; the silence was deafening.

"Are you threatening me, Ivor?" I asked.

"I'm not threatening you," he answered. "What if that's my testimony, is what I'm asking. You still want me as a witness?"

"You're an engineer and a scientist who knows about levees and hurricanes," I said. "You're not an expert on nursing homes and whether they should or should not evacuate, and you wouldn't be allowed to answer that question anyway. The only questions I have for you come right out of your book, and I assume you will answer them truthfully. This conversation is ended." And I hung up. That's not exactly the way one wants to end a conversation with a potentially pivotal witness, but I had no choice.

I found the whole incident disturbingly odd. Van Heerden had been the good guy, the white knight who rode in on behalf of all of us Katrina victims, proving our losses weren't our fault but the fault of the Corps that was supposed to protect us. He was one of the heroes. What caused this unexpected change in his behavior, I wondered. I started nosing around and discovered that Ivor was under tremendous pressure from his employer LSU to shut up, remain quiet, and quit criticizing the federal government. The university was heavily dependent on federal research dollars and feared the flow of them would be cut off if this outspoken, thickly accented Afrikaner didn't shut his trap. LSU's new chancellor was a disciple and protégé of then Vice President Dick Cheney, and van Heerden's criticism reflected poorly on President Bush and the whole Republican establishment. Shut your ass up or you'll be out of a job was the message he got from on high. He was a non-tenured faculty member at LSU, which meant they could fire him at will. He had a wife, a daughter, a mortgage, and bills, and he clearly needed to keep his job, hence, the late-night, menacing phone call.

I called Ivor back several days later and explained that I understood his situation. I pointed out to him that being subpoenaed made clear he was not volunteering his testimony. "It's not your idea," I said. "Tell your bosses you are a reluctant, subpoenaed witness but you have to show up. It's the law. It will give you some cover."

He understood and took some solace in the explanation. "Just let me know when you need me," he said with a tone of resignation in his voice.

He was, I hoped, back in the tent with other supporting witnesses, but I was not sure how it would play out. It was a very small tent. I decided to call him anyway. What we needed from him—the third leg of our case—was an expert's assertion that the flooding, death, and destruction was the sole fault of the U.S. Army Corps, the agency that had built the regional flood defense. We desperately needed him to say that. And so I rolled the dice.

"Defense calls Professor Ivor van Heerden."

First, I qualified him as an expert witness, allowing him to offer opinion, not just facts. In addition to being deputy director of the LSU Hurricane Center, he was the director of the LSU Center for the Study of Public Health Impacts of Hurricanes. He was also an associate professor of civil and environmental engineering. He earned a PhD in marine sciences from LSU and his research had included disaster preparation and response, coastal geomorphology, environmental management, and habitat restoration. When it came to hurricanes, disaster preparation, levees, and habitat, he was clearly the smartest guy in the room—any room. He had been appointed by Governor Blanco to head Team Louisiana, the group of scientists who conducted the state's official probe of the disaster, and his book, *The Storm*, recapped that definitive analysis. With van Heerden certified by the judge as an expert, the jury literally sat up straight in their chairs, leaned forward, and gave the scientist their complete attention. Like a professor teaching an attentive class, he held the jurors in the palm of his hand.

He told them that the levees protecting St. Bernard were built largely of sand from the dredging of the MRGO and lacked a proper protective covering—causing the breaches, dozens of them. The Corps didn't just build the levees from the wrong material, he said, they built them to the wrong height. The levee was built one and a half feet too low because the Corps used the wrong baseline elevation.

"It was gross negligence," he said. "Some of the errors were mistakes that a first-year engineering student wouldn't make."

I let that answer sink in with an extended pause and noticed a juror shaking his head back and forth. If the levees had been built to their design height of 17.5 feet, he said, the remaining six inches of storm surge would have been trapped by a second set of levees and the only water in St. Bernard Parish would have been rain water. St. Rita's, with its slab 4.79 feet above sea level, would have remained dry.

"Are you telling this jury that, if the federal levees had not failed catastrophically, not a single person would have drowned at St. Rita's?" I asked, my voice rising in indignation.

"That's exactly what I'm saying," van Heeden responded.

I turned and looked at the prosecutor's table in disgust, pausing just long enough to let the jury absorb what may have been the most important answer in the entire case. Evidently, I must have paused for effect too long.

"Do you have any other questions, Mr. Cobb?" the judge asked sarcastically.

"I'm sure I do, your honor. I was just looking for one," I said, which bought me a little more time and a chuckle from a juror.

"Were there any more glaring mistakes that the Corps made which contributed to the catastrophic flooding St. Bernard Parish experienced?"

"There were."

According to the conclusions reached by Team Louisiana, the Corps had based its levee design on wind speeds associated with a Category 2 hurricane, not the stronger Category 4 storm as intended.

"The result was that the predicted storm surge elevations were 40 percent too low," van Heerden testified.

"Let me see if I've got this right," I said. "The Corps built the levees out of the wrong material, to the wrong height, with no protective covering, and miscalculated the wind speeds associated with a surge. Did they do anything right?"

"Not that I can think of," van Heerden replied dryly. Ignoring the judge's time clock, I let that answer sink in deeply.

"Are you here today voluntarily, Professor van Heerden?"

"No, I am not."

"Did you want to testify?"

"No, I did not. I was subpoenaed by you and my appearance was commanded, and I wasn't too happy about it. In fact, I was angry."

"Why didn't you want to testify?"

"Because I feared I would lose my job in testifying against the Corps of Engineers."

Conflicted in a battle between his own conscience and his obligations to his family, Ivor van Heerden stepped up, responded to the call for truth, and was, perhaps, the most compelling witness in the case to that point. He was certainly the most courageous. Less than a year later, he was fired from his job by the cowardly and despicable LSU administration. He was fired for telling the truth. Truth and academic freedom at Louisiana State University are like two distant cousins who haven't spoken in years. The scientist who discovered, against overwhelming odds, what the Corps did to the people of Louisiana and who had the courage to speak truth to power, was likely to become a forgotten footnote in the history of a terrible disaster. But he would never be forgotten by Sal and Mabel or anyone else in the hushed courtroom on the day he testified. He was a giant.

We were running out of witnesses and it was about time to have "the talk" with Sal and Mabel. "The talk" was whether they wanted to take the stand and testify on their own behalf. I was completely uncomfortable with taking the lead in this conversation. There are ethical and practical rules that experienced criminal defense attorneys must follow in having "the talk." Bob took charge and I was deeply grateful. He met with them alone. Sometime after "the talk" was concluded, Mabel called me and put me on speaker phone with Sal and asked me what I thought. Through every major decision during the two years I had worked with this couple, whenever we reached a decision point, Mabel would always say, "Whatever you think is best, Jim, that's what we'll do."

I told her that decision model didn't work for this decision. "Only you guys can make this one," I said.

"Will they try to do to me what you did to the governor when she was on the witness stand?" she asked.

"They will try to do that, and more," I told her.

"Then I don't want to testify," she replied.

"Me neither," chimed in Sal.

So this big, momentous decision was reached quickly and relatively easily. After they made it, I told them I agreed with their decision. Law professors and newspaper pundits notwithstanding, it was the right call. Both Sal and Mabel were so fragile and so vulnerable that exposing them to withering cross-examination would have been cruel and unusual punishment. It could also have led directly to their convictions. We all placed our trust in three principles upon which our republic was founded: the presumption of innocence, the right to remain silent, and the requirement that the state prove guilt beyond a reasonable doubt. Many a criminal defendant went down in flames relying on these three principles. We placed our trust in the good people of St. Francisville and West Feliciana Parish. The case was coming to an end.

We had only two witnesses left to call. The state had called forty; we would call but five and three of them were expert witnesses. In a criminal homicide prosecution, this lineup of witnesses was most unusual. John Reed expressed his discomfort with our expert-laden presentation. He was concerned that the jury would think we went out and bought some experts and got them to say things consistent with a not-guilty verdict. In his experience, criminal trials were almost always fact driven, and we had yet to call a single fact witness. That was about to change.

The most empathetic lawyer on our team, John had taken on the job of preparing the only defense witness who was actually at St. Rita's on that fateful August morning in 2005: T.J. Mangano, Little Sal's wife and Sal and Mabel's daughter-in-law. She was incredibly fragile and emotional, but John had prepared her well, working with her for days in the belief that she could be a terrific witness.

"Do you want to call her last or next to last?" I asked. "Do we want her to be our final word?"

"I do," he said. And the decision was made.

It then fell to me to call our third and final expert witness, Dr. Dennis Mileti. Mileti was a retired sociology professor from the University of Colorado, where he directed the Natural Hazards Center. He had been a consultant to the Nuclear Regulatory Commission, the Department of Defense, and numerous other federal departments, as well as a dozen or more state governments. He was *the* guy nationally in the field of disaster management and emergency planning and preparedness. He had authored numerous books, including the definitive textbook on the subject. The court certified him as an expert and so instructed the jury. He was then allowed to give his opinions about the federal and state response to Katrina. He had waited a lifetime to have this big a stage on which to express his professional creed. It was the biggest disaster in the history of the United States, and he was now front and center in the only trial to that point in which an American jury would decide who was responsible and who was at fault. I wanted to start him off with a big, broad question, one which would attract the jury's attention and give him the opportunity to wax eloquent.

"Should *anyone* have died in Katrina?" I asked. My emphasis on the word *anyone* was pronounced, as I wanted to include all 1,600 storm victims, not just those at St. Rita's.

His answer was impassioned: "Absolutely not; *every* death was avoidable."

"All sixteen hundred?" I asked, not quite believing his answer myself.

"That's right; every one of the deaths was avoidable. If adequate emergency plans had been in place and implemented during Katrina, people would have perceived the risk and taken appropriate action to avoid it."

He said the greatest, saddest failing was in not ensuring the evacuation of New Orleans area nursing homes and hospitals, where more than 150 residents and patients died during the hurricane and its aftermath. I pointed out to him that less than a month after Katrina, Governor Blanco marshaled state resources to evacuate nursing homes and hospitals in southwestern Louisiana that were threatened by Hurricane Rita. During her testimony, the governor said state officials had "learned our lessons from Katrina," a statement which drew a sharp rebuke from Dr. Mileti.

"Everything they think they learned from Katrina, the field of emergency management already knew for decades," he snapped. "Had the state exhibited a fundamental, basic understanding of emergency management, not a single life would have been lost at St. Rita's."

Cementing his credibility as a witness, Mileti responded to Cullen's questions on cross-examination. He condemned St. Rita's emergency plan, which relied on Sal Mangano's company and the nine-person van that was supposed to evacuate the hundred-bed nursing home.

"It's not even a plan," Mileti said. "I can't imagine how that would work."

Addressing the concerns of caregivers having to make a life-or-death decision to unplug someone from a ventilator in order to evacuate, Mileti was emphatic. "Such concerns demonstrate that caregivers in nursing homes have too much of an emotional stake in their residents to make the right call regarding evacuation," he said. "That call should be left up to the government."

Noting that the Manganos relied on parish officials to tell them when to evacuate and to provide the transportation, Cullen returned to a familiar prosecution theme: "Whatever happened to personal responsibility? Doesn't it have a role in our society?"

Mileti said the government's primary responsibility is to ensure the public's health and safety, especially during life-or-death situations such as Katrina's approach.

"If you rely too heavily on personal responsibility, it will cost some of your citizens their lives. That's what happened here. Sixteen hundred people died because government failed in its responsibility to protect the public's health and safety. It's really that simple, Ms. Cullen."

He was a powerful, credentialed, impressive witness. We only had one left. Conveniently, her last name was Mangano.

After almost five weeks of trial, the jury was finally going to hear from someone in the family. It wasn't going to be Mabel or Sal, however. It was to be Tammy "T.J." Mangano, Little Sal's wife, the defendants' daughter-in-law. T.J. was an attractive woman in her late thirties or early forties; I didn't have the courage to ask which. She was the mother of two sons, Sal III, a police officer in the New Orleans suburbs, and Tanner, the number-one graduate in his Special Forces boot camp. Later, Tanner would follow in his older brother's footsteps and become a police officer himself. From the moment I had met T.J. two years earlier, it was clear to me she was having an extremely difficult time coping with the tragedy at St. Rita's. Every time I attempted to engage her in a substantive discussion about what happened, she would break down and be unable to continue the discussion. This vulnerability was a huge contrast to her otherwise feisty personality.

In the months after Katrina, the destroyed nursing home was set upon by photographers and TV camera crews who trespassed on private property to take unauthorized photos and videos. I had established a protocol with Little Sal on how to handle these press invasions. Call the sheriff's office; have them arrested for trespassing, with forfeiture of their film, camera, or videotape set as the price of their release. Little Sal and T.J. were infuriated by the trespassers with cameras and at times things got a trifle intense. On one occasion I got a frantic call from T.J. Another snoop had invaded the property, taken photos, and was attempting escape, she told me breathlessly. Little Sal had tackled him and pinned him to the ground in a headlock, waiting for the law to arrive. By cell phone, T.J. was giving me a play-by-play as her husband struggled.

"Sal's got him, Mr. Jim. He ain't going nowhere," she said. "But he won't give up his film. I got a gun on him, too." I was most uncomfortable with this revelation and was about to tell her to go put the gun back inside her house. But evidently the photographer had begun to turn the tables on Little Sal. "Just hold him still, Sal," his wife shouted. "I'll shoot him in the leg." Before I could say no, T.J., *please* don't shoot him in the leg, I could hear the photographer begging her. "F—, lady," he screamed, "I'll give you the damn film, just don't shoot me!" Crisis averted. This was the T.J. who would be our last witness, and with T.J. anything was possible.

She began her testimony by telling the jury that she and her husband lived in a small house within fifty yards of the nursing home's back door. Both she and her husband had worked in the home for years, essentially living there, except when they went to their place to sleep. She told them how she had two children who were raised in the nursing home, how her kids took to the old folks, and how the old folks took to her kids. Everyone was family and her children had "sixty or seventy grandmas and grandpas."

John guided her carefully and skillfully through her testimony. She displayed an encyclopedic knowledge of her residents. She knew their room numbers by heart, which pairs were roommates, what they liked to eat, and whether they took their meals in their rooms or in the dining hall with the others. She knew which ones needed help eating and she described how she and Sal and Mabel and Little Sal hand-fed those who couldn't feed themselves. She then described St. Rita's hurricane preparation planning.

"Little Sal" listens closely as relatives of victims talk to the press during breaks in the trial. Courtesy of CBS News, from *48 Hours: No Way Out* (02/02/08).

They had food, water, fuel for generators, medicines, diapers—everything they needed if they became cut off from the world for as much as two weeks. She described how Mabel was worried that some residents would not survive the ordeal of an evacuation and how they did not plan to leave unless parish officials ordered them to do so.

"When you have to start unplugging stuff, it's a big decision," she said, her voice getting softer. She referred to the medical machines that kept many of her beloved residents alive. "If it's a mandatory evacuation, you have no choice. As much as it hurts to put these people in jeopardy (by evacuating), you have no choice." She testified that ninety-three people had sheltered at St. Rita's that night: fifty-nine residents, twelve staff members and their families, and the Mangano clan. T.J. said she and the staff made ice cream sundaes for the residents who watched a movie in the hours before Katrina made landfall. During the night some windows were blown out and there were some leaks in the roof, but when daylight broke, it appeared that the home had weathered the storm. She described the wall of water six feet high that she saw rushing toward the nursing home when she stepped outside shortly after 10:00 A.M.

"It wasn't some pretty, blue wave of water," she said. "It was muddy brown with trees and bushes mixed in it and animals in front, trying to get out of the way."

She said some of the men went to get boats while the staff rushed to put residents on mattresses wrapped in plastic. They floated, all right—right up to the ceiling. That's how high the water had risen in less than twenty minutes. She described standing in a boat in the wind and the rain, helping lift residents onto the roof after they had been pulled from the flooded home by her Special Forces son, Tanner.

She fought tears as she described her son's heroics. "I would scream for him to stay with me, but he kept going back in again and again, getting more people." Every time he dived under the water to swim back in, she feared it was the last time she would see him alive. Her anxiety was unimaginable.

All thirty-four of the able-bodied people survived the flood along with twenty-four residents who made their way from the roof to the old parish school. During the next forty-eight hours the residents were evacuated by airboat but T.J. and her clan stayed on until they were ordered to leave by a sheriff's deputy. The parish had been placed under a mandatory evacuation order that had come too late for the thirty-five residents of St. Rita's who remained in the building.

"We still had residents inside St. Rita's, the ones we couldn't save," she said breaking down. "I didn't want to leave them there all alone."

I thought her testimony was a *tour de force*, a bravura performance by lawyer and witness. John's sensitivity and his approach were perfect. From an informational and emotional standpoint, it was perhaps the best direct examination of a witness I had ever seen. T.J. held up on cross and finally, the jury had heard from a Mangano. The beauty of this Mangano's testimony was that she wasn't a defendant. What came across most clearly was that T.J. and the entire family cared deeply for their residents and loved them as if they were their own kith and kin. The jury knew nothing of our decision not to call Sal and Mabel. When T.J. finished her testimony, Winsberg turned to me and said, "Who's your next witness, Mr. Cobb?"

I rose from my chair, faced the jury and said, "The defense rests, your honor." There were a couple of raised eyebrows in the jury box. Not calling Sal and Mabel appeared to catch them by surprise. The state had the opportunity to call rebuttal witnesses and chose to recall Brian Jarvinen, the storm surge expert from Miami whom I had named the "Lone Ranger" for his deeply flawed analysis of what happened—a hypothesis supported by no one other than Jarvinen himself. I was thankful they did, because, coming as he did on the heels of van Heerden's compelling testimony, I had a chance to slap Jarvinen around a little bit more. They attempted to call a second rebuttal witness, but he admitted discussing the case with someone else in violation of the judge's order, and the judge kicked him off the stand. It was not the way the state wanted to end their rebuttal, but the evidence was at an end. Closing arguments would follow the next day, the judge would charge the jury with the law, and deliberations would begin. Before dismissing the jurors, the judge told them to pack a bag and bring it with them the next day, for they would be sequestered for the length of their deliberations. The trial had been grimly serious from the start, but now it got even more so. Jurors would spend the next night, maybe more, in a hotel room cut off from their families and the outside world, locked in deliberation and protected by a squad of sheriff's deputies.

Chapter 35: "I'm Going to Be Positive, Judge"

In the two plus years since Katrina struck, I had experienced scores and scores of sleepless nights. None of them were worse than the night before my closing argument. The court had allowed each side a maximum of five hours for the closing argument. John would close first on behalf of Sal. I would follow on behalf of Mabel, splitting my time with Bob, who would bat clean-up. Amazingly, the three of us never sat down in advance and coordinated what each of us was going to talk about. At dinner that night, fueled by our last bottle of Argentinian sauvignon blanc, I came up with an idea that required vetting. The argument I envisioned would be an attack on Foti and the entire prosecution like a pack of hungry wolves, but dressed in sheep's clothing. John liked it and sanctioned it but said, "Whatever you do, don't tell Bob. He might not like it." It was comforting to know that I wasn't the only one who was scared of Bob.

In the early morning darkness of the following day, I took my usual run through the streets of St. Francisville, past the courthouse and the old Episcopal church and graveyard, the final resting place for some Civil War dead. I stopped by Mike Hughes' office on my way back, and he was already there. By dawn's early light we shared a cup of his black-as-ink coffee, freshly brewed. We had participated together in the early morning coffee ritual almost every day for the past four weeks. It was a huge comfort to me, and Mike's gentle manner steadied me each and every day before the bullets started flying. Most of those bullets were aimed directly at my head. On this fateful day, unlike any other, he wished me luck.

"You ready?" he asked.

"I sure hope so, Mike, and I can't thank you enough for what you've done for us as lawyers and for what you've done for Sal and Mabel. We could never have gotten to this point without you."

"Go take a shower," he said. "I'll see you in court. And by the way, kick Foti's ass for me."

Hours later while the jury was deliberating downstairs, I remembered seeing Mike sitting outside the jury room all by himself as if he were ensuring and protecting the sanctity of their deliberations. It wasn't *his* case, but it was *his home town's* case and he clearly wanted to see that justice was done. He was fiercely loyal to the honor and integrity of St. Francisville. With Mike on guard, I was confident no one would attempt to corrupt the process. He assumed this responsibility without discussion and did it all on his own. That was the measure of the man.

Back at the Shadetree Inn, I readied for battle. I chose my armor carefully: blue pin-stripe suit, crisp white shirt, and power tie. For inspiration, while I dressed I blared classical music so loud it rattled the tiny glasses on the room's flimsy shelves. The courthouse was a study in media gone berserk. There were more TV cameras, more still photographers, and more print reporters than ever, including on the trial's opening day. Today, they all sensed, was judgment day. The vultures gathered in the space between Mike's office and the front door of the courthouse waiting to feast on scapegoat. They were circling, waiting for the corpses' last gasps. I hugged Sal and Mabel inside Mike's front room before opening the door and leading the way through the media circus. Mabel held on to me longer than usual. Our two sheriff's deputy escorts joined in the procession. It was a madhouse. Ignoring the shouted questions, I talked about the weather and how hot it was so early in the day.

As we neared the entrance, Paul Ryan of CBS asked, "What music did you listen to this morning?"

I gave him a truthful answer. "George Frideric Handel's *See, the Conquering Hero Comes,* as loud as I could play it," I said.

"You're a piece of work," he said smiling.

"At least I ain't from New York City," I said, winking as I ducked in the front door, escaping the media crush. Standing next to Ryan was Adam Nossiter, the reporter for the *New York Times.* Why not kill two Yankees with one stone, I thought.

The state bears the burden of proof; therefore, it has the advantage of presenting its closing argument first *and* last. Paul Knight, the old country lawyer, would make the state's first closing argument. Julie Cullen, the state's fire-breathing avenger, would deliver the rebuttal, the last words the jury would hear. It was a tremendous advantage, but they bore a heavy burden and I wouldn't have traded places with them. I dearly would have loved to have had the last word, but that was the government's privilege and advantage.

As I entered the packed courtroom through a side door, I was face to face with rows and rows of victims' family members in their reserved seating less than thirty feet from the jury box. They had coordinated their outfits. Hot as it is in South Louisiana in mid-September, every single one of them was dressed entirely in black. As I received a barrage of dirty, hateful looks from the assembled mourners, I wondered which of them had threatened to kill me. From their looks, it could have been all of them. I noticed a more disturbing detail about their attire. They all wore large color buttons, with a photograph of their departed loved one pinned to their outfits. The only color on an otherwise colorless background, these large color photos really stood out. I suspected the state had coordinated the entire presentation and likely paid for it. Before court was garbled to order, we met with the judge in his chambers to handle some matters preliminary to the war's final battle.

"Anything else?" Winsberg asked, putting on his robe and preparing to take the bench.

"I got something, judge," I said. He gave me a look which indicated he was tired of me saying, "I got something." I told him what the audience looked like and asked him to have the family members remove their color-photo buttons from their black lapels. "It is a blatant sympathy bid, designed to influence and intimidate the jury," I argued. "It's bad enough they're all dressed in black, just have them take off their buttons. You wouldn't let them wear a button that said, *'Guilty!'* would you?"

"No, I wouldn't," he said. "But this is different."

"No, it's not," I said. "It's sending the exact same message."

"It's a form of speech. If I made them take them off, it would violate their constitutionally protected right of free speech. Let's go to work."

I wished the court had been as concerned about protecting *our* constitutional rights through hours of unsworn, uncross-examined videotapes of news and weather broadcasts. What about those constitutional guarantees that *we* were denied?

Never raising his voice during slightly more than one hour of argument, Paul Knight dispassionately and methodically denounced the Manganos for not evacuating the home, a theme that had been repeated by the prosecution's forty witnesses.

"Thirty-five frail, elderly, sick souls died on August 29, 2005," he said. "Twenty-four others—mothers, fathers, brothers, sisters—all sick, elderly, and frail, requiring twenty-four-hour medical care, suffered needlessly. And it all happened for one simple, inescapable reason: because they were there. They didn't have a choice to be somewhere else. The Manganos denied them that choice."

Knight told the jury that the Manganos should pay a price for their decision to keep residents at St. Rita's as a hurricane bore down on them. Despite urgent, constant warnings on television news and emergency broadcast alerts, the Manganos made no preparations to evacuate. All of their preparations—buying supplies and medicines, fuel for generators— bespoke their decision to never evacuate, no matter how dangerous the threat. "They're guilty because they made a decision consciously and well in advance not to take these people out of harm's way," he said.

Referring to the testimony of no fewer than three former employees, Knight charged that the Manganos had a financial motive for not evacuating: they didn't want to pay the cost of moving patients and they didn't want to see the flow of federal reimbursements diminish while the patients were absent from the home. Witnesses testified that they had overheard them saying so.

"Let me tell you something," Knight said, his voice rising slightly; "to even factor in cost—$1, $5, $10—is a reckless disregard for those people they were responsible for. Reckless disregard, ladies and gentlemen, is the very definition of negligent homicide."

He pointed out that the Manganos did not *intend* the death of their residents. "Under the law of negligent homicide *intent* is not an element of the crime, nor do we have to prove it," he stressed. "Did they carelessly, negligently, and recklessly allow their residents to die?" he asked. He then answered his own question: "Of course they did; of course they did."

His understated argument was not loud or overbearing but it carried the dispassionate power of calm reason, logic, and the undeniably compelling fact that thirty-five innocents had died. Family members provided, through their audible sobs, the background accompaniment to this old country lawyer's aria. It was a song he sang disturbingly well.

John Reed was up next and went immediately on the attack, disturbing the quiet, dispassionate mood set by Knight.

"If they had built the levees the way they had promised forty years ago after hurricane Betsy, not a single person would have drowned at St. Rita's or in St. Bernard Parish," he began indignantly. He then made an impassioned plea to the jury to spare the couple from being the only two people held accountable for the litany of Katrina errors.

"It's time to heal, time to come together, time to put Katrina behind us. It is time for the government to stop turning on these people. It is time not to add two more victims to the disaster that was Katrina." He let his words sink in. "Why were these two people singled out when so many people made so many mistakes?" he asked.

It was a rhetorical question to which the state had no legitimate answer. John's tone was a little louder than Knight's but it was still relatively calm, reasoned, and passionate. For him, it was all about family: the Mangano family gathering together in the belief that the best way to care for their residents—who were almost like family to the Manganos—was to shelter in place together, as they had always done. "It didn't work this time because the government failed its people so miserably," John concluded. His plea was elegant and eloquent, full of reason and level-headedness. I was up next and given what I had prepared, the volume and tone in the room was about to change dramatically. It was my intention to humiliate and eviscerate this mean-spirited, dastardly prosecution in open court. No one would have to strain to hear what I had to say. I would hold nothing back.

I began quietly, thanking the jury for their patience and attention. Ever mindful of the people of faith on the jury—two Sunday school teachers and a woman who had almost become a nun—I would begin and end my argument with references to scripture. This, more than anything, I would later learn, drove my opponent Julie Cullen stark-raving mad. It would affect her rebuttal to my argument and earn me an enemy for life—another one.

I reminded the jury of our first encounter more than four weeks earlier. The courtroom was packed with prospective jurors, more than 150 of them in lines out the door and down the stairs; they were selected in a careful, tedious process; and many discussed the problems they would face if called to serve on such a lengthy case.

"Do y'all remember?" I asked. There were several nods of agreement among the jurors. "And what strikes me about that day is something we learn in Matthew 22," I said. "Matthew tells us, 'While many are called, few are chosen.' *You*, ladies and gentlemen, are the chosen few. And *you* are here at this place, at this moment in time, called upon to correct an incredible injustice. You have been called. You have been chosen to do exactly that." Had we been in church, I would have asked, "Can I get an Amen?"

Playing on a theme that had recurred throughout the trial, I told the jurors that there were all kinds of words I could use to describe the state's evidence, but I was not sure the judge would be happy hearing that kind of language in court. Turning away from the jury and briefly facing the judge, I said, "I don't want to start out bad. I'm not going to start off bad, so I'm going to be *positive*, your honor, and I'm going to remain positive and avoid startin' out bad."

And I said I was going to use the word positive to keep me on track. I had a power point presentation prepared and the word *"POSITIVE"* appeared on the screen vertically; I would use the letters to fill in my view of the state's presentation and evidence.

"The first letter 'P' reminds me of a word that describes their case . . . *pathetic.*" The whole word now appeared next to the letter "P" on the screen. "It was pathetic that their evidence began and ended with a transparent attempt at sympathy and bias; they showed you pictures of poor, dead old people which proved absolutely nothing.

"'O,'" I said. "It stands for *outrageous.*" And then the word "outrageous" appeared on the screen next to the letter "O." "They say we are guilty because 'they were there.' Really? And, because we didn't watch television. So, now in this country we put people in jail for not watching television? Outrageous.

"'S,'" I said, "stands for *sinful,* for this prosecution surely is a sin." The word "sinful" then appeared on the screen next to the letter "S." "It was a sin for the state to spend the money they spent on this prosecution. A fortune. Sparing no expense, paying witnesses hundreds of thousands of dollars to say things that have nothing to do with this case. Gerontologists, geriatric psychiatrists, and don't forget the Lone Ranger and the tens of thousands of dollars they spent on him. It was also a sin to bring poor Mr. Jack in here, in this terrible heat, to say nothing about the facts. He was only here to appeal to your sympathy.

"'I,' *illogical.* The prosecution is illogical. Is it logical to conclude that these good people would carelessly and recklessly put themselves, their own children, and their precious grandchildren in harm's way? Of course not. It is illogical.

"'T,' stands for *tyrannical,* for this is a prosecution founded in tyranny. You know, we fought a revolution against tyranny, against a concept known as the king's justice. Do you know what the king's justice was? It was anything he wanted it to be. You know why? Because he was the king. Well, we don't have a king anymore, but we do have an attorney general who believes himself king. He has chosen to oppress caregivers in this storm: Sal and Mabel and others. Caregivers who stayed at their post, caring for their residents and their patients. We are now second-guessed, railroaded, and scapegoated by a state government that clearly did not do *its* job. They seek to apply a standard of care against us that they don't dare apply against themselves. That's tyranny.

"'I,' *insulting.* This case, presented by the government, is an insult to your intelligence. In one lawsuit, they sued the Corps saying all the death, damage, and destruction is due to the Corps' 'gross negligence.' They ask for $200 billion, not exactly chicken feed. Yet here, they say the deaths are poor Sal and Mabel's fault. Well, it can't be both, and evidently we have a much higher view of your intelligence than they do. We are convinced that you will not be tricked or deceived into an emotional verdict. That's what *they* want. And it is an insult to your intelligence.

"'V,' *vindictive*. The prosecution is vindictive because they are covering up for their own mistakes and failures. We proved to you that it was the DOTD's responsibility to direct the evacuation and shelter of nursing homes, yet they admittedly did *nothing* to fulfill this responsibility. It is, therefore, vindictive, because they now attempt to blame us for their own admitted failures.

"'E.' And finally, ladies and gentlemen, it stands for *evil*, for this is a prosecution conceived and executed in evil. It is evil because our government cannot do this to these two innocent people in this country. It is evil because they are covering up, aren't they, their own failures, and asking us to pay for their failures. To ask another to pay for your own sins is evil done with an evil purpose."

By the time I was finished, the large plasma screen recapped the whole harangue:

Pathetic
Outrageous
Sinful
Illogical
Tyrannical
Insulting
Vindictive
Evil

I repeated the column of words: "Pathetic, outrageous, sinful, illogical, tyrannical, insulting, vindictive, and, ultimately, evil."

Turning to the judge, with my tongue firmly planted in my cheek, I spread my arms out wide as if begging for mercy and said, "So, you see, judge, I told you I would remain *positive*." The counter-intuitive nature of the argument caught many by surprise, and even though the state objected throughout, it was not the kind of closing argument easily forgotten. At various points, my presentation brought smiles to the lips of some jurors; at other points, they appeared deadly serious. One effect of the argument was undeniable and clearly visible—Cullen twisted in her seat and was agitated and angry. I would find out exactly how angry when she rose to give her rebuttal.

I lobbed a few more hand grenades in the prosecution's direction, but having already characterized their case as everything from pathetic to sinful and evil, as well as outrageous and tyrannical, the jury had a pretty good idea of where I stood. I supported each description with numerous references to the record. I was winding up and wanted to lower the temperature and the volume. I suggested that once they retired, they elect a foreperson and first take a secret-ballot vote to see where they stood. "You might be surprised at the result," I said, "and if not, it will give you a reference point for your work." We would later learn that this methodology was exactly what the jury followed when they retired to deliberate.

I then paused a very long time, my silence commanding responsive silence in the room. I closed my eyes, wove my fingers together as if in prayer and began speaking, my eyes still closed, my head slightly bowed.

"And I am reminded, according to the Gospel of John, that the elders and the Pharisees in an attempt to discredit Jesus brought a woman charged with adultery before him." I opened my eyes and began looking each juror in the eye, one at a time. "For the Pharisees meant to trick and deceive Jesus and embarrass him, for his message of hope and forgiveness was a threat to them all. They reminded Jesus that adultery was punishable by stoning unto death under the Law of Moses and challenged Jesus to judge the woman so that they might then accuse him of disobeying the law. At first he ignored their questions, remaining as he was, seated on the ground. They persisted. 'What say you, Rabbi?' they demanded. Rising up Jesus thought for a moment and replied, 'He that is without sin among you, let him cast the first stone at her.' The people crowded around him were so touched by their own consciences that they departed. The woman was saved. 'He that is without sin among you, let him cast the first stone,'" I repeated for emphasis.

"Ladies and gentlemen, do your duty; Sal and Mabel are not guilty." I then looked each of the six jurors squarely in the eye, one at a time, moving from left to right and said to each of them, "Not guilty." I repeated it six times. "And I thank you."

"Let's take a break," said the judge.

Bob was next and he continued the full-throated assault on the state's case. He ridiculed their reliance on TV broadcasts. He explained the Biblical origins of the term, "scapegoat," and brought it home beautifully to Sal and Mabel. The sins of Katrina had been placed on them, and only them, so that the real sinner, the government, could be absolved. He slowly and carefully explained the law of the case to the jury and how the facts were impacted by that law. His presence and his argument filled the room.

It was time for the last word, the state's rebuttal, and Julie Cullen was hot. At the break, Sal had told me what was to become the take-away quote of the entire trial, "Jim, I don't know what you said to make her so mad, but she was so hot at you, her panty hose were on fire! I was lookin' for a fire extinguisher."

Cullen started by excusing herself from the ritual of thanking the jury. "I've got something much more important to address," she said, "and that's the comments made by these defense lawyers in the last couple of hours." She looked me dead in the eye as she spoke. She went right to it.

"You want to talk about pathetic? You want to know what's pathetic? That these people ignored their responsibility to the most dependent people of St. Bernard Parish, the people that they took in $2.4 million a year to care for. That's pathetic!" Sal was right. Her panty hose were on fire.

"You want to know what's outrageous? To suggest to the family members that their loved ones were safe in a parish surrounded by water when a hurricane was coming directly at them, Category 5 with 200 mph winds." By the time Katrina made landfall, the storm wasn't a Category 5, nor did she have 200 mph winds, but that's the beauty of rebuttal—it didn't have to be true or accurate. Cullen had the last word.

"You want to know what was sinful? To ignore the Sunday morning *Times-Picayune*, the main paper for the greater New Orleans area which read: 'Katrina takes aim.'

"You don't need cable TV for this. You need a brain. You need a heart. You need some senses to pay attention!"

"You want to talk about illogical? It is [illogical] to ignore forty years of public outcry on the MRGO. Lots of problems there. They should have gotten out."

"You know what else is outrageous?" she yelled. "That big, fat fraud of a hurricane plan that they filed back in April of 2005. That's criminal. As Mr. Knight has said, that's when the negligence started."

She was indeed on fire, an avenging angel come to ground on behalf of those who lost their lives and their families. Her speech was classic rebuttal, using my words and turning them on me, shoving them down my throat— or perhaps some other bodily orifice, to judge from the furor with which she spoke. Some thought her rebuttal too strident, too shrill. I did not. She crystalized the state's case and the question the jury now had to answer.

"This is a tough choice. Everything about this case has been difficult to listen to. It's been tragic. It's been very sad," she said. "But you don't leave your common sense at the front door. And you don't leave your common sense at a nursing home when a Category 5 storm is coming towards you. What were they waiting for?" She asked for a verdict of guilty on all counts and sat down confident she would receive one. The jury never took their eyes off her.

Chapter 36: A Room Full of Tears

The judge charged the jury, reading them the law applicable to the case, a law they had sworn to accept exactly as he gave it to them. The jurors, however, were the *sole* judges of fact. It would be their job and their job alone to determine the true facts of the case, apply the law as instructed, and reach a verdict. That verdict would have to be unanimous. As the jury retired to deliberate behind locked doors, they were guarded by three sheriff's deputies. With the jury now cut off from the outside world, the judge lifted his gag order and allowed prosecutors, defense attorneys, witnesses, and the Manganos—anyone who wanted—to speak to the press.

A victim's relative talks to the press about the Manganos. "Dey oughta put dem unda the jail!" Courtesy of CBS News, from *48 Hours: No Way Out* (02/02/08).

"They ought to put dem under da jail," I heard one woman say to the assembled press. She was a survivor, a member of a family that had lost a loved one during the inundation of St. Rita's, and print reporters feverishly scribbled her every utterance.

A man from the group of survivors spoke with equal passion. "Da state clearly proved its case; dees people need to go to jail and pay for what dey done. Dey killed my father," he said, his voice cracking. Prosecutors did stand-up interviews with the assembled TV reporters, eight to ten cameras rolling at a time.

"Jim, you gonna talk to us?" one of the New Orleans TV guys shouted as I walked past the media circus. "I'll talk after the verdict," I said, continuing on to the sanctuary Mike's office provided. What I wanted to say was already rolling around in my head, and I wanted to think about it and choose my words carefully. I wrote only one statement, in longhand, anticipating a particular result. If fate coughed up a different verdict, I was out of luck. With the statement completed and tucked away in my pocket, I beat a hasty retreat to the Magnolia Café, exhausted, shell-shocked, and spaced out. My all-too-brief stay slumped against the Magnolia's back wall was cut short by the sheriff's command to the barmaid, "Tell Mr. Cobb the judge wants him back here *right away.*" I had not finished my first drink and it was much too soon for a defense-friendly verdict. I was virtually certain we had lost and I began to prepare myself mentally for the crushing blow.

Back in the courtroom, the warring sides were separated by the center aisle; soon that aisle was filled with armed sheriff's deputies to prevent any melee between the two groups as the verdict was announced. I had never felt this kind of energy, this kind of raw tension and anticipation in any room I had ever been in. It was a kind of out-of-body experience; I was a participant, but it felt like I was a spectator. Faces on both sides of the aisle were already grim. Some of the victims' relatives were wiping away tears. Everyone's two-year journey was rocketing to a conclusion, one shrouded in the creaky formalities of courtroom procedure. There was a specific role that we, as lawyers for the defense, had to play. Sal and Mabel had been assigned their parts as well. Seated beside me at the table, Mabel was ashen faced. She whispered to me, "I can't do this anymore, Jim." I clutched her hand, gave her a smile, and whispered back, "It's going to be okay."

The judge came in first, almost sprinting to the bench. He read the assembled multitude the riot act, threatening to jail anyone who engaged in an outburst. It struck me that *he* didn't know the outcome either. That outcome is only revealed when the jury hands up a form of verdict, filled out and signed by their foreperson—in this case signed 118 times, one for each of the 118 counts against the Manganos. For a brief moment, we were on equal footing with the judge—none of us knew the outcome. Like everyone else, Judge Winsberg would also have to maintain his composure as he read through the verdict before announcing it, poker-faced, revealing nothing of the outcome.

Suddenly, there were three loud knocks on the wooden door leading to the jury room, a sound as ominous and startling to me as the crack of thunder that, almost simultaneously, had threatened to blow out the courthouse windows. The door swung open, and the sheriff intoned loudly and with great formality, "All rise." Everyone complied.

The judge spoke next: "Everyone be seated." He swiveled his high-backed chair toward the jurors: "Ladies and gentlemen, have you reached a verdict?"

Sheepishly, one of them stood and answered, "We have, your honor."

"Please hand it to the sheriff and, sheriff, please bring it to me." He perused the 118-count form for what seemed like an eternity. My heart raced and I began taking short, shallow breaths. Finally, the stone-faced and inscrutable judge had finished his review of the verdict form. Out of the corner of my eye, I glimpsed my wife, Debbie, her hands folded in prayer. Debbie had come up to St. Francisville early in the morning on the last day. She wanted to be present for all the closing arguments.

"Will the defendants please rise and face the jury." The five of us did so, Mabel clutching my arm with such force that I fully expected to look down and see that blood had begun to spread through the fibers of my already sweaty sleeve. Mabel and I exchanged glances, and her look of confusion and abject fear was forever etched in my memory.

The judge began. "State of Louisiana versus Salvador and Mabel Mangano, on the charge of thirty-five counts of negligent homicide, we the jury find the defendants *not guilty*." The judge turned to other pages. "State of Louisiana versus Salvador and Mabel Mangano, on the charge of twenty-four counts of cruelty to the elderly and infirm, we the jury find the defendants *not guilty*." The judge paused, took a deep breath, and said, "With my thanks, this jury is discharged and so are the defendants. Mr. and Mrs. Mangano, you are free to go."

Was it true, I thought? Did I actually just hear the words, "Free to go?" Was it possible that we had actually prevailed against incredible odds and an unholy alliance of vengeful media and the machinations of an attorney general hell-bent to get himself re-elected? The gentle but audible sobs from both sides of the gallery somehow had the power to confirm that it was true. We had won.

I threw my arms around Mabel and Sal. They collapsed in each other's arms, both sobbing uncontrollably. There were no outbursts, no shouted recriminations in the courtroom, just sobbing. *Everyone* was crying. I sat back down in my chair for a moment. I leaned over, placed the back of my hands against the table and pressed my forehead into my palms. As I cried, all the calamities that had befallen us in the previous two years flashed before my closed eyes: the mud-caked rooms of the nursing home; the bulletin boards with pictures of grandchildren and prayer cards; the misery to which Katrina—and perhaps I as well—had subjected Debbie and the kids. I was overcome. I felt a hand on my shoulder. It was John. I stood up and we embraced. I got control of my emotions, but no words were spoken. None were needed. I met Bob and we congratulated each other inside the rail. I noticed that the jurors were still in their seats; none had moved as they studied the tableau before them, the throng of us whose lives had been changed by the power of their decision.

As I made my way to the rail separating the participants from the gallery, the first person waiting for me was Ron Goux, the president of the Louisiana Nursing Home Association and the man whose recommendation of me to his son had initiated this two-year saga. Ron's face was red, his eyes filled with tears. His handkerchief was red with blood. Evidently, he had cried so hard upon hearing the verdict that a blood vessel burst in his nose. Droplets of blood were visible on his otherwise immaculate white shirt. He was a large man and I could all but hear my back crack as he folded me into a bear hug. He whispered "thank you" through his tears. I finally made it to Debbie whose face was red, eyes glistening. She gave me the most heartfelt hug I had ever received and we just stood there, holding each other, saying nothing, but somehow reprising everything we had been through since Katrina and expunging all the pain we had endured.

On the other side of the aisle, the victims' family members huddled in disbelief, a stunned silence punctuated by deep sobs. It was yet another crushing disappointment in a horrible two years that had only begun with the deaths of beloved elders. And this was likely as wrenching as their first shock because, in an instant, they had been stripped of all hope of vengeance and closure. They were no longer my adversaries. I was swept by unexpected feelings of profound sorrow for their loss and their disappointment.

I went back inside the rail to pack up and leave. To my surprise, the jurors were still in the box. The sheriff approached me: "Mr. Cobb, one of the jurors wants to speak to *you*. Can you talk to her?"

I was reluctant but agreed. "Of course," I said.

The woman was a secretary at the nuclear power plant in town and a devout Sunday school teacher. Throughout the five weeks of the trial, she had had what I took to be a perpetual scowl on her face, directed at me in particular. I thought she hated me. As I approached her, she put out both of her hands and grabbed mine.

"Mr. Cobb," she said, "you are a wonderful lawyer. Thank you for what you did for the Manganos." She was emotional. So much for my ability to read and judge juror expressions—I was 100-percent wrong about her. "May I say something to Mr. and Mrs. Mangano?"

"Sure," I said. "Let me get them for you." I brought Sal and Mabel over, leaving them to speak with this juror and others in the box. I was told the juror wished them well and was sympathetic to what they had been through the past two years. She concluded by saying, "Sleep well tonight and into the future. You are free." It was a moving scene to watch as Sal and Mabel received the best wishes of the six ordinary people who had set them free and ended their nightmare.

The jury was contemplative too, talking about what they decided and why. The fact that Sal and Mabel were the only people charged with a crime played a role in their decision. "We talked about that," the forty-six-year-old nuclear power plant secretary and Sunday school teacher said. "There were a lot of mistakes made and it should have been a lot of people answering for it. So why just these two people?" she asked.

In interviews with the *Times Picayune* and the *Morning Advocate,* jurors gave the world a glimpse into their secret deliberations. As I suggested in my closing argument, the very first thing they did when they retired to deliberate was to cast a secret ballot vote on guilt or innocence, before even discussing the evidence. The vote was 5-1 for not guilty. I was glad I had made the suggestion.

The middle-school English teacher said he was swayed by our arguments that the government was largely to blame for the tragedy because of breached levees and the state's failure to help evacuate nursing homes under a revision to its emergency plan that took place five months before Katrina struck.

"When I first walked in here for jury selection, I was like, 'They're guilty as sin,'" he said. "It was not one particular thing that changed my mind, but the fact that state officials didn't carry out their duties was a big factor." All six jurors were forced not only to spend more than a month away from their jobs and daily routine, but to confront in grotesque detail the aftermath of Katrina, which only peripherally touched their lives in West Feliciana Parish, some one hundred miles north of destroyed St. Bernard Parish. The English teacher said he and his five colleagues were in a no-win situation, knowing they would either convict the Manganos or disappoint the many victims' relatives who had filled the courtroom on the trial's final day, all dressed in black.

The juror who had initially voted to convict was one of several who said he went back and forth between conviction and acquittal as he listened to the attorneys from both sides make their arguments. He was conflicted. Then, he had a revelation, perhaps a divine one: his uncertainty that the Manganos' conduct during the storm amounted to negligent homicide constituted reasonable doubt. He was reminded by his fellow jurors that reasonable doubt was grounds for a verdict of not guilty. In fact, reasonable doubt *required* a verdict of not guilty. The founding fathers and the framers of our Constitution and Bill of Rights had to be smiling down upon this group of six ordinary, American citizens. A jury had accepted and enforced the presumption of innocence, central to our democracy, and required the state to prove guilt beyond a reasonable doubt. This time, the system and its underlying principles prevailed. Although the decision was difficult and painful for all concerned, there was a certain majesty to the jury's verdict. The English teacher said it was the most important thing he had ever done in his life.

As we packed up and got ready to go, the rain was still pounding the courthouse roof and windows. At last, we made our way out to a breezeway

Not Guilty! *Walking from the courthouse to Mike Hughes' office. Mabel's first smile in two years.* Courtesy of CBS News, from *48 Hours: No Way Out* (02/02/08).

to confront the media. As we hit the door and headed for the microphones they had set up, the cameramen took a cue and the gray afternoon air exploded with what seemed like a million strobe and spotlights. I stepped up to the microphones flanked by Bob and John and Sal and Mabel. I reached inside my coat pocket and pulled out the folded paper on which I had written what I intended to say to the media, win or lose. All the television networks were there, as were statewide newspapers, the *New York Times* and the *Washington Post* among many others. I waited until the hubbub had died down and then began to speak.

"Our first thoughts are of our residents and their family members. Not a day has gone by since August 29, 2005, when we have not thought of them, missed them, and prayed for them," I said.

"We are also mindful of all the residents of New Orleans and St. Bernard Parish, some of whom lost their lives, their homes, and their entire city. This was a tragedy for everyone in Southeast Louisiana, the tragedy at St. Rita's, and the sorrow and hurt is not over.

"But the case of the State of Louisiana versus the caregivers at St. Rita's *is* over, and justly decided. God save the United States of America and God save this honorable court."

The author reading his prepared statement after the verdict. New York Times *reporter Adam Nossiter is on the left, taking notes.* Courtesy of CBS News, from *48 Hours: No Way Out* (02/02/08).

I wasn't the only one talking to the media after the verdict. Family members of the victims vented their frustration, anger, and hurt. "They just got away with murder!" said the daughter of a resident who had drowned. "This jury might not have found them guilty, but their maker will!" she said emphatically through tears. Her God was evidently different from the God to whom the deeply religious jury had prayed.

We retreated to Mike's office across the street surrounded by reporters, cameras, and onlookers. Once inside, there were hugs all around and more tears. These were not tears of joy or triumph, for there was neither joy nor triumph in our victory. These were tears of relief, of release from a possible fate that would have ruined three generations of the Mangano clan, destroying their reputation while the family's matriarch and patriarch ended their days rotting in prison.

"What do we do now, Mr. Jim?" Sal asked.

"I'm headed to the Magnolia Café, Sal, but I don't want you guys out and about." I was still deeply concerned about retaliation and retribution. I told him to go straight back to the home they had established in Baton Rouge and to stay inside. We'd speak in the morning, I said. "Get a good night's sleep. Now get outta here before somebody changes their mind!" Sal hugged me and kissed me on my cheek. And they disappeared in the drizzly twilight, free people for the first time in two years. As I watched their taillights fade from view, it struck me that I had helped to save the lives of two deserving people. It was the most intense feeling of satisfaction I had experienced since taking the oath as a member of the Louisiana State Bar, almost thirty years earlier.

Speaking of bars, Magnolia, here we come! As we entered the back room, there was a smattering of applause from those who had arrived ahead of us. My bartender friend came out from behind her perch, gave me a hug and said, "Those people were innocent!"

"I know," I said. I drank more margaritas than I should have, given my level of exhaustion and the long, rainy drive back to New Orleans that still lay ahead for Debbie and me. En route, she worked the cell phone, which lighted up with calls of congratulation. I learned that all the New Orleans and Baton Rouge television stations had interrupted regularly scheduled programming to announce the verdict, live from St. Francisville. It was stunningly unexpected news statewide—its shock value a testament to how completely the media and "General" Foti had hounded the Manganos in a two-year campaign of vilification and character assassination. As we passed the TV trucks heading back to New Orleans, they recognized my car and flashed their lights, blowing their horns in tribute to our success. It was, to say the least, surreal.

And making it home safely and in one piece could be described by another adjective: miraculous. I opened the trunk to take my belongings inside, but I had none. In my haste to get out of town, I had left everything at the Shadetree Inn. For the first time in months, I went under without benefit of pills and potions. I slept the sleep of a man physically, mentally, and emotionally exhausted. I slept like the dead. It was wonderful.

It was not yet 7 A.M. when I was jarred awake by the phone next to my bed. "Who in the hell is this?" I thought. It was the guy from the Shadetree Inn. "Jim, you left all your s— up here, and I already rented the room for tonight. When you comin' to get your stuff?" Thanks for letting me sleep late, I thought.

"Let me wake up," I said, "I'll be there in a couple of hours." I stumbled downstairs, put on a pot of coffee and—further force of habit—walked outside to get the newspaper. All but oblivious to what had happened the day before, and more than a little bit hungover, I had walked back inside before sliding the *Times-Picayune* out of its clear plastic sleeve. There on the front page, just below the paper's banner, was a five-column headline in thick black letters two inches high: "Not Guilty." The subhead on the line below: "St. Rita's Owners Exonerated in Nursing Home Case." Below that was a seven-by-nine-inch color photograph of Mabel, Sal, John, and a shockingly haggard yours truly striding back to Mike's office after the verdict had been rendered. The story headline and photograph took up almost the entire front page above the fold. It was either a very slow news day or, as I preferred to think, the verdict was a very big deal. I was shocked by how drawn and tired I looked in that front-page photo. I was almost unrecognizable, even to myself. That image would stick with me as I began the process of trying to figure out what I was going to do with the rest of my life.

Epilogue

Within days of the verdict I received a phone call from Buddy Caldwell. I did not know him and had never spoken to him before. He was a candidate for Attorney General of the State of Louisiana, running against Foti in an election that would take place within six weeks of Foti's stunning St. Rita's defeat. Caldwell, a district attorney from northern Louisiana, congratulated me on my victory and sought to enlist my support for his campaign. "That was a hell of a piece of lawyering," he said. Buddy was a Tulane grad, an accomplished prosecutor and trial lawyer, and was supported and trusted by people I respected.

"Buddy," I said, "I'd vote for a snake before I'd vote for Charlie Foti, although both are members of the same reptile family." He laughed and said he appreciated my backing. I repeatedly took to the airwaves, fully explaining to talk-radio audiences how abusive Foti and his crew had been of the Manganos' constitutional rights. I told anyone who asked that I was voting for Buddy Caldwell, and a lot of people asked. The media, which had so shamelessly supported Foti, now turned on him in his hour of ignominious defeat.

Six weeks later, Foti ran third in a three-man field. Almost as quickly and contemptuously as he had condemned the Manganos after the storm, he was thrown out of office by Louisiana voters. His persecution of doctors and nurses post-Katrina and his losing prosecution of the Manganos figured prominently in his stunning defeat after a single term as A.G. An incumbent, who wasn't under indictment, running last in a primary, was virtually unheard of in Louisiana politics. Buddy Caldwell went on to win the general election and I served on his transition team. One of his first acts was to go before the Louisiana Nursing Home Association and pledge that he wasn't going to try to put people in the industry in jail for doing the best they could in an emergency. "That's not me," he said plainly.

Julie Cullen retained her job as Director of the Criminal Division but eventually was nudged into retirement. Burton "Crawdaddy" Guidry was let go, went into private practice, and began to make noises about running for attorney general himself. Paul Knight, the old country lawyer, retained his position and continues to this day to prosecute criminal cases on behalf of the Louisiana Attorney General's office.

I told my students that there was a new definition of winning a case. First, your client has to be fully exonerated. Second, your opponent has to lose his job for messing with you in the first place. "*That*, my young friends, is what I call an old-fashioned ass-whipping." Nobody deserved it more than Charles Foti. He has largely disappeared from the public eye. The removal of Foti from office was something that Bob and John and I had spoken about. It was, in fact, one of our objectives. It was a service we performed on behalf of the citizens of Louisiana.

Five years after our time together in St. Francisville, Judge Winsberg remained the Louisiana Supreme Court's go-to guy, their preferred appointee to preside over cases where local judges had recused themselves. It also turned out he had a heart. Remember the unemployed middle-school teacher who said he would be doomed if selected to serve on the St. Rita's jury? Starting out bad, Winsberg refused to excuse him and allowed him to be seated on the jury. What we didn't know was that the judge had worked the phones, contacting the local school board and helping the unemployed teacher find a job, employment he started on the Monday after he returned with the jury's verdict of *not guilty*. What started out bad for the judge and the juror, wound up *positive*. How about that?

Sal and Mabel continued to struggle but never gave up. Slowly but surely, Sal set about repairing his family's homes in the St. Rita's compound. He and Little Sal finished the son's home first. Sal had done the tile work in the kitchen and bath and was extremely proud of it. So one day I took a drive down into the parish to see his handiwork: it was simple, direct, and straightforward, like the man who did it—a beautiful job. Next they repaired Tammy's house, a classic Creole cottage that they restored to its former grandeur. Finally, Sal tackled his and Mabel's home. Putting everyone else first was his way. At last the family was reunited on the grounds where they all lived and worked before Katrina. The nursing home itself stands empty, a gutted shell of a building and a sad reminder of what happened on that terrible August morning.

The Manganos and I had spent three consecutive Augusts and Septembers together in a struggle for justice: 2005, the year of Katrina and their arrest; 2006, the year the grand jury indicted them; and 2007, the year of the trial in St. Francisville that re-established their freedom. We would spend one more August and September together, in 2008, fighting against the insurance company that had denied their claim for wind damage caused by Katrina.

The despicable Lafayette Insurance Company had sent them a check for $1,150 for wind damage to a 30,000-square-foot building, shredded roof included. Their initial offer had been $0.00—a clear strategy to exploit Sal and Mabel's legal troubles and deliver them another kick while they were down. They had figured, stupidly, that a St. Bernard Parish jury would dislike the Manganos more for what happened at St. Rita's than they would dislike the arbitrary and capricious insurer. They figured wrong. In another trial in August and September spanning three weeks and two mandatory evacuations of St. Bernard for hurricanes, the local jury welcomed Sal and Mabel home. I represented them in the suit against their insurer for its failure to pay for damage at St. Rita's and its handling of their claim. My closing argument was another barn burner. I ridiculed the insurer's lame defense that only flooding damaged the building, not wind, by asking, "Do we look that stupid, here in St. Bernard Parish, that you would expect this jury to believe what you just said?" In a case in which we were offered zero, the jury returned a verdict in our favor. The amount? $2.56 million. And we won again when the Fourth Circuit Court of Appeal sustained the verdict. Back in front of our friends at the Louisiana Supreme Court, the justices reasoned we had beaten the poor insurance company so badly that they lowered the amount of the award by $1.2 million. One can always count on our supreme court for a good, juridical laugh. The Cobb family was, unfortunately, the punch line of their joke masquerading as a decision, as they took $400,000 off our family's table with the stroke of a pen. Such a sum would have come in quite handy in paying all our accumulated expenses, not the least of which was repairing our flooded home.

We nonetheless collected the remitted amount and returned a princely sum to Sal and Mabel. It almost got them even with everything they spent defending themselves in the criminal case. Their world was back on an even keel and I was the captain of the ship that brought them through three years of stormy seas. I was assisted in the civil trial by a wonderful young lawyer. His name was Michael Winsberg, and, yes, he was Judge Jerry Winsberg's son.

Sal and Mabel are essentially retired, but Sal is always busy fixing something, helping someone who needs it, riding his tractor cutting grass, and in love with his bulldozer as he moves dirt around and plans for the future. I believe he most enjoys the freedom he has when he's outdoors working on something, the south Louisiana sun on his face, bouncing up and down on that damned tractor or bulldozer, a free man. I remain in contact with Sal and Mabel to this day; we speak often. We go out to dinners as a foursome, almost always to an Italian restaurant with names like Café Giovanni or Tony Angello's. Mabel and Debbie order healthy fare—grilled, fresh speckled trout with a little crabmeat on top or grilled eggplant in a tomato sauce. Sal and I order the same thing every time, regardless of the venue. We both order meatballs and spaghetti, with some crispy, hot Italian bread and a nice, full-bodied Italian red wine, usually Chianti. We are entirely predictable in what we order and are forever joined at the culinary hip. My family views them the same way the Manganos viewed their residents at St. Rita's: They're like family and we love them.

So what happened to me? I returned to my law firm and its business—maritime, insurance defense, corporate law—the stuff that I had done for almost thirty years. But I was conflicted. Other than Susan Henning, I had essentially been cut off from my partners for almost two years as I single-mindedly defended and protected the Manganos. Resentment may have been around the corner, and maybe some jealousy after our unexpected victory. Perhaps my partners felt *they* were doing the firm's business and I was doing *mine*, jousting with this windmill of a case. Because all the fees I received from the case came to the firm, I felt as though what I was doing *was* the firm's business. It was just a different, higher-profile case than we usually handled. The time away and the distance, the lack of confidence and support, and the lack of others' recognition of the amazing result were the seeds of my confusion and discontent.

My partners did not comprehend my zeal to preserve Sal and Mabel's freedom. Maybe that's because none of my partners had lost their homes—and almost everything they owned—to the United States Government's flood of lies, as did the Cobbs and the Manganos. I used to say, "If you didn't get *wet,* you don't get *it*." No amount of attempted sympathy and understanding could bridge that gap. It was a very big part of my mission to put an end to the government's efforts to scapegoat the public; in prosecuting Sal and Mabel, they were prosecuting *me* and everyone else who was a victim. No one else was at fault for *anything*; the government was at fault for *everything*. And somebody had to prove that in an American court of law. It was my calling to be part of a team that proved that point conclusively and put an end to government's assault on its own people. I reviewed my professional options. If I'm going to go out, I thought to myself, that's not a bad note to go out on.

I received several phone calls from lawyers and firms interested in my coming to work with them, capitalizing on the publicly hot hand I currently held. There is an easy path to leveraging this sort of victory, turning it into greater financial reward. I had options. So what did I do?

I quit. I resigned from the firm at which I had been a partner for more than twenty-five years. I declined all offers from other firms and really never engaged them in substantive discussions. To keep body and soul together, I accepted an offer to go in-house and became general counsel to a marine transportation company that I had represented for decades through the firm. Instead of the bright lights of CNN, FOX, MSNBC, and the *New York Times,* I found myself working in a poorly lit and windowless second-floor office next to a warehouse. It was a seventy-minute commute from home—and it was perfect. I became instantly anonymous, disappearing from the public stage.

Everyone is broken by life, but sometimes we get stronger in the broken places. Katrina shattered our lives along with hundreds of thousands of other lives. In taking up the defense of the Manganos, I got stronger in the broken places, strong enough to walk away from it all.

For me, the St. Rita's case represented a dream—a young boy's dream of aiding the oppressed and the helpless. That dream was germinated by Harper Lee's *To Kill a Mockingbird* and took form as I sat in a darkened theater, drawing inspiration from a black-and-white film about a gentle giant named Atticus Finch. As I grew older, I became separated from my youthful dream. Sal and Mabel, by contrast, realized theirs—a dream of operating a nursing home—a dream that turned tragic when they were railroaded and scapegoated by their government and the media in the wake of the worst disaster in the history of the United States. Defending them was not every lawyer's dream—most, in fact, would have run from this case, fearing it was a nightmare. To be sure, our journey together was at times nightmarish, but this struggle on behalf of the innocent and the oppressed, against overwhelming odds, was *my* dream.

Youthful dreams are often misplaced and easily forgotten. When *your* dream calls, will you recognize and remember it? Will you answer its call? Sometimes life comes between us and our dreams. And sometimes we are fortunate enough to be reunited. I was reunited with mine.

Acknowledgments

Writing is a lonely, solitary enterprise, but it is not accomplished all alone. A grizzled, veteran reporter and writer queried me early in this process, asking, "You want to know the two hardest things about writing?" "Of course," I answered excitedly, expecting to receive the keys to the secret kingdom of great writers. He leaned over and whispered, "Starting . . . and not stopping." Truer words have never been whispered. The individuals listed below were absolutely essential to my starting . . . and not stopping.

Michael Zweig, a good friend and superb lawyer at Loeb & Loeb in New York, provided early encouragement. Laura Parker, a great reporter and wonderful writer, and her writer/husband Bill Prochnau believed in the story and urged me to tell it. Judge Jay and Sandy Blitzman of Boston cheered me on. Jim "Nubbin" Davis, a college classmate of forty years ago, longed to tell me an early section was junk, but instead, fell in love with it and clamored annoyingly for more copy as the book progressed. Steve Jacobson, a law school classmate, and his brother Danny, a Hollywood-type with an inflated golf handicap, were very early supporters. Sherrel Jones, Dr. Brobson Lutz, and Penny Bajeux were early cheerleaders, too. Dara and John McDaniel provided encouragement, support, and timely bottles of writer's juice—Bombay Sapphire. New Orleans attorney Joe Stahl, a former adversary who always remained a friend, didn't just provide encouragement but rolled up his sleeves and meticulously line edited the piece. Carter Hooper's hard work and creative mind had much to do with the book's title and haunting cover. Thanks, Carter.

To the folks at Pelican Publishing, especially Kathleen Calhoun Nettleton, who saw the value and the importance of telling this story to the world, my thanks. To my editor, Katy Doll, your attention to detail and the meticulous way in which you have made this book better is acknowledged and greatly appreciated.

I owe a debt of gratitude to the gurus at Clarity Litigation Support, LLC, a terrific New Orleans-based litigation support firm. Eric Draper and their staff helped with technical support regarding the photographs you will find in this book. Thanks, guys.

As with all things of any real importance in New Orleans, there would be no story here without Galatoire's restaurant. It was there that I met John Berendt and, with the assistance of several Sazeracs, told him this tale. He suggested I write something about it. I told him I already had, and he committed the fateful error of saying he'd like to read it. I handed him a pitch piece and within twenty-four hours had received an enthusiastic voicemail, declaring it a great story that could be a book, a movie, or whatever I wanted it to be. This breath of encouragement rekindled the smoldering embers at the heart of this book. Without it, the fire likely would have died, and the book along with it. The generosity of John's commentary and advice creates a debt I can never adequately repay.

In similar fashion, I was fortunate enough to be introduced to Jed Horne by a mutual friend, Jack Pruitt. Jed reviewed some of my copy and pronounced that it was a great story and I appeared to have the skills to tell it. Truth be told, he taught me *how* to write this book *while* I was writing it: a pretty neat trick by a great teacher and an even greater writer. To the extent the prose shines, it is Jed who applied the wax and the elbow grease to make it sparkle after I had hit every mud hole and pot hole on this literary road. Thanks, Jed.

To Sal and Mabel Mangano, my thanks for trusting me to write their story. They have no interest in this book nor have they read in advance any copy or retained any editorial rights. When this book is published, they will read it for the first time. I am solely responsible for the book's content, but it is my fervent hope that they will be pleased with the way I have told their story. I also hope that this will be the first and final exposition of the whole truth of what really happened on that terrible day in August 2005. They remain the two most resilient people I have ever known.

Last, but by no means least, I owe an enormous debt of gratitude to my wife, Debbie. She typed, edited, and reviewed every word of this book and put up with my dictation and scribbles for years on end. Without her patience and good humor, there would be no book—literally. She has another unique qualification deserving acknowledgement: She didn't just type and edit the book—she lived it! My son Christopher provided some early, meaningful edits to the piece while we were on a family vacation to Costa Rica's Pacific coast. *Pura Vida, Chris!* Along with our children, Christopher and Collette, the four of us made it together to the other side of Katrina's devastation. I love you guys very much and could not have accomplished this without your understanding, love, and support.

Jim Cobb
March 2013

Author's Note

The primary source for this book is deeply personal: the experience of living through the extraordinary events now seared into my memory. I also reviewed press reports, conducted dozens of interviews, and relied heavily on the trial transcript. Quoted testimony is verbatim. I chose to remain strictly faithful to the real people and the actual events. That commitment was easy to fulfill. What we went through together had the force—and some of the surreal quality—of great fiction. There was no need to embellish it.

Index